Political Folk Music in
America from Its
Origins to Bob Dylan

Political Folk Music in America from Its Origins to Bob Dylan

LAWRENCE J. EPSTEIN

McFarland & Company, Inc., Publishers

Jefferson, North Carolina, and London

LIBRARY OF CONGRESS CATALOGUING-IN-PUBLICATION DATA

Epstein, Lawrence J. (Lawrence Jeffrey)
    Political folk music in America from its origins to Bob Dylan /
Lawrence J. Epstein.
       p.   cm.
    Includes bibliographical references and index.

    ISBN 978-0-7864-4862-3
    softcover : 50# alkaline paper ∞

    1. Folk music — Political aspects — United States — History.
I. Title.
ML3918.F65E67   2010
781.62'1301599 — dc22   2009054322

British Library cataloguing data are available

Front cover image ©2010 Shutterstock

Manufactured in the United States of America

*McFarland & Company, Inc., Publishers
  Box 611, Jefferson, North Carolina 28640
   www.mcfarlandpub.com*

Political Folk Music in America from Its Origins to Bob Dylan

LAWRENCE J. EPSTEIN

McFarland & Company, Inc., Publishers

Jefferson, North Carolina, and London

LIBRARY OF CONGRESS CATALOGUING-IN-PUBLICATION DATA

Epstein, Lawrence J. (Lawrence Jeffrey)
    Political folk music in America from its origins to Bob Dylan /
Lawrence J. Epstein.
        p.   cm.
    Includes bibliographical references and index.

    ISBN 978-0-7864-4862-3
    softcover : 50# alkaline paper

    1. Folk music — Political aspects — United States — History.
I. Title.
ML3918.F65E67   2010
781.62'1301599 — dc22   2009054322

British Library cataloguing data are available

Front cover image ©2010 Shutterstock

Manufactured in the United States of America

McFarland & Company, Inc., Publishers
  Box 611, Jefferson, North Carolina 28640
    www.mcfarlandpub.com

In memory of my mother
Lillian Scheinert Epstein
who taught me how to live.

Contents

Acknowledgments

It is a great pleasure to express my appreciation to the many people who were kind, generous with their time, and enormously helpful to me as I wrote this book.

I would like to thank the following people for agreeing to interviews, sometimes several of them, and being so extraordinarily intelligent and insightful: Mark Barkan, Dave Berger, Mitch Blank, Ed Blum, Oscar Brand, Paul Breines (e-mail), Cantor Bob Cohen, Ron Cohen, Ed Cray, David Dunaway, the late Mark Eastman, Barbara Gitlow Edge, Mary Jo Guthrie Edgmon, Mary Feidt, Carl Granich, Ann Guthrie, Nora Guthrie, John Earl Haynes (e-mail), Mark Allan Jackson, Danny Kalb, Ann Lauterbach, Peter Lefcourt (e-mail), Robbie Lieberman, Charlie McCoy (e-mail), Charles Miller, David Miller, Tom Paxton, D.A. Pennebaker, Ron Radosh, Millie Rahn, Douglas Rathgeb, Alan Rinzler, B.J. Rolfzen, Suze Rotolo (e-mail), Pete Seeger, Noel Stookey, John Szwed, Jennifer Warren, Josh White, Jr., Peter Yarrow, Izzy Young, and the late Henrietta Yurchenco.

Some of these people provided special help. In alphabetical order, they are:

Cantor Bob Cohen, who knew the folk scene so personally, was indefatigable in sending me materials from all over the place and being incredibly kind as he did so.

In his biography of Woody Guthrie, Ed Cray called Ron Cohen "Folk Music Central." After receiving so much help and material from Ron, I know what Ed means. Whenever I had questions about folk materials, I knew Ron would help. He provided me with hundreds of pages of information about folk music. As if that were not enough, he gave the manuscript a meticulous reading under a tight deadline. While we sometimes had different approaches or interpretations, Ron made the manuscript subtler and more complex.

David Dunaway, Pete Seeger's biographer, sent me original material and provided very useful insights for the direction of my book.

The late Mark Eastman's incredible story of his early encounters with Bob Dylan was truly remarkable. I interviewed him several times about these vital moments in Dylan's life, and Mark was always gracious and extremely helpful.

Mary Jo Guthrie Edgmon, Woody's beloved sister, spoke to me on the phone for two minutes before inviting me over for some food. She has Woody's incredible sense of humor and his warm humanity, and I thoroughly enjoyed hearing her stories of Woody's life.

Mary Feidt, director of the wonderful documentary *Tangled Up in Bob: Searching for Bob Dylan*, provided some important suggestions for people to contact in Hibbing.

Dave Plant arranged for me to get a hard-to-find copy of an article from the Dylan magazine *The Telegraph*.

Ron Radosh, on whom I had to call more than once, has a unique perspective and an incredible amount of knowledge, both of which he was kind enough to offer as I thought through some of the issues of the book.

B.J. Rolfzen, Bob Dylan's high school English teacher, was extremely helpful. He sent me his memoirs of growing up during the Great Depression and answered a wide variety of questions about his teaching methods, the results of which Dylan had so well absorbed.

Betsy Siggins of Club 47 in Cambridge made valuable suggestions.

Jason Smukler, a former student of mine, provided access to information.

Izzy Young's kindness came through all the way from Sweden. He e-mailed and sent me materials and patiently answered my many questions about his pivotal role in Greenwich Village in the 1950s and '60s.

Finally, I'd also like to thank an anonymous source close to Bob Dylan.

People either individually or from various organizations and archives provided much-needed materials or advice. I'd like to thank Ray Allen of ISAM, the Institute for Studies in American Music; Hillel Arnold, formerly of the Woody Guthrie Archives; Peggy Bulger, Director of the American Folklife Center at the Library of Congress (and a former student of mine); Anna Canoni of the Woody Guthrie Archives; Robin Chen, Southern Folklife Collection Assistant at the University of North Carolina in Chapel Hill; Mark Damron, General Secretary Treasurer of the Industrial Workers of the World; Roy Eddey of the New-York Historical Society; Peter Filardo of the Tamiment Archives at New York University; the FBI for calling me to discuss the Freedom of Information Act materials I had requested; Richard Fliegel; Todd Harvey, Folklife Specialist at the American Folklife Center at the Library of Congress; Julie Herrada, Curator of the Labodie Collection at the University of Michigan; Dina Kellans of the Archives of Traditional Music at Indiana University; Sue Kriete, of the New-York Historical Society; Nancy Kuhl, of the Beinecke Rare Book and Manuscript Library at Yale University; William LeFevre, Reference Archivist at the Walter P. Reuther Library at Wayne State University; Zicel Maymudes; Dawn Olejar, Vice-President of Production Operations at CPI-Grand Entertainment; Robert Parks, Director of Library and Museum Services at the Morgan Library; Jeff Place, Archivist of the Ralph Rinzler Collection at the Smithsonian Center for Folklife and Culture; Rob Rosenthal, Professor of Sociology at Wesleyan University; Rodney A. Ross of the Center for Legislative Archives at the National Archives and Records Administration; Natalia Sciarini of the Beinecke Library at Yale; Maggie Skinner,

Manager of Public Relations for the Experience Music Project; Jeffrey Taylor, Director of ISAM; and Doug Yeager of Yeager Productions.

Keith Condon played an unimaginably important role in shaping the book. His constant guidance and help was invaluable. I deeply appreciate his help.

My former colleagues and permanent friends in the English Department at Suffolk County Community College were unendingly kind in patiently listening to my tales about this book and providing much-needed emotional solace and support. All of them were like a wonderful extended family. Some provided materials for this book. David Axelrod found some early folk magazines and recalled his days wandering through the folk clubs. Maury Dean, author of books about music himself, was always a valuable source of suggestions and ideas. Tony DiFranco, my friend and office mate for more than thirty years, had to endure many questions from me because of his intelligence and capacity to explore and explain emotions. Sarah Kain Gutowski provided many valuable insights especially into contemporary music and suggested a very useful documentary and other materials. Doug Howard, the department's Assistant Academic Chair, regularly walked into my office with new suggestions about a particular radio program, or an article or book. Adam Penna found a particularly interesting article and often discussed writing with me. Sandra Sprows, the Academic Chair of the Department, made suggestions for material and helped me think through what I wanted to say about a number of ideas. Sandra Emmachild, who teaches philosophy and Women's Studies courses, used her incredible knowledge of feminist history to answer questions I had.

The librarians at the College have always been admirably persistent and enormously patient in obtaining the many materials I requested. I'd particularly like to thank Marilyn Ventiere, who dutifully e-mailed me whenever new materials arrived from libraries in faraway places; Marilyn Heller, who is in charge of Periodicals; Gail Kunes, who arranged for intercampus materials; and Margaret Blackmore in the Circulation Department. Susan DeMasi, the media librarian, always has useful suggestions for me. Kevin McCoy, the Library's Director during the writing of the book, facilitated help from his staff and gave me specific help about the Wobblies.

Some of the people I interviewed or who provided help or advice might disagree with some of the interpretations I've made or conclusions I've drawn in the book. Their help and advice are not endorsements for the ideas contained in the book. I bear sole responsibility for the content and interpretations contained in these pages.

Doug Rathgeb is a friend of going on half a century. I called him frequently about this book. He always provided enthusiasm and great intelligence in helping me. Indeed, his assistance was indispensable.

My dear friend Assemblyman Mike Fitzpatrick and I traveled all over the country together going to my speeches and sampling America's cuisine. I treasure his support. Mike, his wife, Lorena, and brother, John, are like family.

Don Gastwirth, my invaluable literary agent, deserves enormous credit for this book's birth. His dazzling intellect and warp-speed wit were needed, as was his unbounded concern for me as a writer and as a person.

Don's brother, Dr. Joseph L. Gastwirth, has always provided valuable support and kind words.

My cousins Toby Everett and Dr. Sheldon Scheinert have always been great friends as well as relatives. Their influence goes all the back to our early childhoods.

My in-laws, Harvey and Marsha Selib and Judi Marshall, and their children and grandchildren are wonderful examples of a warm extended family. Indeed, I want to thank all the members of my extended family.

My father, Fred Epstein, was always enthusiastic about my writing. His enormous musical skills didn't make the jump between generations, but at least the interest in music did.

This book is dedicated to my mother, Lillian Scheinert Epstein. She was the one who taught me — and many others — what kindness, wisdom, and love meant. I'm sure she listened to more Bob Dylan records than she wished to hear, but she always found a way to share my enthusiasm and provide a matchless model of what a parent should be.

My brother, Richard, hears all my concerns and always provides great and sage advice. Although he is two years younger than I am, Richard's memory is such that he recalls far more than I do. He provides much-needed and constant support. His wife, Perla, always listens to family tales with interest. I also thank their children: Adam, his wife, Jayne, and their family; and Sondra, her husband, Warren Cooperstein, and their family.

My own four children were particularly helpful with this book. My son, Michael, has the musical talent in the family. His musical knowledge and contacts through his band *The Motion Sick* were extremely helpful. His wife, Sophia Cacciola, provided many needed CDs. My daughter Elana provided CDs as well and on our walks together always listened to my concerns and offered helpful advice. Her husband, Justin Reiser, provided much-needed materials. As a writer herself, my daughter Rachel read my initial proposal and made many valuable suggestions. Her husband, John Eddey, and I have an ongoing conversation about the entertainment industry. My daughter Lisa is a great listener with a quick, creative mind. She knows how to encourage me.

My wife, Sharon, makes all I do possible. She hears all the good moments and the bad ones. She's there on the days when the words flow and on the days when they hide from me. Through it all, she provides constant guidance and loving encouragement. She and my family are the most beautiful music in my life.

Preface

It was the day before Thanksgiving in 1965. I had just arrived home with a new purchase after a dusty journey from college. I was primarily interested in literature, so I didn't buy too many records, but a couple of friends told me this guy Bob Dylan was special. With no knowledge of his work, I bought the album *The Times They Are A-Changin,'* packed it into my suitcase and went home. And so, though exhausted, I was eager to hear the album as soon as I arrived.

I put the record on the phonograph and sat down on the couch to listen. From the opening lines I knew I had entered a stunning and original world. I'm sure I tried my parents' patience that weekend as I played the songs over and over.

Bob Dylan got me interested in folk music. This book stems from that interest. In a way, for me at least, the book is about part of Dylan's musical and political genealogy. This is the story of the birth and growth of the folk world into which Bob Dylan was born and lived and partially left.

It is the story of how some of the greatest American folk singers desperately wanted their country to change in radical ways. They sang with fierce moral voices as they sought to relieve human suffering and transform what they saw as an uncaring society. They envisioned themselves as moral auditors for the angels. They charted the political and social health of America unflinchingly, providing their assessment of where it had gone right and, more commonly, where it was going wrong. They were widely considered to be free-spirited modern troubadours who achieved a special status as heroes in American society.

These folk singers wrote and sang politically charged songs. Woody

1

Guthrie wrote about the deported, the homeless, and the abandoned. Dylan wrote brutal attacks on war profiteers and those who practiced racial hatred or who cheated justice. Buffy St. Marie, Phil Ochs, and Peter, Paul and Mary, among others, sang songs that encouraged draft resistance during the Viet Nam War. Beyond singing, though, the folk singers also engaged in direct political activism. Guthrie and Pete Seeger, for example, helped organize unions and supported striking workers. Dylan sang at civil rights rallies and at benefits for other causes.

The folk singers saw themselves as the vanguard of a changing society. They envisioned a "Great Day Coming," as the title of one well-known folk song puts it, a day marked by the end of the economic inequalities of American life, the elimination of discrimination, and a saner, safer alternative to the Atomic Age, a day and a future guaranteed by people who saw themselves as part of one large communal effort to repair the world. They believed they could accomplish all this through their songs.

The folk singers offered calls to action for young and passionate audiences. The songs initiated conversations between people and their consciences.

But these guitar-toting idealists were not always heroic. Their legacy is more tangled.

Some of them had personal failures. Woody Guthrie, for example, frequently abandoned his family and sought the company of other women during his various marriages. Even his friends sometimes found him difficult to bear.

Additionally, in the 1930s and '40s the folk singers were either Communists or supporters of Communism. I use the term "Communist" throughout the book in as unemotional a way as I can. Terming them "Communists" is not meant to call them names or reduce them to supporters of some evil conspiracy or to ignore complex personalities that can't be understood if they are branded by a single, highly charged political term. I use the word "Communist" descriptively, and I hope I can provide clear reasons why they found in Communism a congenial home, why the horrible circumstances they found in an America suffering through the Great Depression compelled them to seek an alternate economic system. All they ever wanted was a better world for suffering people.

Some of their political insights were visionary, such as in their early, unpopular, and persistent efforts on behalf of civil rights for African Americans, or their genuine concerns for the poor and the mistreated, those unseen or tossed aside or injured by the rich and powerful. But how, I wondered, could those same decent people have supported Stalin, and what did that even mean at the time?

I also wanted to know how they wrote such great songs.

It soon became clear to me that understanding their politics and their music was contingent on understanding their personalities.

I therefore tried in this book to tell the story of these folk singers, to consider their personal circumstances including the complicated politics of their era. I write about their struggles with pain and loss, their songs and how those songs contributed to a developing art form, and how they reacted to the powerful people and institutions that stood in their way. At each point, I tried to tell this story to show it leading up to Bob Dylan and so, at various pertinent points, I illustrate the particular effects on him.

I wrote about how the folk music of rural people became popular through the efforts of the Carter Family and Jimmie Rodgers, about Joe Hill's arrest for a double murder and how the consequences of that arrest affected political music, about Woody Guthrie's attempt to discover the American character on the road and the songs he wrote to comfort the people he saw suffering, about Leadbelly getting out of prison because of a song he sang, about Alan Lomax lugging around a giant machine to record the voices of prisoners, about Pete Seeger's appearance before a congressional committee in search of Communist influences, about the reemergence of the popularity of folk music thanks to such artists as the Kingston Trio, Joan Baez, and Peter, Paul and Mary, about Bob Dylan finding folk music and his eventual angry break with the movement, and about the legacy of the great folk singers.

Why this book now? As a nation we have undergone such recent economic turmoil that it has become routine to compare our situation to that during the Great Depression. Many people are fearful, angry at the greedy on Wall Street, and concerned that our nation's leaders may not be capable of correcting the problems. This book tells the story of articulate artists struggling with just such emotions. A new political generation is emerging, one marked most prominently by the election of Barack Obama, a generation with different experiences and preconceptions, a generation with the idealism of those who have been excluded from power, the sense that the untried can't be worse than the tried. That generation will inevitably explore America's folk music heritage, seeking guidance for those who will write and sing the songs of the new world we are entering.

The book does not provide a complete background history of American folk music. Many significant artists are not included or only briefly mentioned. Many centers of folk music, such as Boston and Cambridge in Massachusetts or Chicago or Los Angeles are given insufficient attention.

Because the focus is specifically on the political or social content of folk music, some extremely talented musicians are not included. Additionally, the story in the book stops in the first months of 1966 when Dylan recorded his album *Blonde on Blonde*. For these reasons, such immensely talented songwriters as Leonard Cohen, Joni Mitchell, and Paul Simon are not discussed.

The political focus has another potential weakness. Woody Guthrie wrote and sang all kinds of songs, including an enormous number of delightful children's songs. Most of the songs Pete Seeger sang were not explicitly political but were drawn from America's great folk heritage. Alan Lomax, the collector and promoter of folk music, had vast musical interests beyond the overtly political music. In emphasizing the connection strictly between folk music and politics, that is, there is a danger of distorting these people's lives and their artistic contributions. Still, the political story is a valuable way to understand how audiences primarily perceived them and how they most profoundly affected their society. It is important, however, to keep their complexity in mind even as their political story is told to prevent thinking of them as caricatures.

Another ongoing problem in writing the book was that many observers had different perceptions. It is sometimes hard to separate the factual from the misremembered or the shaded for personal or political reasons. I've tried to present the facts as they made sense to me, but I realize others will have different memories, conceptions, or interpretations.

I also faced an ongoing dilemma in considering the subjects of the book as a single entity — folk singers — as though they were interchangeable, as though their idiosyncratic personalities could be easily reduced so they fit into some neat common definition. I proceed in the book in a dual track in order to deal with this problem. I describe the folk singers individually, especially those whose talent and influence surpassed others. In particular, Guthrie, Seeger, and Dylan emerge as the central subjects. The folk singers were influenced by the times they lived in and by the political and social views they held during the times I write about. It was difficult to write about their politics because the politics each had was not precisely identical to the politics of the others and because Guthrie and Seeger lived and acted in a social and political world that was partly overlapping but mostly different from a time in which Bob Dylan lived. Guthrie was a genial man filled with humor; his prairie socialism and Communism was different from Seeger's more studied, more ideological approach to politics in general and Communism in particular. Dylan's politics emerged from the personal and the raucous society of the 1960s. His politics were left-wing, at least for a crucial time in the early 1960s, but then he later rejected politics or had views scattered across the political spectrum.

It is also true that these individuals saw themselves as being part of the same leftist political tradition and the same musical tradition. The political tradition was rooted in faith in the common people of America and a view that their rights were important, that there needed to be a level playing field for the poor, that the rich and powerful too often ignored or exploited the poor, that the weak in society deserved to have a voice, and that those who adhered to this tradition intended to provide it in songs.

What differentiated the folk singers as a group, what separated their political tradition from liberal or progressive movements, is that most of them didn't believe the capitalist economic system could accomplish these goals. Their radical tradition called for fundamentally changing that system.

Their common political tradition explains their attachment to a common musical tradition, one that came from ordinary people.

Because of these shared traditions, I will include general comments about the folk singers as a group, always trying to be aware of the possibility of distorting them as individuals by offering a generalization that oversimplifies and is overly neat. I will write not only about their common outlook, social relations, and cooperation but also about their competition, rivalry, and conflict.

I also wanted to turn the spotlight around from the stage and focus it on the audiences who listened to the folk singers. I examined who those audiences were and tried to get at the reasons for their attraction to the singers and the complex, frequently emotionally intimate relationship that emerges between folk singers and audience members. The folk singers saw the audience members as potential new recruits or already determined radicals seeking renewal. But such a view made many of the folk singers oblivious to the changing musical tastes of American audiences. They were, for example, blindsided by the resurgence of rock and roll after the arrival of the Beatles in the United States. Dylan was the first to recognize the true implications of the new British sound.

The audience members themselves attended the concerts for various and complicated reasons. Some were there because they liked the tunes. Some saw themselves as rebels but could only act out that identity at a concert where they could separate the couple of hours there from reality and believe they were rebelling. Even the genuine radicals were frequently in transition within generations, going from immigrant to assimilated in the '30s and rebellious teenager to young adult in the '60s. The songs were useful for their stage in life. As they changed, many chose to keep the songs but separate them from the rebellion.

Finally, in addition to the singers and their audiences, their enemies played a major role in their story. These enemies included J. Edgar Hoover, Senator Joseph McCarthy, the House Committee on Un-American Activities (widely known as HUAC), various people and publications that sought to prevent them from getting employment, and people who picketed them or even physically attacked them.

If the folk singers made some political misjudgments, their enemies made mistakes as well. In general, all their enemies overreacted to the supposed threat the folk singers posed. The various people and groups that successfully sought to prevent the folk singers from working seriously miscalculated the long-term effects of their misguided efforts. The FBI sought to suppress dissent during war, but the folk singers were not spies or genuine dangers to American liberty. They were entertainers. HUAC went after entertainers primarily because doing so got them good press, not because such an effort aided the fight against Soviet spying.

These efforts by their enemies understandably made heroes out of the folk singers and provided an alternative narrative to the more troubling one involving their political views.

The story of the folk singers' attempt to change the United States is filled with wild characters and high drama.

I also want this book to be a celebration of folk singers and their songs. I want to entice readers to go to old records, to CDs, to Internet sites, and anywhere else they can go to hear the music I write about.

That is what I intended. But it is time to hear from the folk singers themselves. I hear the first chords of their music.

One

Music from the Mountains: The Birth of Popular Folk Music

Woody Guthrie was furious. He was about to be fired from the radio show he loved just for standing his ground, just for singing the songs that told the truth about the country. But Frank Burke, his boss, was angry. Burke had been upset since August when the Soviets signed a non-aggression pact with the Nazis and then became absolutely enraged when Hitler invaded Poland on September 1. Through the whole fall of 1939, Burke had warned Woody about singing those pro–Soviet songs. There were lots of great songs to sing, music from the people, the traditional songs.

Woody — it is a mark of his character and cultural imprint that it is awkward to address him as "Guthrie" — loved those old songs. He wasn't objecting to them as music. He had heard them as a child as his mother, Nora, cuddled him in her arms. Woody had learned that music could not only be about tragedy but also could cushion the pain itself. He had heard his mother singing plaintive Scotch and Irish ballads. She sang "Gypsy Davy," "Barbara Allen," and many other songs her own mother had taught her. Even as a child, as he would be for his entire life, Woody was attracted to rhymes. The unexpected affinities between two or more seemingly different words were enchanting. They provided an order missing from the mess and chaos of life. The rhymes hinted at an unseen place, a land of language, a retreat where fear was calmed by the distractions of beauty and order.

His mother's songs had put him to sleep and kept him cheerful. They stirred him with their sad tales of love gone wrong, or romantic outlaws, or bone-chilling recollections of natural disasters. Once Woody and Charley, his father, were in the yard when they heard the wind and watched as the whirling dust mixed with chicken feathers, rocks, and other loose material. Then the rain came sweeping across the sky and pelted them. Nora ran for a neighbor's storm cellar and called after Woody and Charley to go there too. Charley hoisted Woody on his shoulders and slowly made it to the cellar. The terrified Woody ran to his mother and begged her to sing "The Sherman Cyclone." As scary as the lyrics were, Woody felt his fear draining. Music could do that for him.

Charley also loved to sing when he worked. He enjoyed playing his banjo and guitar. The family gathered around the piano and, as Nora played, they all sang the lonesome cowboy wails and the soul-saving gospel tunes. It wasn't long before Woody began creating words to the songs and hearing tunes in all the sounds around him.

The folk music his parents sang and that Woody began to sing himself was simple music created anonymously and played by and for common people. The music was most often performed together by family or community members rather than presented to an audience. Folk songs were transmitted through sheet music, broadsides, and songsters, but mostly they were memorized and passed along orally. Inevitably, the traditional songs were changed in the transmission to mirror the circumstances, such as occupation and social reality, of the singer.

That oral transmission inherently included a filtering process. The ballads that survived were characteristically under an octave so that most people could sing them. They had to be memorable both to entertain and to ease passing them along. To aid the memory, the ballads told terse stories in a telegraphic style with one major plot point of the lyric leading almost immediately to the next without meandering or including extraneous elements. The images had to be vivid, the characters recognizable. The inflection of the voice, the facial expressions, the physical gestures, and the tone the singers put in their voices all worked with the guitar or other instrument for an overall performance.

Those accompanying instruments were crucial. Six-string guitars had originated in southern Europe in the late 1700s and quickly found their way to America. After the guitars became mass-produced, they were cheap enough for southern musicians to afford them. Along with the traditional fiddle and banjo, the guitar became a standard instrument. Some scholars think black railroad workers traveling throughout the South spread the guitar's popularity. The guitar was a crucial addition because the sound was rhythmically attractive and soft enough to allow singers to accompany the instrument. While any noise-making object (pipes, drums, flutes, washboards, mandolins, whistles, and so on) was used in the South to make music, the guitar and banjo developed as the most popular.

Beyond the ballads from the British Isles, American folk music had another crucial source. The black slaves who had forcibly been kidnapped and taken to America brought with them their own music and a formative version of both banjo and drums. The spirituals, field hollers, and work songs — all created before emancipation — were in the air.

The spirituals were a prototype of protest songs in their yearning for freedom from enslavement such as in their identification with the Hebrew slaves in Egypt. Songs like "Swing Low Sweet Chariot" were used as signals that all was clear when slaves sought to escape. "Wade in the Water" was a virtual how-to guide to evading re-capture after the escape.

The traditional folk music Woody heard from his family was not commercial and so was not copyrighted. It stood in direct contrast to popular music, which was intended to be sold to a particular audience for a profit and was made available through mass media, most particularly the phonograph and radio. The invention of such media was the gateway to making the folk music the Guthries and other rural families loved widely available.

On December 22, 1877, the *Scientific American* reported that thirty-year-old telegraph-operator-turned-inventor Thomas Alva Edison had invented a machine that could mimic natural sound. However, it wasn't until the Edison Standard Phonograph, costing $20, was introduced in 1898 that average Americans began in large numbers to buy this piece of musical magic for their homes. They had become used to the contraption in various hotel lobbies, saloons, and phonograph parlors where, for a nickel placed in the slot, they could hear a musical number. Now that the phonographs were widely available, people wanted songs that spoke to their everyday needs, their romantic dreams, and their troubled lives.

People turned to the tunes of Tin Pan Alley, music specifically aimed at urban, economically secure, white America. It was widely assumed that the poor whites who lived in rural America and the even poorer blacks simply would not buy enough records to make such products commercially viable. The country folks, having no popular songs aimed at them, relied for their music on singing at home, in houses of worship, in smoky bars, private parties, stage shows, and county fairs.

Then radios became widespread in the 1920s, and suddenly the music business almost died. Sales dramatically flattened as people gathered around the new technological marvel. After all, the music on radio sounded much clearer than on a phonograph. Additionally, the radio was far more convenient — listeners didn't have to jump up every few minutes to change a radio as they did a record. And, best of all, once a radio was bought, all the music on it was free.

Record companies, in an understandable panic, had to rethink their entire sense of marketing. A desperate idea emerged: instead of creating large numbers of records for a rapidly disappearing mass audience, they would create a more limited number of records for a carefully defined, more numerically limited audience. Most critically, they had to look for new record buyers with musical tastes radio music couldn't satisfy.

Two identifiable previously overlooked audiences — blacks and poor whites — were suddenly attractive consumers. But the companies faced a continuing problem: how to label the new music. The music for blacks was called "race" music. The music for poor whites was called "hillbilly" music.

Having latched onto what they considered a clever marketing gimmick, the companies suddenly found themselves in desperate need of artists to perform on the records.

The companies developed a method to identify local talent. Scouts recorded local musicians and forwarded the best material to the companies that might then sign the singers to a recording contract. One such scout found himself in Bristol, Tennessee, on a hot August day in 1927.

In many ways, modern American culture was born in 1927. It was the year Babe Ruth swatted sixty home runs, Charles Lindbergh flew solo across the Atlantic, *The Jazz Singer* became the cultural boundary between silent and sound films, Norma Talmadge and Douglas Fairbanks stepped in the wet concrete outside what was then known as Graumann's Chinese Theater and the tradition of hand and footprints outside the theater was started, the Harlem Globetrotters were organized, the Academy of Motion Picture Arts and Sciences was founded, and Sacco and Vanzetti were executed. In music, the year was equally momentous. The poet Carl Sandburg published *The American Songbag*, the first popular collection of folk songs. The year 1927 was also the year that the great modern founders of popular country music — the Carter Family and Jimmie Rodgers — were discovered.

Woody Guthrie loved the new commercial music. And the Carter Family and Jimmie Rodgers were the ones who affected him the most. They showed that poor folks could sing and record and find a big audience. Before them, Woody's notion of singing just involved doing so for family and friends. But they provided a crucial vision of a wider world for Woody.

A.P. Carter lived in Poor Valley, Virginia, in the shadow of Clinch Mountain. It was a place as tough as its name. In the middle of the Roaring Twenties, Poor Valley was isolated from the flappers and the Fitzgeralds. The mountain folk were patriots, in part because however poor they were no one could take their country from them. They were willing to work hard and suffer in quiet dignity because of their optimism that each day would be better and their certainty of reaching Heaven as a final reward after their hardscrabble life. They had God and family, and so had no need for politics and big speeches like the city folks did.

A.P. was a lonely, stubborn, driven man with a tremor that caused his hand to shake for his whole life. He also had a quiver in his voice, a distinctive sound revealingly called a "tear." He wandered by himself, always thinking of music that somehow could heal his loneliness. He loved the music from the mountains, the stories of salvation from above and love while on Earth, the plaintive tales of the forgotten, the criminal, the cowboy, the killer, and the fighter. He wanted to bring the music down from the mountains into the lives of others.

His wife, Sara, had been orphaned before she was five. She intuitively grasped the pain in the ballads A.P. collected and sang them with an unforgettable voice. But, unlike her husband, she did not want a musical career. She had none of A.P.'s restlessness or drive and instead wanted a quiet home life.

Maybelle Carter was Sara's first cousin besides being married to A.P.'s brother. Maybelle had an extraordinarily distinctive self-taught guitar-playing style — known eventually as the Carter Scratch — which sounded as though two guitars were playing together, one doing a melody and the other chords.

It was August 1, 1927, and the next few days turned out to be the most important ones in the history of what later came to be called country music. Ralph Peer, on a search for hillbillies who could sell records and make him money, listened carefully to the Carter Family and was deeply impressed by the clarity of A.P.'s bass voice and even more by Sara's incredible lead vocals. A woman singing lead was itself amazing, and the exciting way the sixteen-year-old Maybelle — eight months pregnant — worked her guitar fascinated him. The group's touching harmony came through as it rendered "The Poor Orphan Child" and three other songs. The next day they recorded a couple of other songs, including "Single Girl, Married Girl."

Ralph Peer had known the moment he heard Sara's voice that he had a gold mine. He made sure the traditional songs that A.P. gathered and re-worked were copyrighted in A.P.'s name. Peer eventually started a music publishing company and made a lot of money by attracting singers who wrote their own songs. The ability to write the songs, therefore, made even a great singing talent much more attractive. This business fact was crucial in the emergence of later folk singers.

The Carter Family's simple renditions, the care with which they collected the songs from back porches and open fields, and the genuine love of the music which came through on every take gained them a huge following and made their influence seminal.

Their timeless lyrics were unflinching in the depiction of an orphan's pain, the treachery of unfaithful lovers, the endless expanse of lonely nights, the despair accompanying an empty wallet, and the hell created by living with an uncaring partner. Their message was crucial for their times. Suffering through the Great Depression, the Carter Family's audience could feel the pain virtually coming through on the records or the radio. The Carter Family felt so much pain but had so much religious faith that they gave audience members a hope for Heaven and emotional permission to express their own pain unabashedly.

While the Carter Family are considered among the founders of country music, they are also a crucial part of the folk music tradition. The term "folk music" has several different meanings. First, it refers to the traditional or roots music that the Carter Family sang. "Folk music" later became associated with people who sang songs with political or social importance. The old folk songs the Carter Family sang were then separated from that political folk tradition and considered country music. But the early folk singers, folk collectors, and audiences sang, gathered, and listened to the folk songs sung by people like the Carter Family. Popular folk music just like popular country music begins with them.

In particular for folk music history, the Carter Family made the vocals in the song as prominent if not more so than the instrumental backing, whereas in the old-time music they inherited the vocals were of secondary importance.

Two days after recording the Carter Family, Peer was still in Bristol when he recorded a thin young man a month away from his thirtieth birthday but already struggling against the tuberculosis that would kill him in just six years. Jimmie Rodgers, who had worked as a brakeman on the railroad until his health forced him to focus on singing as a seemingly less strenuous vocation, only had one original song. Still, Peer was impressed by the voice, especially that distinctive yodel, and the promise the young man made that he had plenty of songs within him aching to come out.

Rodgers was friendly and optimistic, filled with the Southern oral traditions, and its racial language. Indeed, he performed in blackface and developed an incredible talent to sound black. He couldn't read music, but the raw authenticity of his voice was unwavering. He also was a hard worker, struggling with his sister-in-law, Elsie McWilliams, to craft the right words and the right sound. If Rodgers needed help in writing the songs, he was nevertheless an editorial genius. He knew what worked when he heard it.

Rodgers was nicknamed "The Singing Brakeman." The former job was part of his allure. The railroad train was a potent symbol of freedom, its whistle a plaintive sound of escape for those trapped in a backbreaking job or soul-breaking marriage. His job on the railroad had put him into contact with the young, desperate hoboes who sought refuge in the boxcars. It made him a constant traveler and added to an already restless spirit. Despite the job, though, he always was a neat dresser and, perhaps to offset the incredible smells he encountered, he took to carrying a small flask of perfume in his vest.

Rodgers carefully crafted a hard-bitten persona. He created "Jimmie Rodgers." People who listened to his records had the impression that Jimmie Rodgers was always hungry for an eager woman and a speeding sundown, that his wife spent time with too many shiftless rounders. Rodgers sang about being in jail, gambling, parental love, and all kinds of romantic relationships. Like A.P. Carter, Rodgers made the lyrics crucial. Audiences didn't even mind that Jimmie Rodgers had a taste for fancy cars and expensive hotels. They wished they were in his place. Finally, audiences had great sympathy for him because of his tuberculosis. Rodgers's death of the disease in 1933 at the age of 35 only added to his legend.

People listened as Rodgers painted a picture of hope. But he didn't sing about Heaven; his paradisal destination was California, where the water tasted just like cherry wine. People sat on their porches nodding, as though Jimmie knew a hard-bitten life firsthand and could be counted on to be honest about California. His alluring description of the state convinced many to head there to live.

Between them, the Carter Family and Jimmie Rodgers defined country music's roots and almost by themselves transformed what became country music into a major business. Additionally, they ended the long tradition of anonymity among folk song's creators and transmitters. They had names and faces. Just as American audiences had discovered stars among actors, so a uniquely American quest to crown the famous turned to folk music.

But however famous the Carter Family or Jimmie Rodgers became, neither wrote explicitly political material. The Carter Family music was personal, familial, and communal. The woes they sang about stemmed from the human heart, not from the economic system of the country. Similarly, Jimmie Rodgers stayed away from broad social issues. The only possible exception in Rodgers is in what is generally considered his first song "The Soldier's Sweetheart," in which Rodgers wrote about ending the "awful" war in Germany. This song was written after Rodgers's friend Sammy Williams was killed in France. The loss did not move Rodgers to adopt any political positions, so it seems clear that this song was because of an isolated harsh emotional experience and did not lead to the development of a political ideology that injected itself into his songs.

Indeed, it makes more sense to see the Carter Family especially as part of a conserving tradition, one that sought to maintain family and communal values from the onslaught of the Jazz Age. It is unsurprising, therefore, that Henry Ford, a social reactionary, was attracted to American folk music. He saw the music as a way to return to the era before Jewish and other immigrants had adversely affected the American Anglo-Saxon culture, before modern art and dance and music corrupted the country. Ford organized a dance orchestra and fiddling contests. He recorded mountain folk music. He suggested to Thomas Edison that the inventor record square dance music. Ford could not foresee how the folk music he considered as conserving older traditions would be embraced and used by the radical political left.

But most people listening to the Carter Family and Jimmie Rodgers did not think of the songs as political in any way. Instead, the Carters and Rodgers (along with blues singers aiming at black audiences) allowed ordinary people, people without power, money, or influence in the society, the chance to hear their emotions expressed through art. It was a heady experience, and they reacted by buying a lot of records. The descendants of slaves, along with farmers, cowboys, sailors, and many others, rejoiced in hearing their feelings put into songs.

Commercial music in some sense stole musical traditions for a profit. But doing so also preserved the songs by making them widely available. Freezing the flowing stream of traditions and making these traditions commercial allowed the songs to be examined and to be mixed with other styles. Woody Guthrie was among those who listened to and absorbed the new songs.

But the memorable melodies and the stirring stories were not enough for him. As he traveled, he saw despairing people living under bridges. He shuddered as the cries of starving children shook his conscience. As much as he loved those old songs, they told of private pain, not the widespread agony he witnessed. They were not enough for him anymore. History had given him new stories, and he had to sing about them.

But Woody didn't abandon those traditional songs from his family or the phonograph or radio. He took their melodies and reworked them, writing new lyrics to describe the harsh world he saw.

As he had traveled and wrote his songs Woody had learned of another songwriter, someone who took familiar tunes and applied tough-minded political lyrics to them. Joe Hill reinforced Woody's own musical instincts. The Carter Family and Rodgers had taught him it was possible for someone like him to sing songs for a wide audience. Joe Hill taught him that he could write hard-edged lyrics. Hill's work was a rougher music, stirring those who lived in squalor and struggled to find work. Hill looked for a language to describe the degrading lives these workers led. He deliberately wrote provocative songs from the gutter. The songs were sung on

17

the picket lines and in the union halls. They ripped the lies off the pretty picture painted by Tin Pan Alley and took music into the grittiest city streets and the most despairing hobo camps.

Joe Hill's political kind of songwriting tugged at Woody with urgent immediacy.

The story of Joe Hill's fame and influence began with a double murder.

Two

Music from the Gutter: Joe Hill and the Roots of Twentieth-Century Political Music

John Morrison hauled a sack of potatoes down the center aisle of his small grocery store in Salt Lake City. His seventeen-year-old son, Arling, wearily swept the floor. Another son, thirteen-year-old Merlin, headed to the storeroom in the back of the store. It was almost ten P.M. on a Saturday evening, January 10, 1914, and the Morrisons were preparing to close for the evening.

Suddenly two gunmen dashed inside. Their felt hats hung loosely over their foreheads and red bandanas covered their faces. Both waved pistols. One of the gunmen immediately screamed out and shot the elder Morrison, who fell behind the counter. The gunman then briskly strode across to the counter, leaned over its edge, and shot John Morrison a second time.

The startled Merlin hid behind shelves in back, sticking his head out to witness the horrific scene. Arling grabbed the revolver kept in the icebox, ran over to the scales, and fired, wounding one of the bandits. The gunmen then turned to face the young man and coolly shot him three times before fleeing without taking any money.

Merlin dashed out from his hiding place and hysterically dialed the police. His father had formerly been on the force, and so the response was quick.

Arling died immediately, but somehow John was still alive. He was rushed to the hospital at the police station but died shortly after he arrived.

19

The police meanwhile had to deal with a single, young eyewitness in shock. He wasn't sure exactly what happened as he told the story and, over time, changed details of the crime repeatedly. He wasn't even certain that his brother had fired a shot, but a weapon was located next to Arling and the weapon's chamber had an empty cartridge. No bullet was ever found in the store, leading police to accept the version that the killer had been shot and left the store with the bullet in him.

Sometime between 11 and 11:30 that night, a man named Joseph Hillstrom, also known as Joe Hill, pounded on the door of Dr. Frank McHugh. The doctor, a Socialist, had met Hill and was aware of his membership in the radical group known as the IWW, the Industrial Workers of the World, or Wobblies, and his stirring, funny song parodies. The doctor screamed, wanting to know who was knocking at that late hour. Hill said he had been in an accident.

The doctor examined Hill, who had a bullet wound in his chest. The bullet had entered Hill on his left side and exited near the shoulder blade. Both shirt and undershirt were soaked with blood.

Hill told the doctor that he and a friend had gotten into a fight over Hill's supposed insult of his friend's wife. The friend had shot Hill but was sorry, and Hill said he didn't want to involve the police.

Dr. McHugh began helping Hill get his clothes back on when a revolver still in its holster slipped out of Hill's clothing onto the floor. The stunned doctor did not get a good look at the weapon and did not ask about it. After attending to the wound, the doctor arranged for Hill to be driven home. On the journey, Hill threw the revolver away.

Several days later McHugh returned from a trip and read about the murders on the same night he had patched Joe Hill. McHugh alerted the police, who arrested Hill for homicide.

That arrest and Joe Hill's subsequent trial and execution made the wandering laborer world famous. To some his name would go down as a cold-blooded killer aligned with an anarchist movement devoted to destroying America. To others he was a martyr, an innocent, hard-working, brilliant songwriter railroaded for his political views. Somewhat lost in this tug-of-war over the real Joe Hill was his significant contribution to American music and politics.

The man eventually known as Joe Hill was born Joel Hägglund in Sweden on October 7, 1879. After Hill's mother died in 1902, he and a brother immigrated to the United States. Hill became a vagabond, wandering the land and finding jobs where he could. He was a factory worker in Chicago and a longshoreman in California. He fought in the Mexican revolution and loaded sugar in Hawaii. He was in San Francisco for the 1906 earthquake. He changed his name, perhaps like some others to evade an employer's blacklist of workers who might cause trouble.

He joined thousands of other hoboes moving from town to town searching for some wages and a temporary home. Being a hobo was not the romantic life that was sometimes portrayed. The hoboes had their own culture. They, like Gypsies, left signs on a wall or fence to tell the next hobo coming along what to expect at a particular place. An X, for example, meant "all clear." An open hand indicated the people there were friendly. The hoboes also had their own language. A lot of that language involved trains, their main means of transportation. A "peddler" was a slow freight or local train, one easier than others to hop. To "flip" was to jump on a moving train. Jumping off such a train was called "hitting the grit." "Bumpers" were the riding space between freight cars.

The hoboes wandering across America could not always find work. Hungry, angry, and in despair, some of them turned to begging and others joined together to commit crimes, typically robbery. Whether Hill was ever involved in such activities or not, by the time of his arrest he had two scars on the right side of his face (possibly from fights), one scar on the back of his right forearm, and another on the left side of his neck. His tall, tough body was a battleground of the class war in which he volunteered to fight.

Hill was a quiet man. He didn't smoke or drink — believing the sale of liquor to be a scheme by the capitalist class to poison workers — but was renowned for his ability to cook Chinese food. He wasn't attracted to Lincoln Logs or Ouija Boards or ballroom dancing, all popular during the second decade of the 20th century. He famously didn't like discussing his own background, speaking instead even to his buddies only about organizing workers into One Big Union. He saw life as a brutal struggle, and the IWW provided a community and a channel through which that struggle could be undertaken. The intense hatred toward social inequalities filtered through the vision provided by the IWW may also have provided Hill with a justification for illegal activities. Harry K. "Mac" McClintock, a Wobbly who knew Hill and admired him, nevertheless claimed he was a thief: "I believe he was a crook and made a lot of scores."[1]

Joe Hill's America was brimming with economic distress and worker unrest. The country's rapid industrialization, the unhealed scars and demographic losses of the Civil War, the immigration of millions of poor workers at the end of the 19th and beginning of the 20th centuries, the economic dislocations — such as the Panic of 1893 — and enormous gap between the wealthy and the poor all led to social discontent.

This gap between rich and poor was especially stark. Workers labored for 60 to 80 hours a week. In the last part of the 19th century, the average wage was $10–12 for that long week, or about $500 a year. Andrew Carnegie earned $25 million in 1900. By 1910–1920, the wage had risen to $750 a year — when there was work. Approximately 2,150,000 Americans were unemployed, often replaced by machines. The top-fifth of the country lived comfortably, while the bottom four-fifths barely survived. There were 92,407,000 Americans who had a life expectancy of 48.4 years if they were male and 51.8 years if they were female. Thirty million people a week attended movies, but the cinematic romances didn't seduce them; only one in a thousand marriages ended in divorce.

The workers looked for a political alternative to loosen the industrial vise squeezing them. The Socialists sought the workers' support, though they were themselves splintered. Some, like Eugene V. Debs, believed in the American political system and that progressive reforms could ameliorate the deplorable lives of workers. Other Socialists did not believe there could be a compromise between workers and capitalists and therefore called for a change in the society itself. Both of these groups organized workers into unions (2.1 million Americans were union members in the 1910s). Strikes were the favored means of confronting labor problems. There were 1,204 strikes during the decade.

Still other radicals, including the Industrial Workers of the World, believed that dividing the workers by craft into separate unions didn't make sense and that there should be a single union to confront capitalism. The IWW members were nicknamed Wobblies. The "Wobbly" designation, by oral tradition, came from a Chinese restaurant owner in Alberta, Canada, who enjoyed his IWW customers enough to say, in broken English, that "Eye Like Eye Wobbly Wobbly."

The Wobblies favored direct action — including strikes, propaganda, boycotts, sabotage, and physical confrontation — to make workers' lives decent. They were opposed to any political actions, putting their faith instead in general strikes. They argued against all collective bargaining agreements, seeing such contracts as simply surrendering to the capitalists.

The Wobblies were fighting against machines as much as they were fighting against their bosses. Indeed, the word "sabotage" comes from the French "sabot." "Sabotage" became a word either when workers threw a wooden shoe (sabot) into machinery to wreck it or when workers cut the wood (also named sabot) that connected a railroad line to its ties.

Joe Hill supported active damage and consciously withholding hard work and efficiency as vital means to express worker discontent. He joined the IWW sometime around 1910. The Wobblies reflected his view of human nature, clear from the letters he wrote in prison and his songs.

For example, in a 1914 letter Hill wrote: "Self-preservation is, or should be, the first law of nature. The animals, when in a natural state, are showing us the way. When they are hungry they will always try to get something to eat or else they will die in the attempt."[2] In an earlier letter, Hill had said that human nature was simply "animal instinct"[3] and could not be changed. In a January 1915 letter he wrote: "The thing the matter with the 'Underdog' today is that he has drifted too far away from nature. The instinct that forces the animals of the jungle to make a bee line for the eats when hungry, has been chloroformed almost to death in the underdog by civilization and any old thing that has a tendency to arouse the instinct would be beneficial to the revolutionary movement."[4]

But what really made the IWW attractive to Joe Hill was its particular approach to music.

During the 1910s, when Joe Hill was writing his song parodies, American music focused on the most popular trend of the era — ballroom dancing. Restaurants even started to put in dance floors. Audiences loved "Alexander's Ragtime Band," "You Made Me Love You," and "Danny Boy," among others.

For the Wobblies and other radical union members, though, such music was anathema. They focused on singing rousing political songs such as the "Internationale."

Like many other organizations, the IWW tried to spread its message. Mostly it used stickers, leaflets, and pamphlets. But the Wobblies also used songs to buoy spirits on a picket line, raise money at their meetings, steel themselves at trials or in jail, or feel as one in a union hall or a meeting.

They sang in boxcars as they traveled. They sang in fields and bunkhouses, behind bars or standing on soapboxes.

Songs of protest were not new with the Wobblies. Such songs had appeared as early as the Revolutionary War when William Billings adapted tunes from famous hymns to provide new patriotic, anti–British lyrics. The Hutchinson family, among others, wandered the country during the 1840s singing songs for women's suffrage and temperance and against slavery. And there were labor songs, almost all of which used a familiar tune with words adapted to the particular struggle.

For the Wobblies, though, songs were a particularly potent means of organizing, for the songs united workers who spoke different languages and came from different countries. The core Wobbly idea of One Big Union by definition required a unity that transcended national, racial, and religious differences. Such a unity was uniquely found in music.

The Wobblies used a song card, a four-page brochure, in which they printed songs of revolution such as "The Marseillaise" or "The Red Flag" and which they sold for a nickel. New songs became popular and were added, soon making a bulging brochure.

A Wobbly named James H. Walsh not only fostered the creation of the first *Little Red Song Book* (1909) with its distinctive red cover, but he also developed a way to respond to the Salvation Army. The Army frequently was hired to disrupt IWW street meetings with loud music. Walsh had a simple idea: use the music against the Army by composing new lyrics. Mocking Salvation Army songs had its origin in burlesque theaters, and migrant workers frequently went to churches for meals accompanied by hymns, so Walsh knew his audience would recognize the songs and laugh at the very attempt to satirize them. Additionally, music was the means of entertainment workers were familiar with in the era before inexpensive movies, radios, and the still-novel phonograph.

Joe Hill's Wobbly songs were more cynical than those of other songwriters. He thought workers weren't very smart and needed to be informed in a way that reached them. As he wrote in a 1914 letter to the Wobbly periodical *Solidarity*: "A pamphlet, no matter how good, is never read more than once, but a song is learned by heart and repeated over and over; and I maintain that if a person can put a few cold, common sense facts into a song, and dress them [the facts] up in a cloak of humor to take the dryness off of them, he will succeed in reaching a great number of workers who are too unintelligent or too indifferent to read a pamphlet or an editorial on economic science."[5] He believed that workers needed to be manipulated to emancipate themselves. In a 1915 letter he compared them to slaves who resisted efforts to be free.

Hill's patronizing attitudes, in part at least, were grounded in reality. Many of the workers were immigrants. A quarter of immigrants were illiterate and most of the others had to struggle with English. It was much easier for them to sing songs that could be easily learned and that could be sung boisterously to release the turbulent emotions they felt. The relatively sedate experience of reading would not meet their emotional needs. They knew they were hungry, and they needed to tell the world about it.

However he had to do it, Hill was determined to inflame the workers to fight the capitalists at every turn by creating simple, repetitive songs based on popular tunes.

The songs, he knew, were one of the few weapons at his disposal to fight the far more powerful bosses. Hill was discovering the crucial insight that guided generations of political songwriters and singers: American audiences could be moved, influenced, and roused to political action by song better than any other way. Songs could be written with a message and be entertaining. Such songs affected people emotionally and got them to see a better world and to undertake actions and confront powerful people when their common sense might otherwise inhibit such behavior. Songs could create heroes and brand villainous opponents. Songs could band people together to make them feel that they were not alone, that united they could accomplish what they couldn't do individually.

Joe Hill was writing for hoboes and workers. Typically, they had little education and poor job skills; they were Emma Lazarus's "wretched refuse" floating down America's mainstream. They had no political allies or abilities on their own to garner political support. For them, the songs were their only hope and only weapon. It took decades before protest songs, cloaked in folk music tunes and commercially available, found audiences that were larger and more educated.

The precise order of some of Hill's compositions is not clear. "The Preacher and the Slave," his popular parody of "In the Sweet Bye and Bye" was included in the 1911 edition of the *Little Red Song Book*. Hill wandered into the IWW Hall in Portland, Oregon, one day in the fall of 1910 already carrying the song. There were Wobbly Halls in many Western cities that provided a place for the drifting workers, a stove to heat some Mulligan stew, and, invariably, a collection of songbooks or books by such authors as Marx, Darwin, or Tom Paine.

Hill gave the song to the secretary of the IWW local branch, and this secretary gave it to Mac McClintock, a Wobbly busker, or wandering entertainer. McClintock began singing and the place erupted. After some revision, the song was turned into a leaflet and during the local's second street meeting McClintock became the first singer to offer the song in public. The local made $30 by selling the pamphlets for a dime each. Soon the song found its way into the IWW songbook.

"The Preacher and the Slave" — the street corner evangelist and the struggling worker — were, in Hill's view, in direct conflict. The preachers, he wrote, ignore the hungry, promising salvation instead.

Hill's attack on religious figures was typical for him. He believed that bosses on their own couldn't withstand the united working class. The capitalists survived, in Hill's view, only because they were helped not only by preachers or Salvation Army bands but also by scabs who crossed picket lines to work and by indifferent workers. It was those who enabled the capitalists who irked Hill the most because he thought that either they had chosen indifference over action or were on the wrong side in the great struggle. Precisely because the capitalist couldn't be persuaded, Hill focused his tough-minded satire on those he thought might be shamed or convinced by his songs.

Joe Hill wanted women to be in charge of organizing other women. He thought women were even more exploited than male workers and saw them as willing to fight for the cause. As Hill wrote in a letter supporting the enrollment of women into the revolutionary struggle: "The idea is to establish a kind of social feeling of good fellowship between the male and female workers, that would give them a little foretaste of our future society and make them more interested in the class struggle and the overthrow of the old system of corruption."[6]

These attitudes were reflected in several of his songs. In "The White Slave," for example, Hill writes of a procurer who approaches a young woman who worked in a laundry but who has to sleep in the cold on a park bench. Promising her money, the man lures the woman into a life of prostitution. As the song continues, five years have passed, and the woman's health has vanished.

Hill even found a living embodiment of his model for women revolutionaries in Elizabeth Gurley Flynn, a rousing speaker and tireless organizer for the IWW. She visited him in prison and corresponded with him. In her honor, Hill wrote "The Rebel Girl" as a tribute to the working woman.

Hill also wrote anti-war songs and romantic ones, among others, but the biting satires were the most popular and enduring. That is, Joe Hill was widely known among the Wobblies at the time of his arrest. He soon became an international figure.

Hill's trial began on June 10, 1914. The Wobblies were convinced that a grand conspiracy had been organized to convict Hill, and indeed there was widespread anti-union sentiment in Utah at the time of the trial. Additionally, the evidence used to convict Hill was circumstantial and weak. A key witness may have been coached.

Hill had frequent opportunities to explain his gunshot wound. His defenders noted that it was not even certain that the weapon in the store had been fired, but, if it had been, the bullet would have been in the killer's body because if it had exited it would have been found in the store. However, when Dr. McHugh examined him, Hill had no bullet still in his body. Several witnesses at the trial did testify that Hill's appearance was similar to a man they had seen entering the store. One witness even claimed to recognize Hill's scars. This powerful testimony might be considered conclusive except that these witnesses had a similar chance to identify Hill both when he was arrested and at his preliminary hearing and had not. That is, their statements changed in a way that hurt Hill. Finally, there was another suspect in the case, in some ways a suspect more plausible than Hill. Frank Z. Wilson had recently been released from prison. John Morrison had once arrested him. The police originally thought the John Morrison killing was for revenge, especially since no money was taken. Additionally, using a photograph for identification, one witness claimed to have seen Wilson on a streetcar and bent over, perhaps drunk or perhaps in pain from a bullet. When the police arrested Hill, they originally thought he was Wilson. After Hill's arrest, the police ceased to search for Wilson, who was never located.

Given these inconsistencies and clear potentially exculpatory evidence — all of which raise reasonable doubt — it is fair to wonder why the jury convicted Hill. First of all, the jury couldn't believe that an innocent man wouldn't simply provide an alibi for the time of the shootings and an explanation for the wound. No one ever went to authorities to provide such an explanation — no woman who was the supposed object of Hill's attention and no man who supposedly shot him. The jury evidently found it impossible to believe that — given Hill's impending death sentence — such witnesses wouldn't come forward. The jury looked at the other evidence: Hill's gun that dropped while he was being examined and his choice to throw the weapon away. Lastly, Hill had said he wanted to take the stand to prove his innocence, and then when he had the chance refused to do so. That looked deeply suspicious to the jury.

But there were extra-judicial factors at work as well. Hill was a member of the Wobblies, by all accounts a radical group. He was an immigrant in an era when immigrants were deeply mistrusted. He was a vagabond when living in one community to raise a family was the norm.

Whatever the mix of all these in their thinking, it took only a few hours on June 27 for the jury to find Joe Hill guilty and sentence him to execution. On July 8, the judge wanted to know if Hill preferred death by hanging or rifle fire. Hill responded: "I'll take shooting. I'm used to that. I have been shot a few times in the past, and I guess I can stand it again."[7]

As Hill sought a new trial and new counsel made a motion for one, the Wobbly bard stayed in jail and wrote more songs.

At first, Hill did not want to involve the IWW in his case, thinking any money raised for his defense could be better used elsewhere. However, by mid–April 1914, Hill changed his mind and the union began to inform its members of Hill's plight and to raise funds.

Once Hill was convicted, though, the Wobblies began efforts in earnest. They urged members to write to Utah's governor for a new trial. Perhaps because of Hill's popularity as a songwriter or the seeming inadequacy of the evidence or the romantic aspects of Hill's refusal to name the woman he claimed could save him or a combination of these and other reasons, the response was immediate and widespread. Wobblies and then others began sending in letters of appeal and contributing to the defense fund.

Meanwhile, Joe Hill prepared to die. He sent a telegram to the Wobbly organizer "Big Bill" Haywood: "Don't waste time mourning — organize!" In the same telegram he asked Haywood to have him buried outside the state that was going to execute him because "I don't want to be found dead in Utah."[8]

Hill was taken from his cell early on the morning of November 19, 1915. He sat outside on a chair and was strapped down. A target was placed over his heart. Five men with rifles faced him. Four of them had live bullets and one weapon contained a blank.

The sheriff began the proceedings. "Aim!"

Joe Hill screamed out to his executioners: "Yes, aim. Let her go. Fire!"[9]

The sheriff ordered the men to fire.

Joe Hill was pronounced dead at 7:42 A.M.

Hill's body was sent to a Salt Lake City funeral home where it was viewed by large numbers of supporters. Haywood arranged for the body to be shipped to Chicago where three thousand people attended the funeral services.

Hill's body was cremated. One year to the day after the execution, Haywood gave away envelopes containing small amounts of Hill's ashes. Eventually the ashes were scattered in 47 states — all that were then part of the United States except for Utah — as well as in all countries of South America and in parts of Europe and Asia.

Joe Hill had died, but his legend had been born.

The person most responsible for Joe Hill's legend was Joe Hill himself. Even the use of the name "Joe Hill" as opposed to other names he had used was a shrewd calculation for it was an easy name to remember and more euphonious than his real name. At some point he realized — with complete accuracy — that he could have a powerful effect on the labor movement as a dead martyr believed to have been murdered by a conspiratorial group of religious figures, bosses, and the unyielding power of the state. This was not a martyr complex on Hill's part; he made a rational calculation of how to use his own life on the IWW's behalf. In effect "Joe Hill" was an identity he created in prison: a victim, a man who would die before betraying a woman's honor or bowing to an unjust legal system, a man languishing in jail, losing weight, hoping for help from other workers. Grafted onto his songs, this romantic image was irresistible for the IWW speakers and organizers who portrayed Hill as a doomed victim of the system the Wobblies wanted to replace. The various political and legal blunders by Utah authorities supplemented Hill's conscious efforts and the IWW's political calculations.

In death, Joe Hill transcended his own existence and became a symbol for his followers of how society railroaded working stiffs, how an artist was assassinated by the cruel taskmasters of capitalist society. People sang his songs and felt anger at authorities who, if they framed Hill, could frame any honest worker.

Sometime around 1930, a writer named Alfred Hayes — who later received an Academy Award nomination for co-writing the script for the Italian neo-realist film *Paisan* — composed a poem titled "I Dreamed I Saw Joe Hill Last Night." During the summer of 1936, Hayes was a staff member at Camp Unity, a Wingdale, New York, retreat run by the Communist Party. The camp had scheduled a campfire meeting aimed at memorializing Joe Hill, and Hayes needed a song for the occasion. He took his poem and handed it to the camp's musical director, Earl Robinson, who grabbed his guitar and Hayes's poem and strolled into a tent. Forty minutes later he emerged with the song. He sang it that night. Several weeks later the poem appeared in a Communist newspaper, the *Daily Worker*. It was the song, more than any other factor, that kept Joe Hill's name alive. Paul Robeson and Pete Seeger were among those who sang it. Joan Baez famously sang the song standing on center stage at Woodstock in 1969.

The song would be invoked again by Bob Dylan. It is unclear when Dylan first heard of the Wobblies. Dylan grew up in Hibbing, Minnesota. The IWW, with their famed red badges, had marched in North Hibbing in the early 1900s and were there at the 1917 May Day picnic. Additionally, Charles Miller, Dylan's twelfth-grade history teacher, taught about the town's mining heritage, the labor struggles the miners had, and the Wobblies. In 1961, soon after arriving in New York, Dylan asked Izzy Young at the Folklore Center about Joe Hill, and Young gave Dylan pamphlets to read. Dylan went into the back of the Center and absorbed the story. Reading, Dylan concluded that Hill didn't commit the crime. Dylan planned to write a song about Hill, perhaps titled "Scatter My Ashes Anyplace but Utah." But Dylan didn't write about Hill. Instead, he wrote his first major song about another hero — Woody Guthrie. Even with that, there was an additional connection to Joe Hill. Dylan's "Song to Woody" starts out with words remarkably similar to lines that begin the thirteenth verse of Woody Guthrie's song "Joe Hillstrom."

Ironically, Dylan eventually did write a song very much like "I Dreamed I Saw Joe Hill Last Night." But Dylan's song, written in 1967 at a time in which he was repudiating the folk purists who had so consistently booed and rejected him, was titled "I Dreamed I Saw St. Augustine." This song was a direct slap at Hill's anti-religious attitudes and the legacy of the song among leftists. In the song, Dylan expresses sadness and guilt about killing the memory of St. Augustine — that is, the very religious tradition Hill and at least the Communists detested and tried to replace. By the time of his 2004 autobiography, *Chronicles: Volume One*, Dylan was ready to recall his youthful vision of Hill as romantic hero.

Joe Hill was sad-eyed, but he was also dry-eyed. He decried the conditions he saw all around him and issued battle cries through music for workers to take up the IWW's revolutionary cause. He was a prophet not in the sense of believing he was speaking for God or as someone capable of predicting the future. Instead, his role of prophet was as an inspirational songwriter and fighter for a cause. He connected politics to song.

Joe Hill made a significant contribution to the creation of the idea of songwriter as political hero. Hill was the prototype of an American tradition that included Woody Guthrie, Pete Seeger, Leadbelly, Joan Baez, Bob Dylan, and many others.

Hill taught all of them how to construct the persona of a protest singer hero. His life, political beliefs, and music were inseparable. He was the sort of lone-wolf, fierce individualist refusing to bend to any authority save humanity. He provided a model, in his case as a literal outlaw, to stand outside society to examine it. If Hill didn't record songs himself, he nevertheless taught those who sang their own songs that music could have a profound effect.

Hill, though, had limitations as a model. His supposed mythic martyrdom to capitalism is questionable. While he suffered from a serious injustice — he was found guilty on insufficient evidence and should have had a re-trial — it is as likely that he was guilty as that he was innocent, a fact that severely limits the power of his story. He lived in a very different America than the one the later folk singers inhabited, a land chastened by a Great Depression, challenged by the rise of the Communists, a land in which a president re-organized government and where music became commercial. Hill could not, by definition, see the world quite like they did, or see solutions in the same way they did. His plans were too vague; they simply involved organizing workers into one big union, confronting the capitalist bosses, and taking over. He didn't develop a system to provide any useful lessons. He mocked the spiritual instead of grasping its power in workers' lives.

31

It was Joe Hill who, for good and bad, first defined the modern role of the political folk songwriter. And so the later folk singers embraced him, or more precisely his story. Indeed, without them, it is likely that the story of Joe Hill would have been lost to history. In that crucial sense, Joe Hill never did die.

Woody Guthrie, for one, kept him alive by singing his songs, by absorbing his vision. Unlike Hill, though, Woody had grown up in America and instinctively knew its people. He had a deeper attachment to the land and the folk and the music that filled empty nights in many American homes.

But Woody had learned a crucial musical lesson from Hill: the mixing of popular tune and radical lyric. Woody's unparalleled songwriting skills helped give birth to a new American tradition, one that seized the name "folk music" from its traditional owners and re-made it as politically left-wing. This new "folk music" tried to force America to change its ways. Even that failed attempt made America face itself in new and sometimes unsettling ways.

Woody, then, knew the traditional and the political traditions. Even as he had to decide whether to stop singing the political songs as his boss at the radio station wished, his own life up to that moment reflected both of those traditions and his own brilliant addition.

Woody Guthrie took the traditional tunes to write political songs. His unique addition was to do what Joe Hill didn't — perform the songs he had written. Woody Guthrie, that is, was the first to embody the idea of singer-songwriter as a rebel hero in the modern world.

But it took much tragedy for Woody to make that leap. His journey began in a small Oklahoma town with the death of a child.

Three

Hard Luck Days: Woody Guthrie's America

Woody Guthrie's intense empathy for the suffering, especially the suffering of children, came from searing personal experiences, beginning with the tragedy of his sister Clara. He sang so he wouldn't cry about her.

Clara was almost eight years older than he was. She was constantly in motion, the brown ringlets of hair she had dancing around as wildly as her feet did. Little Woody was like that too, hopping around like a cricket. In late May 1919, when Woody was five, Clara and her mother, Nora, got into a fight. The girl was forbidden to go to school. She was forced to remain at home, supposedly to help with the ironing.

Somehow her dress caught on fire. Clara ran screaming from the house and circled around it twice. Nora was immobile; it was a neighbor who finally caught Clara and smothered the fire in a blanket. The fire had burned Clara down from her neck all the way to her knees.

Hearing what he always thought of as the sad song of the fire whistle, Woody rushed home from his grandmother's house, stared at his sister's charred flesh, inhaled the smoky odor coming from her, and started to choke up.

Clara, who had lost all feeling in her body, looked at him. "Don't you cry. Promise me that you won't ever cry like your old Daddy did. And Mama. And your old brother Roy. It doesn't help. It just makes everybody feel bad."[1]

Woody said he wasn't crying, though the words were braver than the boy. He stood and watched as his sister's head tilted off to a side. Clara, who sang with him, played with him, and took care of him, had died.

Maybe the fire had been an accident. Maybe, in anger at her mother, Clara had deliberately poured the oil and set fire to her dress. There were those who, despite Clara's admission to a local newspaper [she was able to speak to a number of people before she died] that she had started the fire, continued to believe that Nora had set her own child on fire. Many in Okemah, Oklahoma, vividly remembered that before Woody's birth the family home had caught fire the day after it was built. Woody himself had heard rumors that his mother had started it.

It was only later when Woody stared at his dead sister through the glass lid of her coffin that he briefly broke his promise. And then he stopped crying. And he kept his promise. His younger, beloved sister Mary Jo recalled, "I've never seen him cry."[2]

Woody was deeply influenced not only by his family but also by his surroundings in Okemah, Oklahoma. Oklahoma had become the 46th state, admitted to the Union only in November 1907, fewer than five years before Woody's birth.

Woody was on the edge of American culture in Oklahoma. He had one foot in it and one foot outside it. He could understand it like a native but analyze it with the objectivity of a foreigner. He could love it but feel distant from it. It was, that is, a perfect place for the nurturing of someone to question the culture and love it at the same time.

Okemah gave Woody a chance to get to know hard-working people who too often found an enemy in fate, who lost their homes to bankers and their lives to poverty and disease. Woody met the drifters, the men in town for an oil boom, and the wandering cowboys. These men who had no home understood the boy who was so often on his own. They told him wild stories of outlaws that they knew, of suffering and love, and endless tales of unmerited pain. It is unsurprising that Woody always reflexively embraced the cause of the underdogs he met or read about. As Mary Jo notes, "He never did want to have more than anybody else."[3]

The pain in Woody's own family grew worse. His father, Charley, brought home food for the family, and Nora threw it out to the dogs. In the morning she'd start to do laundry in a #3 washtub and the children would come home from school to find it still there. She chased her son George around the house with a butcher knife because he wouldn't get into a cold tub of water to take a bath. Nora was unable to bear criticism and would begin to cry when her husband berated her. She had a terrible temper, and Woody never knew what mood she'd be in when he arrived home.

Then, in late June 1927, Charley napped on the sofa, a newspaper stretched across his chest. Nora, alone with her husband, strode over to his sleeping body and threw a kerosene lantern on him, setting him on fire. He awoke, stared at her wild eyes, and ran outside to roll around on the grass. A neighbor covered him with a blanket.

Charley was adamant that the horrible truth would never get out; he had always protected his wife, and he would continue to do so. Woody tried to explain the incident by saying his father wanted to kill himself because of economic difficulties. But Charley's silence didn't fool anyone. Charley was a stoic; his laughter and his smiling, his eternal optimism, his refusal to complain, and his desire to prevent his children from worrying could not mask the awful truth. Nora's mother and brother immediately had her admitted to Central State Hospital, a facility sixty miles from Okemah. The hospital housed those with mental illness. No one knew that she was really suffering from Huntington's disease (then also known as Huntington's chorea), an inherited neurological disorder that caused strange bodily movements, a loss of physical coordination, and impaired mental skills. It was a horrifying disease — for which there is still no cure — that Woody inherited from his mother.

Woody greatly missed his mother — he missed combing and brushing her hair, hearing her sing, and the simple knowledge that she was within reach — but he didn't miss the constant vigilance required in case a fire began or the uncontrollable temper evident as she threw dishes.

Charley left his home in 1927, heading to Pampa, sixty miles northeast of Amarillo in the Texas Panhandle, to live with his sister while he recovered. Woody stayed with various families or was on his own. He made money when he could cleaning spittoons or whatever lowly job came along. He once lived by himself in an old piano box on a hill.

By the summer of 1929, the undersized, curly-headed wisp of a seventeen year old began exploring the road. The tales of the hoboes had made the travel sound alluring. Woody traveled to Houston, eventually reaching the Gulf of Mexico. He hoed figs for some friends, and then, as though rehearsing for his future life, he returned home.

But the trip, brief as it was, was important. Woody began to discover his crucial place. Thoreau went to the woods to find nature's truths;

Flaubert traipsed through the French language looking for the precise word that provided an artistic truth superior to other kinds; C.S. Lewis first sensed God while riding his motorcycle to a zoo. Woody Guthrie found his truth in people who had been neglected and injured by society, and he discovered they weren't only in Okemah. It was on the road that he learned the lessons from his family and community applied to a wider world.

And travel let him hide from pain. What he couldn't find satisfying in a fixed point — in a settled family life with a steady job — he found in motion. From then on, for the rest of his life, Woody rambled, sometimes without informing his family or friends. Woody had a homeless soul. He was a spiritual orphan who went looking for storms. He drank the wild wind and slept in the dust. The very land became part of his being. He loved people but often had trouble getting along with them. He told the truth and disappeared. He escaped confrontations by leaving.

He found a strong sense of freedom in the traveling. He had no responsibilities to others. He could go where he pleased, eat and sleep when he could. He listened carefully to the roar of the train, the squeak of newly cleaned dishes, the sigh of the hobo finishing a meal. His travels let him hear the soundtrack accompanying the lives of the American poor. It was on the road that Woody saw that while he always could leave, most people had to stay in place, too often spiritually murdered and financially ruined by the force of nature, which couldn't be controlled, or by the greed of people, which could be challenged. His politics emerged simply from looking around with a profound sympathy.

After arriving home, Woody got a letter from Charley. Woody was wanted in Pampa to help run a rooming house. Charley had judiciously left out the minor detail of the various women on the top floor of the house or the oil boomers who inhabited the "cot house," renting cots for a quarter for eight hours.

In Pampa a druggist named Harris offered Woody a job dispensing root beer for $3 a day. Woody later commented, "I told him I had intelligence enough to do that."[4] Woody's job was a bit more expansive, though. Harris Drugs surreptitiously sold its customers liquor bottles from under the counter, and Woody learned to do that as well. One day he found a battered guitar in the back room. Finding he needed help, Woody turned to his Uncle Jeff, his father's brother, who was an accomplished musician.

Jeff taught Woody chords, and, slowly, Woody learned the basics of the six-string guitar. Woody always favored the simplest of songs. "If you use more than two chords, you're showing off,"[5] he was later fond of saying.

Woody's musical development continued when he met Matt Jennings in study hall. Woody would sneak off to the library to read books and then impress his friends with bizarre facts and stirring stories. The red-haired, freckled Jennings loved music and soon he, Woody, and a third boy they knew, Cluster Baker, formed the Corncob Trio and sought places to play and music to learn. They played at dances, met and flirted with young women enchanted by the music and stories, learned how to entertain crowds, and developed identities as singers.

The Jennings family lived in two cottages. One of them had a phonograph and a large pile of 78s, and the Corncob Trio began to hang out there playing the records over and over again. Guthrie played the Carter Family's "Bury Me Beneath the Willow" and Jimmie Rodgers's "T for Texas" constantly, absorbing the rhythms and sounds.

In the Carter Family, he found the tunes to which he could put his own words. In Rodgers, he found a persona, a writer of original songs, an artist who sprang from the people and sang their own thoughts and feelings back to them.

The Corncob Trio used the Carter Family as their model as they sang the gospels and ballads that their neighbors recognized, loved, and from which they drew comfort. Woody drawled funny stories between songs, slowly developing a performance style. His wry humor, much in demand because of its resemblance to that of Woody's fellow Oklahoman Will Rogers, pleased the audiences. Woody regularly listened to Rogers on the radio and absorbed the same attitude as Rogers had: Don't trust the owners but instead side with the weak, trampled upon, unemployed common people of the country.

Woody didn't just go over to see Matt Jennings for the music. He also fell in love with Jennings's sister, Mary. In 1933, the twenty-one-year-old Woody and the sixteen-year-old Mary were married, over the strenuous objections of her parents who didn't like Woody's not having a job and not being Catholic. Woody tried to earn money. He'd paint signs when he could, but he just didn't want to hold down a regular job. Mary later said, "Woody wasn't ever easy to live with. He always more or less did what he wanted to do."[6]

Whatever forces he felt inside him, they were powerful. He needed a way to get them out. He tried writing stories for *True Story* magazine, but he couldn't sell any. He liked painting but that wasn't enough. Music became his solace.

Woody Guthrie began writing down the songs that came to him. He was struggling to find a way to give voice to his impulse to do good and to reconcile that impulse with his artistic temperament and abilities.

He found material for his songs by listening to the stories of the streets and prairies, of the oil workers, and miners he met. As he traveled, he took out his notebook and jotted down funny lines or acute observations uttered by those he met. He organized those lines and incorporated them into his songs. Therefore, just as the tunes he sang were familiar to his audiences, so, too, were the sentiments in the lyrics. Woody didn't tell people what to believe. He listened to what people had to say and observed how they lived. His songs reflected the deepest truths of people's lives. The politics he put in his songs had a language grounded in the conversations at a dinner table or a campfire.

In 1935, he typed fourteen of his songs and had them put into a pamphlet. Even then, Woody's political views were clear. In one song, "If I Was Everything on Earth," he wrote that if he were the president he'd offer groceries at no cost, provide clothing, and shoot any oil boss responsible for poisoning creeks where people went fishing. The title is revealing. Woody wanted to fix the whole world. It wasn't enough for him to lead an ordinary life, even one that was relatively happy. He had the aching need to correct wrongs, to feed the hungry and to heal the wounded. He needed to tell people just how to do that, as though he were a special messenger delivering the truth to a world breathtakingly deprived of the common sense to discover those answers on their own. Woody was a prophet-in-training. Even then, he could not tame his tongue. He took pride in its wildness.

The song also shows the first phase of Woody's political songwriting: he described what he saw as the sorry state of the society, as do other songs in the pamphlet, such as "Old Rachel," which laments the poor having to hand over property to the banks.

Nineteen thirty-five was also a crucial year for the southern patch of the country Woody inhabited. Two principal factors were the ongoing effects of the Great Depression and the Dust Bowl.

The Great Depression was particularly painful not only because of lost jobs but also because of bank failures. The banks had loaned money to brokerage houses that used the money to purchase stocks. When the value of the stocks collapsed the houses could not repay the loans and many banks declared bankruptcy. There were 800 bank failures in just two months of 1931. That meant that all the money the poor farmers and workers had saved vanished. There was a chain reaction: the lost money meant businesses had to close and mortgage payments could no longer be made.

Americans were devastated. Herbert Hoover's campaign slogan of "two cars in every garage" was satirized as "two families in every garage." The income for farmers fell 50 percent between 1929 and 1932. There was fear and hunger.

B.J. Rolfzen, who eventually became Bob Dylan's influential English teacher at Hibbing High School, grew up during the Great Depression, a time he depicts in his privately printed memoir *The Spring of My Life*. He vividly recalled the homeless men who arrived in his town daily, riding the freight train and looking for work. The men would leap from the train, amble down the track to an area known as Bums' Nest, and sit on rocks or stumps under the willow trees. Rolfzen visited them frequently, staring at the forlorn men waiting to eat the stew, filled with vegetables the hoboes had begged for, being cooked in a washtub. Rolfzen recalled that the men sometimes came to his house for food, and his mother never turned them away.

Rolfzen's experience was not unique. At the height of the Great Depression, there were 250,000 teenagers living on the road along with millions of adults. Most of the teens had been sent away by their parents who couldn't afford them, although some were drawn by the seemingly romantic notion of riding the rails.

They learned to spot the bulls, the railroad detectives, and to stand just outside the yard and start running as the train went slowly past them. They developed the skill of holding on to the grabiron with one hand, and then, still running, wrap their other hand around it. Only then could they step up onto the boxcar. Once inside the boxcar they sat with perhaps twenty other men. (Some women did ride the rails, but doing so was exceedingly dangerous for them. They were subject to sexual assault and robbery.) They inhaled a lot of smoke. Some coughed up the black coal smoke.

When they got to towns, they wandered and begged. Some became "kneeshakers," men who sat on the back porch of a house eating food off a tray. Some lucky few were invited to eat inside the house. They lived in dangerous hobo jungles, where fights were common. Some hoboes were killed for their shoes. Prostitutes came to the jungles and charged fifty cents for services provided.

Woody Guthrie saw his friends and neighbors lose their homes to the bank. In Pampa, the oil delayed the effects of the Depression, but the boom eventually ended, and the workers drifted away. As he traveled, he saw the anguished families living under bridges or in cardboard shacks. He heard angry complaints but also acceptance in the silent sighs of the suffering. He took to hitchhiking instead of riding the rails because doing so was safer, though he knew no one was really safe in such an uncertain world.

Unsurprisingly, people sought answers. They wanted to know why their lives had been upended. They went to fortunetellers. They consulted horoscopes. They peered deeply into glass balls searching for a revelation. They read tea leaves and palms. A million and a half people a year sought advice from the popular astrologer named Dolores.

An increasing number of people also began to question the legitimacy of the government and the nation's economic system. After the stock market crash, President Hoover had assured Americans that the free market system would right itself. Capitalism's unseen hand would cure the nation's ills. But that hand didn't only seem invisible; it seemed immobile.

The wealthy, the corporate titans, and the bankers, admired during the booming economy of the 1920s, were suddenly cast as villains. John D. Rockefeller paid $6,278,000 in taxes while miners earned $10 a week. The twelve million poorest families had the same worth as the top 27,500 American families. In such an atmosphere, some people viewed other societies and other economic systems as better than America's. In 1932, Americans overwhelmingly threw the Republicans out of the White House and elected Franklin D. Roosevelt in hopes that reform could come from within.

Beyond the profound economic, social, and psychological effects of the Great Depression itself, another sort of disaster struck Woody Guthrie and his neighbors directly.

The origins of the Dust Bowl were economic. During the First World

War, farmers in such states as Oklahoma and Texas had used grazing land to grow cotton and wheat that earned them high profits. Farmers tore up the sod that retained moisture in the soil, preventing its erosion. Combined with the overgrazing of cattle on the land and the coming of a succession of dry seasons from 1933 to 1935, the land became desert as the storms took away the topsoil. Families scattered across the country. In the five years following 1934, almost 350,000 families left their farms and homes. Many from Woody's home state, dubbed the Okies, were lured west by the visions sung by Jimmie Rodgers, by the ads of the fruit growers, and by the romantic notion of California as a land where dreams that had died could be re-born.

Dust storms were common enough, but Woody never saw any of them like the Palm Sunday Black Duster, the one that hit Pampa on the late afternoon of April 14, 1935. To Woody, standing outside Pampa, the dust storm heading his way looked like the Red Sea about to swallow the Israelites. The pitch-black dust cloud was a thousand feet high. There was no wind, just the inexorable rolling of the dust.

Woody and Mary had a dozen or so people in their tiny house. The dirt came in around the windows, under the doors, through unpatched spots in the wall. All the people put wet rags and handkerchiefs to keep the dust from their nostrils and mouths. A lit light bulb looked like the tiny end of a burning cigarette. People were scared. Woody heard a common reaction: many thought they were going to die. They turned to each other and said words of good-bye.

When it was over, a reporter from Washington, D.C., called Oklahoma and Texas "The Dust Bowl," and the name stuck. In Pampa, the town motto of "where the wheat grows and the oil flows" was sardonically altered by adding "and the wind blows." Woody eventually added to that with his line: "And the farmer owes."[7]

Woody reacted to the tragedy in the way he had learned and had always done: he sang. In this case he wrote a song titled "So Long, It's Been Good to Know You" that emphasized the need to move. Sometime before 1937 he wrote "Do Re Mi," about migrants turned back at the California border because they didn't have sufficient money when they tried to move. Slowly, his accumulated songs were painting a portrait of despair.

Besides using the tunes he learned from his family and the popular folk singers, Woody began to write songs in the popular talking blues

41

form. Sometimes ascribed to African roots or minstrel shows, the form was developed by a humorous pipe-smoking man from South Carolina named Chris Bouchillon who recorded "Talking Blues" in April 1926. The recording director liked Bouchillon's pleasant voice but realized that it sounded better when the musician was talking than when he was singing. Therefore, the director made the suggestion that Bouchillon talk while playing his guitar. Guthrie used talking blues as a way to de-emphasize the beauty of a voice in favor of the impact of the words and to speak with humor in what appeared to be singing.

Woody rambled more and more, grabbing his paintbrushes to make some money, strapping his guitar around his body to be available for making music. One day, the hunger for a new territory found a clear destination: California. Migrants had gone there; it was the journey of a people, and Woody needed to take part in it.

And so either in late February or early March 1937, Woody's brother-in-law Fred commandeered the family beer delivery truck and drove Woody twenty-five miles south to Route 66. Woody stuck his thumb out, trying to get a ride toward better days.

Woody reached the Golden State at the end of the winter. Under the stars California looked beautiful but when the sun shone itself on the poor and the miserable, Woody couldn't turn his head. He came to believe that decent people should be ashamed of the world. He stopped to talk to people living in houses made of orange crates. He saw the goons hired to beat people senseless. He went to the migrant camps, thick with flies and desperate with worry. He sang for the workers, playing the tunes they knew from home and songs he had written about their plight.

The half a million Okies and others who had moved west frightened many Californians. The newcomers were seen as intruders: dirty, poor, uncivilized.

The Okies were also upset. At home, people worked together. There had been petty fights, jealousies, and spats. But here, in what was supposed to be heaven on earth, people formed sides.

You were with the workers or the owners. You were with the poor or the rich. You were a capitalist or not. These were strange words to Woody. He had heard them in the hobo jungles uttered by men from an organization called the Industrial Workers of the World. Those stirring words made sense. Suddenly the swirling feelings he felt — the raging anger at injustice and the powerlessness to relieve suffering — found a political language that Woody could share with others.

Woody Guthrie was three years old when Joe Hill was executed, and now Hill's fame had found its way to the seething young man, furious at the police and the farmers and the government, at everything and everybody who disliked or meant harm to his people. Woody heard the song parodies; he listened to Hill's humor blended with seriousness to the marriage of familiar tunes with simple but searing lyrics that talked about the plight of the workers.

The songs about the Dust Bowl tumbled out as his political education expanded. But Woody was not Joe Hill. Woody was not a violent person. He didn't deliberately sabotage the way Hill did. Any humor Hill had was hard-edged. Woody's humor was sly and natural. Woody thought in a funny way that Joe Hill would have believed insufficiently revolutionary.

Joe Hill could write songs, and Woody saw that a political movement embraced and needed those songs. But the Wobbly approach was not for him. Woody still needed a comprehensive vision and a movement that would channel his political impulses. He knew where to get the music and where to get the words. But what were the right words? What was he aiming at?

In Los Angeles, Woody teamed with his cousin, Jack Guthrie, a self-styled singing cowboy. On July 15, 1937, Jack and Woody auditioned for Frank Burke, the short, stocky, white-haired politically liberal owner of radio station KFVD, and the two were hired to begin four days later, though without pay. Soon Jack was concerned about providing enough money for his family — in sharp contrast to his cousin's lack of a sense of familial responsibility. Jack returned to construction work. Maxine Crissman, a slim, husky-voiced friend of his, took his spot. Woody nicknamed her "Lefty Lou from Ole Mizzoo" — Lefty from her childhood nickname because she was left-handed (and perhaps because he wanted to make a political statement) and Lou because it rhymed with Mizzoo, and she was from Missouri — and the two attracted an audience of displaced Okies, farmers, and people in the country and mountains outside the city. Woody wrote a theme song, spun outrageous and funny tales, and didn't hesitate to provide political and social commentary. He crafted his persona — the rube, the bumpkin, the poor country Everyman with a guitar and a high tenor voice and a down home vocabulary and syntax, and an itch to stick it to wealthy tycoons and politicians.

Although he now had a contract that gave him $20 a week — enough to send for his family — Woody's money flowed away from him in the dusty bars where he bought drinks for those who looked like they needed a drink to get through the night and gave money to those who looked like they were losing their battle with hope.

Woody's radio career had profound influences on him. His success — the letters and dollar bills he got from fans, the support and enthusiastic encouragement from Frank Burke, the fame, the growing sense that he could write songs people wanted to hear — all congealed into a vocational identity. He loved how women he met and seduced were taken by his singing. Woody could measure his songs by the depth of a woman's smile.

And Woody's politics were about to change. He was about to find the language and the movement for which he had been searching. He began staying at the station after his show to hear the one that followed it. That program featured Ed Robbin — a former social worker and gambler — who besides his radio show was the Los Angeles correspondent for *People's World*, the Communist newspaper on the West Coast.

One day in January 1939 Woody approached Robbin and said, "Why don't we go out and have a beer together after your program. I usually stay around and listen to you anyway."

"Sure, Woody, let's do that."[8]

The two did go out. Robbin, assuming Woody was singing just cowboy songs, was surprised when Woody asked him to listen to the program, and Robbin agreed. Woody asked Robbin about Tom Mooney, who was then prominent in the papers.

Mooney was a labor leader who had been accused of planting a bomb that killed people during a 1916 parade in San Francisco. He had just been released from prison after serving 22½ years in prison. Robbin explained the whole story.

Soon after that talk, Mooney appeared on KFVD where Ed Robbin interviewed him. On the day after the interview, Robbin listened to Woody's program. Woody sang a ballad about Tom Mooney. Then he sang some of his ballads about the Dust Bowl, interspersing comments between songs.

Impressed, Robbin saw Woody after the program and asked him who had written all those songs. Robbin found them sympathetic to agricultural and other workers, class conscious especially in his outlaw songs. These songs were steeled with a pro-union sentiment, able to stir audiences with recognizable tunes mixed with well-crafted lyrics, and able to make a hero out of a rebellious Communist leader.

Woody told him, "Some of them I wrote, and some I picked up here and there and changed or just re-wrote, and some are old folk songs."[9]

Robbin immediately invited Guthrie to dinner and then read through a folder of songs that Woody had brought him.

Reflexively, Robbin said, "You know, Woody, there is a big rally for Tom Mooney tonight in downtown Los Angeles, and I'd very much like you to come there and sing this ballad to Tom Mooney, if you're willing to do it."

"Sure, why not?"

"Well, I would like you to know, Woody, that this is sponsored by the Communist Party, and it's a politically left-wing gathering."

And in what would be his trademark way of dismissing mention of the Communist Party, of pretending he wasn't quite sure what this Communism was really, Woody responded by shooing away any controversy: "Left wing, right wing, chicken wing — it's the same thing to me."[10]

With that casual quip, Woody Guthrie linked his fate with the Communist Party's for the next several decades. He had found like-minded people who could offer a group to which he could belong, a revolutionary language to help him understand the world and use in his songs, and an audience to appreciate his music.

Woody's arrival could not have come at a better time for the Communists. Independently of him, some supporters of the Party, most crucially Alan Lomax and Pete Seeger, were discovering in traditional music a new understanding of proletarian culture. They were collecting the old folk songs and re-interpreting the entire tradition in a political fashion. They were preparing for a singing movement that they hoped would end the horrors of capitalism and make America part of a better world.

But Woody's attachment to the Communist cause also soon brought him into a consequential conflict with his boss.

Four

Which Side Are You On?
The Left Discovers Folk Music

Woody Guthrie went to the rally for Tom Mooney, sat on the stage, and promptly fell asleep. Ed Robbin poked him at some point past eleven o'clock. Most people in the audience were preparing to leave. They had come for the stirring speeches, not to hear some hillbilly singer. The Communists were serious, after all. Entertainment was for bourgeois tastes. But Woody's long tales, his pungent, catchy tunes, and his undeniable authenticity were magnetic. The audience was impressed.

For the Communist Party, the discovery of Woody Guthrie was the turning point on a long, uncertain journey. The Party had not always been appreciative of traditional American music.

American Communists emerged from the Socialist Party of America, which in 1912 had 118,000 members; Socialist publications reached 2 million readers. Eugene Debs, the Party's candidate for president that year, got almost 6 percent of the vote. Socialists were elected to 1,200 offices, including 79 mayors in 24 states.

The attractions of Socialism stemmed directly from the rapid expansion of American industry and the growth of corporations (forcing smaller businesses and farmers out of the market) after the Civil War. The new machinery took the place of many skilled laborers and required a rapid expansion of jobs requiring fewer skills. These unskilled workers competed for low-paying jobs. When workers sought to organize, their efforts were sometimes met by brutal resistance from employers anxious to maintain high profits. The pool of unskilled workers increased multifold with the rise of immigration in the years from about 1880 to 1920. The economic disparity — the seeming plutocracy that was developing — engendered a lot of hostility.

World War I and the Bolshevik revolution in Russia in 1917 profoundly affected the future of the Socialists. They opposed American entry into the War, but not sufficiently so for their left-wing. In a factional dispute, the mainstream of the Party expelled the left-wingers.

These internecine disputes occurred just as the Palmer raids were taking place and American radicalism was viewed with deep suspicion. In such an environment, the left-wingers who had been expelled formed two organizations: the Communist Party of America and the Communist Labor Party. Eventually, the two parties merged, and in 1930 settled on the name of Communist Party of the United States of America (CPUSA).

Party members, broadly speaking, shared goals such as transforming the American economic system from a capitalist system — in which the means of production were generally in private hands — into a Communist system in which the means of production were commonly owned. They favored the elimination of private property. They thought that profit-seeking eroded cooperation. They believed individualism undermined a nation's common effort and that consumerism fed capitalism. They eyed the leaders of American capitalism — the bankers, for example — as the enemy. The common people — the members of the lower social class, or proletariat — were the heroes. Their culture, it would eventually be argued, was more authentic than the artificial money-oriented culture created by the elites.

In part because so many members of what would become the CPUSA were foreign-born and had an unenviable grasp of English, the Party avoided America's song traditions. Instead, the Party developed workers' choruses that sang revolutionary songs mostly in the different languages spoken by the new immigrants.

The choruses provided communal support to their various ethnic groups. But, by their nature, they sang mostly foreign songs in foreign languages. This rendered the choruses incapable of reaching wider audiences, of fomenting the call to overthrow capitalism.

While supporters of the CPUSA came from a wide variety of groups, American Jews were, for decades, depicted as members of or sympathetic to the goals of the Party. Relatively few Americans, relatively few immigrants, and relatively few Jewish immigrants actually joined the Party.

Most Jews who favored social change advocated by the radical Left became avid Roosevelt Democrats.

But because Jews were so associated in the popular mind with radical politics and therefore became a symbol of the attractions of socialism broadly speaking and Communism in particular, it is worth recounting the reasons why such an ideology was appealing.

While these reasons apply specifically to Jewish immigrants, some of these reasons had resonances with other groups as well.

- Given their history, Jews felt an intense emotional identification with the poor and powerless. That part of Jewish moral tradition embedded in the Prophets instilled a sense of having an obligation to take care of the entire community, not just the self.

- The immigrant neighborhoods where Jews grew up were the centers of radical activity.

- The Jewish immigrants who left Eastern Europe (where two out of every three Jews remained) were younger, less religious, more adventurous, and more intellectual than those who stayed behind. They were, that is, a perfect audience for new ideas.

- The Jews had no real political history. They had always found themselves in fear of and in opposition to governmental authorities, neither part of the government nor friendly to it. They had always been powerless. The de facto leaders of the Jews during the era of absolute monarchies were a small number of Jewish financial counselors or bankers. The mass of Jews had no economic role, no stake in the society, no control over their own lives. They had no political traditions or identities as they entered America.

- As the threat of European anti–Semitism grew, American Jews saw the Soviet Union as a bulwark against Nazism.

- American Jews were wanted by the left-wing, and repulsed by the Right. American conservatism of the era was commonly anti-immigrant, the home of anti–Semites, and isolationist when such a view amounted to pushing European Jews into the deadly arms of the Nazis. That is, many Jews did not find an alternative to the Left. They knew that the influential anti–Semitism of some on the Right, exemplified by such people as Henry Ford and Charles Lindbergh, prevented them from becoming full Americans. Ironically, they saw in the transformation of the country a chance to become full economic participants in the American system.

As Jews and others flirted with the various parties of the Left, the Soviet Union was changing in ways that would crucially affect the American Communists. In 1929, Stalin engineered a forced collectivization program combined with an effort to industrialize the country. Stalin ordered Communist parties throughout the world to reject alliances with non–Communist groups. The practical result for the CPUSA in terms of culture was that doctrinaire politics was to be injected forcefully into all aspects of ideology. In 1931, for example, the Workers Music League was established to coordinate the various choruses. The League determined to provide the choruses with appropriately revolutionary music.

For help, the League turned to the Pierre Degeyter Club (named after the *Internationale*'s composer) in New York, or, more particularly, to a musical collective that emerged from and was a section of the Club. The Composers' Collective included composers who had received classical training. They included such musical luminaries as Marc Blitzstein, Aaron Copland, Charles Seeger and Ruth Crawford Seeger (Pete Seeger's father and stepmother), and Elie Siegmeister. The Collective usually met once a week during the late afternoon in some loft in lower Manhattan. Each member gave a quarter at the meeting to purchase songbooks and pay for the rent.

Not all members of the Collective were members of the CPUSA. As would be true throughout the history of the Party, not everyone could adhere to its discipline. Indeed, the vast majority of even those who joined the Party eventually quit, some very soon after joining.

Those who didn't join refrained for a variety of reasons. Some wanted to protect their jobs or families. Some wandered among the ideologies of the Left and never felt quite at home residing permanently in any single ideology. Those who had general sympathies for the CPUSA but didn't formally join eventually became called by the awkward term "fellow-travelers"; the French had a more euphonious term for such supporters: *communisants*.

Theodore Draper, a prominent historian of Communism, makes a useful distinction: "It is best to think of Communism as a movement rather than merely a party, a movement of which the party constitutes only a part."[1] Not all of the party members were Stalinists. Some were a mixture of Socialist and Communist. Some Stalinists stayed out of the party so they could operate without the taint of membership. And outside the Party, there was a wide range of support for the Communists among, for example, intellectuals. Many members of the movement outside the party could not define "dialectical materialism," much less make it through *Das Kapital.* Therefore, language in describing members of the Communist movement is always imprecise. Sometimes "left-wing" is useful because of its scope, but there were bitter divisions among Socialists, Communists, Anarchists, and others.

Not all members of the Communist movement initially cared for folk music. The Composers' Collective members were among those who were originally suspicious. They were serious classical composers who, like many urban intellectuals, disdained the culture of the farms and small towns of the South and Midwest. They were hardly alone in such an attitude. Sinclair Lewis joyfully mocked the Babbitts of America. Sherwood Anderson, H. L. Mencken, and other writers similarly felt disgust for what they viewed as the uncultured and narrow-minded middle class.

Unsurprisingly, the high-minded Collective musicians, who had no sympathy for popular culture, could not produce music with widespread appeal. The workers they were writing for didn't grasp dissonance or complexity in music. The music was hard to play, and so even if they had liked it the workers would not have been able to reproduce it.

Charles Seeger, who through his influence had a profound effect on the development of folk music, only slowly came to see the value of such music. Various friends changed his views, as did visits to the Collective by Aunt Molly Jackson.

Jackson was a Harlan County, Kentucky, songwriter well known in Communist circles. Her mother had died when Molly was six. Molly hated her stepmother and was so wild that her father had her put in jail. Having learned folk songs from her great-grandmother, Molly used her brief confinement to compose a song about being released.

She became a midwife at twelve (which gave her the nickname "Aunt" because older midwives were traditionally called "Granny"). She married at 13 — though her brother claimed she had been married once before then.

Jackson's life in Appalachia coincided with the rise of mining. Coal interests, usually from outside the region, bought up the land and transformed it from farming to camps for miners. The camps developed into company towns. The coal companies controlled the towns. They built poor housing and didn't spend adequately on safety measures in the mines. The miners were forced to shop at a company store — there were rarely competing stores in the town — using scrip that the company provided. As captive consumers, the mining families faced high prices that, combined with the low wages, made simply feeding their families an agonizing struggle. However, mining families endured because there was constant work removing the bituminous coal from the mines. Those workers who tried to organize were fired and removed from the company town.

By the late 1920s competition from other fuels depressed the coal market. The companies fired some workers and lowered the barely adequate wages for the remaining workers. Sensitive to perceived injustice, ornery, and quick-tempered, Molly Jackson found this situation intolerable. She once held a pistol on a clerk at a company store until he let her take food to her neighbors' hungry children. There are many other stories about her, but not all can be independently verified since she did not resist inventing her past. She wanted to be seen as a Robin Hood, a savior of the downtrodden, and she did not shy from exaggerating her various efforts. She also began composing songs about the miners' plight, making up words to familiar tunes.

The Harlan County miners struck in 1931. This was hardly unusual. There were an enormous number of strikes after World War I because costs went up along with an unemployment rate that was accelerated by the return of soldiers and the disbanding of war industries. In Harlan, the company thugs brought in to attack the strikers hadn't counted on the tough miners. Fights and bullets became so common that the area became known as Bloody Harlan.

The National Miners Union — a Communist organization — was among those groups that came to Harlan to lead the strikes. The NMU's efforts were based on lots of experience. They provided free food and clothing and organized meetings to get miners to organize. Most miners were deeply religious and scared of "Reds," so the NMU met with limited success. Aunt Molly Jackson was one of those successes. Whatever else she did to aid the miners, one activity was to write songs about the struggle.

Jackson's song efforts were not the first done by a woman on strike. Ella Mae Wiggins was one of her predecessors. Wiggins had helped lead a strike in Gastonia, North Carolina. The 29-year-old textile worker had nine children. When her children got whooping cough, a foreman refused her any time off. She quit the job, but then had no money for the children; four of them died. Wiggins continued in the struggle when strikes began. She wrote songs such as "Mill Mother's Lament" and sang them at meetings. The company hired men to shoot at the trucks of those on strike, and on September 14, 1929, Wiggins was on the way to a union meeting when she was shot through the heart.

Additionally, Bloody Harlan produced other songwriters. Florence Reece's husband was a strike leader. The town sheriff came to the Reece home with a group of men to hunt down Sam Reece. He was not at home, but Florence and her seven children were there and watched as the men looted the home. Not long after, Reece ripped a sheet from the family calendar hanging on a wall and wrote the lyrics to "Which Side Are You On?" She adapted the tune from the hymn "Lay the Lily Low" and created one of the most famous songs about labor struggles. The simple question raised by the song's title — which, repeated four times, formed the song's chorus — was meant to force the workers to make choices.

Incensed by the treatment of the miners, a group of writers generally sympathetic to the CPUSA came to Harlan County at the beginning of November 1931. Theodore Dreiser headed the group, which included such well-known writers as John Dos Passos, Samuel Ornitz (author of the acclaimed immigrant novel *Haunch, Paunch and Jowl*), Sherwood Anderson, and Lewis Mumford. On November 7, Aunt Molly Jackson appeared before the group to testify about the miners' conditions. As part of her testimony, she sang "Kentucky Miner's Wife" (also known as "Ragged Hungry Blues"). When Dreiser published the committee report — *Harlan Miners Speak* — he printed the lyrics of Aunt Molly's song in the front of the report.

By the end of 1931, Aunt Molly Jackson had headed to New York to raise money for the miners and meet some of the leaders of the CPUSA and their sympathizers. Even there, Aunt Molly was still a tough character. (Henrietta Yurchenco, a radio producer and ethnomusicologist who knew Jackson in New York, called her "a terror."[2])

Jackson only slowly influenced Charles Seeger. When Jackson attended the Collective's meetings, she sang some of her Kentucky labor ballads to them. They found her songs musically immature. When she heard their efforts at proletarian music, she was equally aghast.

Meanwhile strikes across the nation were widespread. In 1932 auto workers, tree pruners, California pea pickers, and airline pilots were among the workers striking along with the miners. In 1933 California farm workers and workers at Hormel Meat Packing were just two groups of strikers. In 1934 rubber workers, textile workers, and Minneapolis Teamsters conducted strikes.

Some on the Left were holding a death vigil for capitalism, but those who did underestimated the nation's steely resolve. In reaction to the Great Depression and the wave of strikes, Congress passed the National Labor Relations Act in 1935. The NLRA provided protection for workers to organize and collectively bargain. The Supreme Court declared the act unconstitutional in 1937, but in 1938 Congress provided for a national minimum wage and a 40-hour workweek. Child labor was banned.

Indeed, over time, Franklin Roosevelt's New Deal initiatives convinced many on the Left that the government was willing and able to help workers and correct what the Left perceived as the excesses of capitalism even while doing so on a nationalist rather than an internationalist basis. The New Deal effectively brought in many on the Left who might otherwise have affiliated themselves with socialist parties, including the Communists. The New Deal could so effectively compete emotionally with totalitarianism because it, too, offered soaring promises and delivered social transformations, engineering miracles, and film, theater, music, and art that trumpeted triumph and a mastery of the modern world.

But in the heady days of 1935, the air was crackling with revolutionary fervor. It was in such an atmosphere that the Soviet Union tried a new tactic, one that would finally connect folk music to leftist politics.

On August 20, 1935, the Seventh World Congress of the Communist International (Comintern) announced a new policy called the Popular Front. This movement urged the unity of all anti–Fascist groups. Its slogan in the United States was "Communism is the new Americanism."

The Popular Front was also a way for Joseph Stalin to consolidate his power. The act of framing the new policy as anti–Fascist gained Stalin additional sympathies and cloaked for many the true nature of his regime or provided adequate moral cover for them to ignore the lethal excesses of his exercise of power in the name of defeating the Fascists. Stalin knew opponents of the Soviet Union could now be branded Fascists or, later, supporters of the ultra–Right.

Additionally, Stalin wanted to temper internal leftist criticism. That criticism increased after the Moscow show trials and the murder of his political opponents. The three trials, held from 1936 to 1938, accused a total of 54 defendants. Confessions were forced, and all of the defendants were found guilty of trying to murder Stalin and return the Soviet Union to capitalism. The 16 defendants in the first trial were all executed. Thirteen of the 17 defendants in the second trial were executed; the remainder were sentenced to labor camps where all died. All leading defendants in the third trial were also executed.

Stalin has his supporters for the trials. In the May 3, 1938, issue of *The New Masses*, 136 people signed "The Moscow Trials: A Statement by American Progressives" in which those who signed expressed their support for Stalin's efforts and their belief that the defendants had sought to undermine the Soviet experiment in Communism. Signers included writers Lillian Hellman and Dorothy Parker and the actor John Garfield.

The practical effect of the Cultural Front in the United States was the reaching out to non–Communist organizations and the attempt to make Communism more American. The New Deal suddenly was embraced. Efforts to form unions with non–Communists increased, especially with those unions associated with the Congress of Industrial Organizations (CIO). The Communists now sought coalitions with some of the parties, unions, and people they had previously attacked.

Cultural alliances were among the new efforts. The goal was to present Marxism through culture. Artists, writers, and intellectuals — whether Party members or fellow travelers — were sought. And so were musicians.

The Collective's efforts to foment revolutionary fervor were replaced with a desire to embrace traditional American music, to see what was common between Communist and non–Communist Americans in the joint struggle against Fascism. Folk songs were seen as vital precisely because of their unifying effects. Folk music was the music of the proletariat, untainted by the commercial poison of capitalism. Folk music was familiar and available; precisely because it wasn't commercial music and mostly not copyrighted it could be adapted for political use. The apolitical music of the non-urban folk tradition could be transformed into music suitable for indoctrination. "Folk music" now had political overtones.

With folk music ideologically acceptable, the Collective and others sympathetic to the Communists and interested in promoting music had to locate authentic folk songs and singers who could perform them.

To find such songs, they relied on a variety of song collectors.

The academic collecting of folk songs had begun with a Harvard professor, Francis James Child. This sail maker's son, friend of Oliver Wendell Holmes and Henry James and William James, Harvard's first professor of English, and a renowned Chaucer scholar, left his lasting impression through his four-decade-long fanatical pursuit of ballads. In 1857–58 he published eight volumes of ballads. But Child had an even larger vision.

He wanted to collect, with all their variants, every single known British ballad. Child's monumental work *The English and Scottish Popular Ballads* (5 volumes, 1882–98) includes 305 ballads and commentaries. The book, popularly known as the Child Ballads, became a crucial source for folk song revivalists. For example, on her first album Joan Baez followed academic tradition and gave the number of the ballad such as "Mary Hamilton (Child 173)."

George Lyman Kittredge was Child's student and eventual son-in-law. Kittredge collected song texts and explored folklore, but his major contribution was as a teacher to John A. Lomax. While there were several significant song collectors, John Lomax and his son Alan were the ones who had the most critical influence on the development of folk songs on the political Left.

John Lomax developed an early interest in cowboy songs, a passion not shared by his professors. One of them at the University of Texas at Austin said the songs were not worthy of Lomax's efforts, and the impressionable student went behind his dormitory and burned the songs. He eventually made his way to Harvard's graduate school where Kittredge embraced his song-collecting efforts. In 1910 Lomax published an anthology of frontier songs, the first of two books of cowboy songs. He was increasingly anxious to preserve what he thought of as valuable folklore material that would disappear unless otherwise collected.

On June 7, 1932, as he wrote in his autobiography *Adventures of a Ballad Hunter*, Lomax began the most vital effort of his life. "One morning I drifted into the offices of The Macmillan Company ... Mr. H. S. Latham, a big, healthy, wholesome man, who I knew slightly, received me with gracious courtesy. I told him that for years past I had hoped to edit

55

a volume of American folk songs."[3] Uncertain, but fond of Lomax's earlier collections, Latham asked to see samples. Impressed, he promised to present the idea before Macmillan's Editorial Council and tell Lomax the fate of his dream. Lomax got a letter two days later along with a contract for the book.

Armed with the contract, Lomax knew he needed more folk songs. He first went to Harvard's library and then to the Archive of American Folk Song, which had been established in 1928 at the Library of Congress as the official repository of American folk songs.

Robert Winslow Gordon, who headed the Archive, had also studied folklore at Harvard with Kittredge. Gordon convinced Carl Engel, the head of the Library's Music Division, to establish the Archive. Gordon had, with limited funds, begun a collection, including field recordings done on wax cylinders.

Gordon was eventually fired, but the Archive agreed to provide Lomax with recording equipment. Lomax would, in turn, travel and record songs that would then be included in the Archive. Over time, Lomax would provide more than ten thousand recordings.

John Lomax set out to collect folk songs for his new book in June 1933. A month later he was named Honorary Consultant to the Archive of American Folk Song. His stipend was $1 a year.

Eighteen-year-old Alan Lomax accompanied his father on the trip. Alan had already gone on a collecting trip with his father and brother Johnny from June to mid–August 1932. Alan had attended the University of Texas at Austin and then went to Harvard from September 1931 to June 1932 before going on the trip. After the 1932 trip Alan had not returned to Harvard because of low grades, insufficient funds, his general distrust of getting wisdom from dusty books rather than traveling, hard labor, and other work he did himself, and a sense that his burning belief in Communism would hinder his academic career. It was the trips with his father that would allow him to see his role in support of the Communist movement.

Father and son packed a couple of army cots, cooking materials, food, and eventually a 350-pound Dictaphone recorder that, because of its handle and with some considerable exaggeration, was termed "portable." The recorder had two batteries, each 75 pounds, cables, a microphone, and a large number of aluminum and celluloid disks. They also carried their long-standing political dispute. John, traditional and conservative, railed against Alan's Communist friends and beliefs. Both men were large, powerful, and filled with sturdy egos, argumentative temperaments, and Southern, courtly manners.

Disdainful of popular culture, with its purported contamination of the genuine roots of traditional music, the Lomaxes went to where they thought the radio had not replaced the banjo playing after dinner on the back porch. The Lomaxes therefore sought out lumber camps, ranches, plantations, and, especially, the penitentiaries and prison farms in the South that — because of strict segregation — held exclusively African American inmates. The Lomaxes wanted music that law-abiding, God-fearing black folks wouldn't sing either because their churches thought of it as sinful or because the folks were scared to find out if singing the songs really could lead to hellfire.

John Lomax wrote to various wardens. When he got approval to record, he and Alan auditioned the prisoners in the striped uniforms. They tried to look for places where the sound would be better, such as barns where the hay blocked outside interferences. After selections of the singers were made, Alan operated the recording equipment as the prisoners repeated their songs for the device. Alan was stunned as he listened to the prisoners. The young man had heard symphonies, chamber music, and even a bit of jazz, but none of it seemed as important to him as the authentic sounds he heard coming from the inmates.

From July 16 to 20, 1933, the Lomaxes recorded at the Louisiana State Penitentiary in Angola. At first, the prison staff was suspicious, carefully searching the men and their car. The guards were amazed at the reason for the visit. The Lomaxes wanted to record while the inmates worked, but that request was denied.

A prison official led one of the inmates to meet the two strange men who wished to record. Because one inmate, Huddie (pronounced Hughdee) Ledbetter, was so talented, it is likely that he was one of the first recorded on July 16, a Sunday morning with a gray sky and a steady drizzle.

Ledbetter got the nickname Leadbelly not only as a variation of his name but also in tribute to his toughness. According to one story, another inmate in Angola had used a knife and attempted to slice Ledbetter across the throat and indeed left him with a scar. Leadbelly acquired his mythic status among the inmates when he took his attacker's knife away and almost killed him with it.

The nickname, though, could have come earlier, since Leadbelly had a long record. In 1915, Leadbelly, then 27, was arrested in Marshall, Texas, for an assault either on or about a woman. He was convicted of a reduced charge of carrying a pistol and sentenced to a month on a chain gang. Leadbelly escaped after three days and took an assumed name. On December 17, 1917, someone shot Will Stafford, the husband of one of Leadbelly's cousins. Leadbelly was arrested and, under his assumed name of Walter Boyd, he was convicted of homicide on June 7, 1918, and sent to the Texas penitentary at Sugarland (another place where he might have acquired the nickname). His sentence was commuted on January 15, 1925, by Governor Pat Neff; Leadbelly had composed a song in the governor's honor and reaped freedom as a result. On January 15, 1930, Leadbelly was arrested again. He had been listening to a Salvation Army band, began to do a soft-shoe dance, and was shoved by three white men trying to get him off the sidewalk. Leadbelly drew the penknife he always carried for making slides on his twelve-string guitar and cut the arm of one of the men. On February 20, after a one-day trial, Leadbelly was convicted of assault with intent to kill and sentenced to Angola for five to ten years.

Standing in front of the Lomaxes, Leadbelly played his guitar and used his deeply affecting baritone voice. Leadbelly sang seven songs starting with *The Western Cowboy* and *Honey, Take a Whiff on Me*, a song about cocaine. Leadbelly continued on until the disc's first side was filled.

As the second disc was being prepared, Leadbelly began to sing a waltz. His voice became higher so that he seemed almost a tenor. The Lomaxes listened. The song, *Irene*, was so thrilling to them that the Lomaxes recorded it three times. Eighteen years later, in 1950, six months after Leadbelly died, that song, re-titled *Goodnight, Irene*, and with its line asserting that he'd "get" Irene in his dreams altered to the prediction that he'd "see" her there, was sung by the Weavers and became the most popular song in the United States.

Leadbelly didn't write *Irene*. He learned it from his uncles. It seems originally to have derived from a waltz written by the African American composer Gussie Lord Davis in the 1890s and meant for popular consumption, such as in the then-popular minstrel shows.

Leadbelly was released from Angola on August 1, 1934. He wrote to

John Lomax seeking a job. On September 24, the two men met at a hotel and Leadbelly became Lomax's driver and recording assistant. In September and October the two journeyed through the South, mostly to prisons. Leadbelly was, beyond his normal duties, extremely helpful to convincing some of the prisoners to sing.

John and Alan Lomax's book, *American Ballads and Folk Songs*, was published in October 1934. Throughout 1934 and 1935, Leadbelly continued to get recognition for his talent and for his incredible story. Most significant was the January 3, 1935, story in the *New York Herald Tribune* with its headline "Sweet Singer of the Swamplands." Leadbelly was now well known, if neither wealthy nor nationally famous.

The Lomaxes and Leadbelly parted ways in 1935, although Leadbelly continued to rely on Alan Lomax for encouragement and career opportunities. Leadbelly would play a prominent role in folk music circles in New York City during the 1940s.

The Lomaxes' book with its collection of folk songs and the emerging stories of collecting techniques made John Lomax an even more important person. Charles Seeger, just beginning to develop the folk consciousness that would sweep through the political Left, went to Washington in November 1935 to work in the Resettlement Administration, which sought to help displaced farmers. His first action was to find a machine to record rural folk songs.

Seeger was determined to meet John Lomax. They were introduced by Harold Spiacke, the chief assistant to W. Oliver Strunk, who had replaced Carl Engel as chief of the Music Division. (Strunk's father, William, wrote the first edition of the book *The Elements of Style*, later revised by E.B. White.)

In 1936, Alan Lomax went to Washington and became the Assistant in Charge of the Archive of American Folk Music. In 1937, John appointed Alan as Acting Curator of the Archive, with the express purpose of cataloging the records.

In June, Alan invited Leadbelly to sing some songs for the Archive and asked the singer and his wife to stay in the Lomax apartment near the Supreme Court. Leadbelly was awakened the next morning by a loud argument between Alan and the landlord. The man was profoundly unhappy to learn that the temporary guests were black. The Jim Crow segregation laws were in effect, and legally the landlord could create considerable trouble. Alan placated the landlord by telling him the guests would move. Leadbelly was also with white people, including Kip Kilmer, son of the poet Joyce Kilmer. They couldn't find any place that would rent housing to both blacks and whites, and then they couldn't even find a restaurant where they could all eat together. They joked that Washington was a very bourgeois town. Leadbelly didn't know the word but liked its sound. The end result was one of Leadbelly's most famous songs, "The Bourgeois Blues," first recorded in December 1938.

While Leadbelly didn't think of himself as primarily a political singer, he was understandably outraged not just by segregation but by prejudice. He wrote, for example, about the Scottsboro Boys and created a campaign song for Wendell Wilkie in the 1940 presidential race against Franklin D. Roosevelt. Though he wrote relatively few political songs, he did perform at Popular Front events and found acceptance among the folk crowd. The singer Ronnie Gilbert perfectly summarized why someone like Leadbelly would gravitate to the political life. There, Gilbert said, he "would have found friendship, understanding of his and the life that oppressed people anywhere would have to face. He would have found a sympathetic ear and he certainly would have found a deep appreciation for his music and who he was. For his dignity and an appreciation for what he was doing."[4]

Alan Lomax was one of the most appreciative. But the driven, impatient young man saw himself as having an even wider mission.

With the Cultural Front providing him ideological support and with his efforts, his father's, and those of other collectors having resulted in the locating of thousands of traditional songs, Alan Lomax knew it was time to take the next step.

He was a defining figure in the folk song movement because he knew that even with those songs, the Communists needed new songwriters and new singers who would promote the causes embraced by the Left. For him there was a clear connection. Capitalist society needed to go. His contribution would be to change the capitalist culture. He would do this by promoting folk music, literally the music of the folk, those mythic rural peasants who worked hard so that the owners and investors could live off their sweat. Lomax wanted to replace the mind-numbing culture that capitalists produced, culture aimed at making people accept their plight and accept capitalism as permanent. He knew that old folk music was the true voice of the masses and new, more explicitly political, folk music could educate the masses, help them interpret the nature of their oppression and make them prize social justice above social tranquility.

One way to see Lomax is as someone who understood all folk music as political on one level or another. According to this interpretation, he fervently believed that songs could move the already politically committed — those interested, for example, in socialism, civil rights, labor unions, and, depending on the era, peace — to give more money, volunteer more often, be willing to do more than they thought they could, and feel their beliefs more sharply.

And folk music did not need to be explicitly political in the way Aunt Molly Jackson sang.

The genius of his approach is that even seemingly apolitical music could take on a political purpose. Any traditional folk music promoted the common folks over the elites. That is why Lomax never wrote down his political views. He could promote them without endangering himself. This concern about self-endangerment came in part from concern about his father's views. Additionally, according to his FBI file, while at Harvard Alan had been arrested on May 12, 1932, for demonstrating outside a courthouse to oppose the deportation of Edith Berkman, a Communist Party activist. He was charged with disturbing the peace and fined $20. Alan went on his first scouting trip with his father and brother the next month. No doubt his father saw in the trip a chance to keep Alan away from his Communist friends and offer him an alternate world, not realizing that Alan would ultimately connect the two worlds.

Lomax engaged in a wide variety of efforts. He always worked tirelessly on trip after trip to collect material.

On December 23, 1938, he helped record the first of the two "From Spirituals to Swing" Carnegie Hall concerts presented by John Hammond. The concerts helped bring gospel, blues, and jazz music mainstream recognition. Hammond was, like Lomax, a talent scout and promoter who would have a primary influence on American music through his discoveries or promotion of such musicians as Count Basie, Leonard Cohen, Bob Dylan, Aretha Franklin, Benny Goodman (who married Hammond's sister Alice), Lionel Hampton, Billie Holiday, Bruce Springsteen, and Big Joe Turner, among many others. Hammond, the great-great-grandson of Commodore Cornelius Vanderbilt, dropped out of Yale, voluntarily withdrew his name from the Social Register, and sought to use his money and connections to promote all kinds of African American music and to effect racial justice however he could. The "Spirituals to Swing" concerts were sponsored by the pro–Communist publication *The New Masses*, although Hammond himself was suspicious of Communist Party sincerity in their support of racial harmony. He wrote for the magazine, arguing against discrimination, including in the music industry. When no one else agreed to be the sponsor, Hammond reluctantly accepted the offer of the magazine, but made it explicit that the concert could not be a venue to promote any political ideas.

Soon after the concert, Hammond invested in the first integrated nightclub, Café Society, which opened in Greenwich Village by Barney Josephson. A second "uptown" branch on 58th Street opened in 1940. The Café, which sought to end racial discrimination in its treatment of customers, used many of the acts that Hammond found and used at the "From Spirituals to Swing" concerts. It was at Café Society, for example, that Billie Holiday first sang "Strange Fruit," a powerful indictment of lynching blacks.

Alan Lomax continued his own efforts. In 1939, he reached an arrangement with CBS radio's "The American School of the Air," a program broadcast at 9:15 each weekday morning and heard in about 100,000 classrooms, averaging about 3 million listeners daily. Lomax created a "Folk Music of America" segment that aired each Tuesday for twenty-six weeks. The program had a different theme each week. For example, on the February 20, 1940, broadcast the theme was "Negro Work Songs." Leadbelly was among the guests.

Lomax spent time with the folk singers, listened to their problems, and provided counsel. He taught them songs. He helped nurture their intellectual instincts. He had learned music theory and history from Charles Seeger. This, combined with the collection experience he got from his father, his knowledge gained from listening to so much material, and his institutional affiliation at the center of American folk music gave him a vision from atop the folk music world that the singers didn't have, that no one else had. This perspective helped him see where those singers fit, how he could help advance the careers of those he wanted to help, where the movement was, and where, in his opinion, it should go.

Alan Lomax was the great impressario of the folk song movement. If Woody Guthrie was the writer, Alan Lomax would be the collector and publicist, a man who with his family, personal, and institutional connections was seen as an authority on folk music. He would, sometimes through his radio shows, sometimes behind the scenes, endlessly promote the cultural products he believed would lead to a better world.

Having helped discover and promote Leadbelly to the public, Lomax took upon himself the task of finding other singers, encouraging them, and helping them develop their careers, and getting their songs before the public. Like some strategic master builder, he did this with single-minded devotion and brilliance.

Sonny Terry was one of the singers he helped. Lomax met Terry, a blind harmonica player, at the first of the "Spirituals to Swing" concerts and recorded him for the Library of Congress the next day. Terry was blind from two childhood accidents. For two years after the second accident he stayed in his house out of shame. Only the wailing and shouting accompanying his harmonica playing gave him solace. On it, he could mimic the cries of the train whistles and the animals. As a teen he wandered from town to town, showing up on paydays and playing his music. One day he was in Wadesboro, North Carolina, visiting his brother when he met Blind Boy Fuller, by then a successful recording artist. Fuller invited the youngster to record. Only a year later, John Hammond, searching for performers for his concert, had come to North Carolina to invite Fuller. But Fuller was in jail, and Hammond heard the amazing work of Sonny Terry.

Alan Lomax had many great successes in finding, developing, and promoting talented folk singers. For the promotion of the folk song movement his greatest success was helping the man who would, more than anyone else, make folk music popular.

Pete Seeger's life was far removed from Woody Guthrie's hardscrabble existence. Seeger's family ancestry went back to the *Mayflower*. His uncle, Alan Seeger, a poet famous for "I Have a Rendezvous with Death," died during World War I. If Joe Hill had been born in a foreign country and Woody Guthrie in a state that had only recently been admitted to the United States, Pete Seeger's family was deeply rooted in America.

In 1914, Charles Seeger, then teaching at Berkeley, decided to explore radical politics. He gave a talk about Wagner during the 1848 revolt to a club run by the IWW. They mocked him for being naive. He marched with the Wobblies but never formally joined. Just like Woody Guthrie,

Charles found a more congenial politics as he began to follow the Russian Revolution.

It was natural in such an environment that by thirteen Pete subscribed to *The New Masses*. Pete Seeger became a radical not because he saw his people become victims as Woody had but because of his upbringing and his own study.

He devoured novels about Native Americans. He liked the idea of early peoples, pristine, untouched by human civilization. He thought, "We don't realize how much we lost when we became civilized. We lived in small tribal groups. We all did a little of everything.... Singing was one of the things nearly everybody did.... Then along comes the agricultural revolution. Now there's a class society. The aristocracy could have music made for them. And then when cities really developed people found they could pick up coins singing in the street. This is the first pop music."[5]

In the summer of 1936, seventeen-year-old Pete Seeger stayed with his father in Washington, where Charles had gone after departing the Composers' Collective in New York. Pete met his father's friends, including Alan Lomax. At the time the Lomaxes had arranged for Ruth Seeger, Pete's stepmother, to transcribe Library of Congress recordings.

Pete listened attentively, but he grew increasingly frustrated with his four-string banjo playing as he tried to replicate the sounds he heard. His father suggested trying a five-string banjo and seeking advice from Bascom Lunsford, a famous banjo player in North Carolina. Several weeks later father and son headed to the Ninth Annual Folk Song and Dance Festival in Asheville. Mesmerized, Pete listened to the banjo pickers, the old men who had spent dying summer evenings on the back porch drinking lemonade or moonshine, swatting away flies, and playing and singing to ease their burdens.

Pete Seeger made his decision: He would learn, no, he would master, the five-string banjo. And he absorbed another crucial lesson: The popular songs on the radio weren't the only music available. The songs his stepmother transcribed were made real to him in the North Carolina hills. This music breathed in and let out the real air of the nation. As his father was discovering, this was the people's music; the proletariat sang with a banjo or a guitar on a porch, not from some microphone high above a city street.

Seeger went off to Harvard on a scholarship, read Spengler and

Goethe, but found his real interest came from music or books like Carl Sandburg's *The People, Yes.* He became increasingly interested in politics and increasingly uninterested in the life of scholarship. He wanted to be a journalist, and Harvard, which didn't teach the subject, wanted him to master sociology. He got angry when the famed scholar Pitirim Sorokin answered Pete's query about why there was a necessity to use big words by telling the young student that it was crucial to be impressive. Pete's poor grades resulted in a loss of his scholarship.

He knew it was time to bust out, to get started in the world. He preferred his ambition and optimism to the shrewdness of obtaining a Harvard degree. He keenly felt that it was a greater risk for him to remain in a safe haven than to venture forth into a dangerous and uncertain world. In April 1938, just short of his 19th birthday, Pete Seeger crossed Harvard Yard, saw John Kennedy, another member of the Class of 1940, rushing along with his personal secretary, and wandered away from the traditional route to a good life.

Seeger headed to New York, determined to be a journalist, but he could not get a job. He tried painting. His art teacher told him to stick to the banjo. His aunt got him some singing jobs, but they didn't pay much.

Alan Lomax called one day to invite Seeger to meet Leadbelly, then in the city. The guitar playing entranced Seeger, who had met few black men in his life. Leadbelly began giving him lessons.

Lomax, only a few years older than Seeger, but bolder and worldlier, advised Seeger to turn to folk music and backed up the advice with a plan. Lomax suggested Seeger come to the Archive of American Folk Song in Washington to catalog and transcribe songs in the archives. Reality had its own way of pointing toward a future, and Seeger saw all the signals: More and more he looked to music as his livelihood.

Lomax could only pay fifteen dollars a week, but for the puritanically frugal Seeger, it was enough. And so during the winter of 1939-40 he got the kind of education a college couldn't provide. Day after day, he imbibed the music almost no one else had heard. He discovered a world, one populated by song characters he treasured. He had found his direction home.

He aided others as he made his own journey. And early in 1940 he met Woody Guthrie, a man who changed his life just as he would change Woody's.

Back in California, Woody had begun performing in union halls and at rallies after appearing at the concert for Tom Mooney. He also wrote a newspaper column titled "Woody Sez" for the *People's World*.

Ed Robbin became Woody's booker, mentor, and friend. Slowly, Woody, mostly a social isolate, found his social circle among the Communists on the West Coast. Robbin introduced Woody to the actor Will Geer, a friend from Robbin's college days, who eventually gained national fame as Grandpa on *The Waltons*. Geer, a bi-sexual, had been introduced to Communism by his longtime lover Harry Hay, who eventually played a crucial role in gay history by founding the Mattachine Society in 1950. Geer, in turn, introduced Woody to many of his acting friends. It was at Geer's house that Woody first met Cisco Houston.

Cisco — he was born "Gilbert" in 1918 — took his nickname either from a small California town or, more likely, from the famed Cisco Kid, a Western hero originally created by O. Henry, and a nickname Woody heard him use. The name change may have been made to hide the radical past of "Gilbert Houston." Houston had nystagmus, which made him unable to see what was in front of him, although his peripheral vision was decent. His color blindness once cost him a job in a pickle factory; he couldn't distinguish the colors of the various labels. During the Great Depression, after his father had abandoned the family, Houston and his brother began a desperate life traveling, struggling to find work of whatever kind. He was a cowboy and a lumberjack. He worked farms and served as a "barker" standing in front of a burlesque house trying to lure customers inside.

As he traveled and worked, Houston learned all kinds of songs. Even as a child he had been interested in music, and now he was absorbing all that he could.

At 20, he was in Los Angeles, and his good looks helped him decide to be an actor. He located a theater group that considered itself "anti-fascist," a useful euphemism then used for leftist and pro–Communist groups. It was there that he had met Will Geer.

Geer invited Woody to sing with him on weekends in the migrant camps established by the government. Cisco Houston and others sometimes went along. Geer wanted to help the Communists organize the workers. A deal was struck. Geer paid for the gas and some food along the way, and Woody drove his 1931 Chevy.

As he sang for them in the camps, Woody heard the migrants sing a beloved old hymn "This World Is Not My Home," made famous by the Carter Family who recorded it as "Can't Feel at Home." Woody was shocked as he grasped the song's message in a new, political way. The hymn offered religious solace and a message to ignore the woes of this world, accept them without protest, and simply wait to die and go to a better world that would be the migrants' real home. This was not the message he thought migrants needed to hear, so he took the tune and added the words he thought more properly belonged, words that spoke of homelessness and fighting the law.

Seeing all the suffering migrants each week made Woody angry over and over again. Woody concluded that only the Communists were willing to stand up for the working people, to fight back against the bankers.

But his full political understanding of Communism was incomplete. He was still writing about individual heroes, not the working class as hero. In March 1939, for example, Woody wrote about the outlaw Pretty Boy Floyd. Prohibition — by then almost a decade old in the United States — had unintentionally made real-life crooks into folk heroes. In Woody's decidedly a historical version, Floyd was a Robin Hood, forced into an outlaw's life and someone who helped people. They were not at all like the bankers who robbed people in their own way.

Woody would never fully resolve the tension between the admiration for an individual struggling and the more ideological assertion that people had to join together to effect political change. Just as a description of the society was the first phase of his writing, the focus on individuals as capable of solving society's problems can be seen as the second. But individual outlaws are captured or killed. There was an inherent logic to Woody's position and it drove him to the Left. As Woody's political affiliation to the Party grew closer and closer, there came a crucial turning point both for Woody and all the people in the Communist movement.

On August 23, 1939, Joachim von Ribbentrop, the foreign minister representing Nazi-led Germany and Vyacheslav Molotov, the Soviet Union's foreign minister, signed a non-aggression treaty, familiarly known as the Hitler-Stalin Pact. The agreement proclaimed that the Soviet Union would not intervene if Germany attacked other nations, and the Nazis promised not to invade the Soviet Union. In practice, the Pact allowed the Soviets to occupy the eastern half of Poland, one-sixth of Rumania, and the Baltic States of Estonia, Latvia, and Lithuania. Assured that he would not have to wage a two-front war, Hitler waited barely a week before invading Poland on September 1 to trigger World War II.

The Pact also provided that the Soviets would supply Germany with raw materials, shipping it by rail because of the British sea blockade. From the beginning of World War II until the Nazis broke the treaty, Stalin provided the Nazis with 1.5 million tons of oil, along with grain, rubber, phosphates that were crucial for explosives, timber, and other materials.

The reason that the Hitler-Stalin Pact is so important for the story of the folk singers is that until the Pact it is possible, at least up to a point, to appreciate the lures of Communism for American artists and intellectuals in the 1930s. The daily visible devasting human effects of the Great Depression, the brutal beating and shooting of striking workers, the stark disparity between rich and poor, the maddening corporate callousness evident in indifference toward the plight of the poor, the excitement of a new ideology that seemed to be working in the Soviet Union, the interpreting of history both in the Soviet Union and in a depression-soaked America as heralding the collapse of capitalism, the thrilling chance to take part in the building of a new and better world, and the need to unite against Fascism all constructed an understandable ideological home for some.

It should be noted, however, that such attractions were limited. The excitement among the intelligensia never translated into national electoral victories. Despite electing numerous local officials, the Socialists and the Communists, separately or combined, did not do well in presidential politics. As it turned out, the Debs 1912 campaign was the most successful. In the 1916 presidential election, the Socialists got 3.10 percent. In 1920, with Debs again as the candidate, they got 3.41 percent. In 1928, Norman Thomas (who was the Socialist candidate for president from 1928 through 1948) got 0.73 percent of the vote. Given the effects of the Great Depression and the agitation of the Socialists and Communists and their sympathizers, American voters might have become attracted to their candidates. However, in 1932, Thomas only got 2.23 percent of the vote (although that small percentage included 884,885 voters) and William Z. Foster, the CPUSA candidate, got 103,307 votes, or 0.26 percent. (Some prominent American writers supported Foster. They included Sherwood Anderson, Erskine Caldwell, Malcolm Cowley, John Dos Passos, Theodore Dreiser, Upton Sinclair, Lincoln Steffens, and Edmund Wilson.) In 1936, with

Communists in a post–Popular Front world generally supporting Roosevelt, Thomas got 0.41 percent of the vote.

Americans generally didn't trust ideologies that had their genesis on foreign soil, especially when those ideologies were hostile to religion. Neither of those inhibiting factors, however, affected intellectuals. They, after all, lived by, for, and off ideas, and most of those ideas had come from Europe. They lived in a world after Darwin, Dostoevsky, Nietzsche, Bergson, Freud, and Einstein, and many of them increasingly viewed religion as pre-modern. Few Communist supporters, that is, felt much cognitive dissonance prior to late August 1939.

There is an ongoing dispute among scholars of the CPUSA about the relationship between rank-and-file members and the Soviet Union. Everyone seems to agree that the CPUSA leadership supported the Soviets. Some scholars believe the rank-and-file did as well, while others claim that people on the Left who were members of or sympathetic toward the CPUSA had very little to do with the Soviet Union, that their interests and energies were devoted primarily to American domestic problems.

One cautious approach is to note that those who did care about the Soviet Union could have found many troubling signs. There was, for example, a famine in the Soviet Union in 1932, but Stalin blamed reports of such famine on capitalist propaganda. Reports of visitors did not make the situation clearer. George Bernard Shaw came to visit during the worst part of the famine and tossed his food out the train's window before crossing into the Soviet Union, so convinced was he that there would be no shortages. Indeed, while eating at a restaurant catering only to foreigners, he looked around and asked, "Where do you see any food shortages?"[6]

The world now knows that Stalin was responsible for the murder of millions of people. Although the figures are difficult to determine and in dispute, it seems clear that in 1937, the worst of the years of terror, seven million Soviet citizens were arrested, perhaps one million eventually executed and two million were put in camps, half of whom died there. By the end of 1938 about eight million were in camps.

Still, the full horrific extent of Stalin's murderous regime was not at all clear then.

Pro-Communist Americans who cared about the Soviet Union may or may not have followed stories of the Soviet Union in the media. They may have limited their sources of information to Communist publications in the United States. However, even if they had read every story about Stalin published in the *New York Times* in 1937, they wouldn't have had a clear picture. On March 9, they would have read about orders that the Communist party had to increase its democracy. On March 28, they would have read a story on Page One with the headline: "Stalin Calls Halt on Fulsome Praise," with the sub-heading: "Cracks Down on Flattery of Him and All Other Soviet Leaders as 'Complacent.'" On June 13, they would have read how Stalin honored his mother in a ceremony. On September 16, they would have read about how the Soviets had raised the educational level of students.

There were, of course, also stories about the terror and about the struggles between supporters of Stalin and Trotsky. There were reports of executions and imprisonments, but stories of famine, relocation, mass imprisonment and execution could not be found.

Given all that, there is some excuse for those who sympathized with the Communists. They may have been ignorant of a sufficient number of facts to be horrified.

The Hitler-Stalin Pact ended any excuses for ignorance. Perhaps that is why the initial reaction to the Pact among American Communists was shock. How, they wondered, could the Soviet Union, the fiercest opponent of Fascism, the model of a new world, make a deal with the brown-shirted Devil? In the United States, the Communists suddenly found themselves aligned with the isolationists, some of whom were on the far Right, some of whom were anti–Semitic, and some of whom didn't believe, for ideological or economic reasons, that the United States should get involved in another European war. Charles Lindbergh was the most famous proponent of isolationism on behalf of its most prominent organization, the America First Committee. Established on September 4, 1940, the Committee was funded by some of the very business leaders the Communists detested. The Committee was chaired by General Robert E. Wood, the head of Sears, Roebuck and Company. Henry Ford and other tycoons either joined or supported the work of America First. The Committee's approximately 800,000 members also included two future presidents, John F. Kennedy and Gerald Ford; a future Supreme Court Justice, Potter Stewart; people from the entertainment industry, including Walt Disney and Lillian Gish; and writers including E.E. Cummings, Sinclair Lewis, and a young Gore Vidal, then one of the few pro-isolationist students at Choate.

Frank Lloyd Wright donated to the Committee but was denied membership because the group thought his moral behavior was questionable.

CPUSA members left in large numbers. Numerous Jewish supporters of the Party departed, as did an enormous number of writers. Whittaker Chambers viewed the Pact as the decisive moment in his turn away from Communism. The Party, after the Pact, attracted only a thousand new members a month, a quarter of the pre–Pact numbers. The Popular Front activities ended, replaced by cooperation only with other pro–Soviet Communist groups. Radicals and liberals, who had worked together, were suddenly at odds. The CPUSA support for Franklin Roosevelt dissolved into mocking him as a war-monger.

And the folk singers saw artists who refused to go along. Charlie Chaplin was "horrified by the Soviet-German pact,"[7] according to Dan James, Chaplin's assistant on the film *The Great Dictator.* Chaplin had finished writing that film, which mocked Hitler, but had not yet begun shooting the picture when the Pact was signed. Had Chaplin, a man of the Left himself, chosen the path of the folk singers, he would have simply abandoned the project. Instead, Chaplin began his shooting on September 9, or almost immediately after the invasion of Poland.

Woody Guthrie, Pete Seeger, and all the folk singers Alan Lomax discovered, whether fitfully or enthusiastically, continued their allegience to the Communists.

It was the Hitler-Stalin Pact that caused Frank Burke, Woody's boss, such concern. Woody staunchly defended the Soviets on his radio show. Burke asked Woody to temper his support. Woody flatly refused. Burke didn't want to fire Woody. He liked the funny young man from Oklahoma. All he asked was that Woody sing the songs the listeners wanted and stop supporting the Soviet Union on the air. The tensions continued until November 30, 1939, when the Soviets attacked Finland. A Gallup Poll revealed that 99 percent of Americans supported Finland. Frank Burke was among the majority. He could take it no more. He confronted Woody. This was the moment of decision.

In the end, though, Woody simply had no choice. He always had to do what he thought was right, independent of any personal economic consequences. As much as he loved the songs his boss wanted him to sing, they had in his view been overrun by history. Woody Guthrie surrendered his livelihood and his microphone.

It is reasonable under the circumstances to wonder why, to wonder what kind of man Woody Guthrie was. Like all human beings, and maybe in an even more exaggerated case all artists, Woody was a contradictory person. It is misleading to add him like some newly netted butterfly to a collection with a label. He, as Bob Dylan would later be, was constantly on the run from being pinned down. He needed to be free to keep exploring the world in his own way, which was writing, whether songs, books, articles, letters, or just notes. Words sprang out of him like some Oklahoma oil gusher. His speech came out like talking blues.

His search began with a childhood curiosity that never ended. After his family fell apart, the constraints that bound most young people simply disappeared. As his daughter, Nora, notes: "His curiosity wasn't naturally inhibited by family, by religion, by education."[8] He allowed no fences to restrain his roaming. His soul had its own passport to cross the borders that made others halt. He wanted to see all that the world had to offer. He felt burdened by reality's refusal to let him escape the boundaries of nature and the human condition.

He constructed a hayseed persona to present to the world in his writings, in his play-acted thick Oklahoma accent when he needed to use it, and in many other ways. The persona helped him identify with ordinary people. It gave him an advantage over others who misjudged him as an unlettered rube. It let him judge people by how they reacted to him as someone (at least seemingly) poor and uneducated. It added to the sense of authenticity that especially Eastern audiences craved. It enabled him to keep the most precious part of himself private, masked by the hillbilly front. It gave him a new identity as "Woody Guthrie," master folk singer, a man who knew that guitars don't lie, a man who sang truth to power. He was no longer Woody Guthrie, skinny pint-sized kid from Okemah whose mother had died in a mental hospital.

Parts of Okemah stayed with him always. He had a deep love of the natural wonders of the country. Its beauty awed him, and when he saw its valleys, mountains, and skies as belonging to and shared by all the people, not just owned by the rich who bought the land and then kept others off it, he had his complete vision.

Woody retained a great faith in Jesus as a healer (he called Jesus a doctor in letters to people and often included references to God). Marjorie, his second wife, was Jewish. When hospital officials asked what they should fill out under "Religion" on the birth forms for Woody and Marjorie's children, Woody insisted on "All." When the officials hesitated, he told them it was "All" or "None." His spirituality was reflected in his attitude toward government. He thought a government should display deep love, affection, and tenderness toward its people. At its best, it should share nature's bounty and governmental largesse with all the people.

He identified with Jesus as a rabble-rouser on behalf of the poor, as someone with a gritty determination to rectify wrongs done to the downtrodden, and as a believer in love as the ultimate answer. He even wrote a song titled "Christ for President."

Woody also believed that Jesus was an early Communist and would be one again if he were alive in the 1940s. In Woody's view, the most important person who ever lived was also the poorest. The sentiment poured out into the song "Jesus Christ" in which Woody imagines that the same sad fate that befell Jesus for defending the poor would occur again if He showed up in New York City.

In some sense, Woody wanted to be Jesus with a guitar. But that identification did not mean that Woody was religious in a traditional way. He saw the people in charge of the church, the very people who were supposed to embody Jesus' teachings, as corrupting the message. He detested people who used religion for their own purposes rather than to help the needy.

Woody wasn't always easy to live with. He ate over a sink while others were at a table, or repeated annoying lines over and over, or didn't take baths, or slept in a bed with his boots on, or just was ornery and confrontational. Woody gave people a lot of trouble; some of them enjoyed it and some couldn't live with it.

Woody assertively chased women whether or not he was married at the time. It was as though he felt that only by being faithless could he escape the mundane and grasp the tragic or that the farthest corners of his soul could only be reached as he observed his own reactions to each new romance. He was once briefly jailed for writing obscene letters to Lefty Lou's sister. He tried to justify his behavior by claiming a belief in free love. As an artist, Woody saw himself as released from the bourgeois morality of American society.

He wanted to live the Protestant American Dream: sin, suffering, and salvation. He testified in his songs as a sinner trying to do better in life.

There are, of course, non-religious explanations for his aberrant sexual behavior. It is unclear, for example, to what extent the Huntington's disease that would kill him affected his behavior. It may have affected his frequent drinking, or his inability to stay in one place, or his sexual escapades. There is also a psychological explanation offered by Diane Kovacs, a marriage and family therapist, who suggested that in constantly going from woman to woman Woody was really looking for his mother.[9] It is not surprising, given this explanation, that Woody used to sit and brush Marjorie's hair as she played the piano just as he had done for his mother.

Beyond religion, Woody had a homegrown Socialism. He hated the greedy. He never learned to trust money. As Pete Seeger said about Woody, "He felt there was a great tendency once you got working for money to do what money wanted you to do and not what the truth wanted you to do."[10] The suffering he saw tested Woody's optimism, but it was the optimism that won out. Woody believed there was a better way, that ordinary people would triumph, that people were born to be winners. His prophecy was of a better world, and it infuriated him that not everyone was working toward it. He ached for that world.

Woody's Socialism was all-embracing and filled with love. But that part of him lived alongside another part, one that drew sharp battle lines, that still loved the poor but believed no one could extract compassion from a banker's heart. Woody saw that tension, one of many he lived with, but the tension was part of his life and work. His songs tried to harmonize what life couldn't.

Like Joe Hill, Woody believed, based on ample personal evidence, that life was a constant struggle. As he wrote in a July 15, 1946, letter to Moe Asch, who had recorded his songs: "I have always said in my songs and ballads that this old world is a fight from the cradle to the grave. I have never sung nor made songs just to entertain the upper classes, but to curse their ... reckless racketeers, and to warn the nervous ones that live and die by greed."[11]

Woody Guthrie found the Communist Party so attractive for a lot of reasons. He saw them organizing the desperate workers. Their way of thinking was congenial to his own. He thought they were creating a heaven on Earth, that he was going straight ahead in history's direction. They gave him recognition. Better yet, they gave him paying audiences, crucial for someone who didn't have access to popular record labels. They told him he was a genius. They gave his talent and his life a direction. They were young, and he was young. He saw the Communists — as he saw blacks, migrant workers, and Jews — as outsiders, despised by the society, in need of love and support and help. This added to the Party's attraction.

As Ed Cray, Woody's biographer, notes, "He put aside his judgment for that of the Party because the party was doing other things that he valued even more."[12]

Woody could never be a doctrinaire Marxist or sit still at cell meetings or even reliably attend regular sessions. As his daughter, Nora, says about the Communists, "They were so well organized, Woody couldn't work with them. He preferred to be the soundtrack for the movement."[13] That's why he noted in his date book on July 19, 1942, that "when three Communists meet, the fourth one ought to be a guitar player."[14]

After Woody left his radio job he decided he would be that guitar player. He drove his family back to Texas to their ramshackle home. But he couldn't take the noise, the pressures, the sense of being away from the fight. Will Geer was acting in New York. Union Square in that city was the place where the radicals always held their largest rallies. He knew he would find friends and audiences there. Woody Guthrie knew it was time to go back on the road.

But he didn't know that what he would hear on the trip East would anger him enough to write his most famous song. Or that he would turn out to be the crucial folk song writer and performer the left-wing folk song community so desperately needed, someone who had suffered with the workers, someone who could proclaim the union movement throughout the land. He didn't know that when he finally met Alan Lomax and Pete Seeger he would help give birth to the folk song movement.

Five

The Endless Hootenanny:
The Birth of the
Folk Song Movement

Early in January 1940 Woody drove his car through a blizzard to Okemah, sold the car to his brother for thirty-five dollars, and used the money to buy a bus ticket to get as far toward New York as he could. The money got him to Pittsburgh, and from there he hitched and rambled until he caught a ride from a forest ranger. Sitting in the back seat, with the animal skins and the traps, Woody had time to think.

The snow and the wind had made getting rides difficult, but what really bothered him was that, even on his way to Okemah, in almost every car he traveled, every diner where he ate chili and sipped coffee, and every roadhouse where he stopped to throw back a shot of whiskey the radios and jukeboxes kept playing Kate Smith's rendition of Irving Berlin's patriotic song *God Bless America.* The jukeboxes especially were in thousands of bars. Once prohibition had been repealed in 1933, the cocktail lounge and bar owners couldn't resist the sales pitch: The customers got cheap entertainment and the owners had a new source of revenue.

Woody felt surrounded by exactly the kind of song he hated, one that made people think they didn't have to worry because God would take care of them. He mistrusted any songwriter who had never seen a dust storm, or stayed in some four-bit flophouse, or begged for a meal. Grimly, he determined that he would write a response when he could.

Exhausted and grimy, Woody finally arrived in New York on February 16 and made his way to Will Geer's apartment. The actor and his wife took him in and let him sleep on the living room couch. Woody, they learned, was not housebroken. He smelled like someone who had been on the road, and Herta Geer was concerned about germs affecting her new baby. Woody kept odd hours. He borrowed Herta's guitar on the promise to take care of it but then refused her request that he put it in a case when it rained. He brought back to the apartment newly made buddies he'd found in the bars where he swapped stories and songs for drinks or some money.

It took a week of such behavior for the Geers to act. Herta wrote Woody a letter gently asking him to leave. She placed it on his chest as he slept. She walked to the living room when she heard him awaken. They stared at each other. They spoke some empty pleasantries and then Woody scooped up Herta's guitar and left.

Woody moved into a fleabag hotel, fancily named Hanover House, at the corner of Sixth Avenue and 43rd Street.

It was time to answer Irving Berlin.

He took a piece of loose-leaf paper and jotted down the title for his new song: "God Blessed America." Alternating between writing down the words in pen and strumming his guitar, he began the song. He stopped, unhappy with the flow of words, and then continued.

Woody found his tune from the Carter Family's "Little Darlin,' Pal of Mine." In turn, the Carters had adapted it from a Baptist hymn titled "Oh My Lovin' Brother." Happy with the tune, Guthrie churned out five more verses, including one left out of most versions because of its explicit opposition to private property.

There was one other protest verse about people at a relief office. When he finished, Woody put a note at the bottom of the page—"All you can write is what you see," signed the page "Woody G., N.Y., N.Y., NY." and put down the date, February 23, 1940.[1]

Then he put the song away for four years.

Meanwhile, Will Geer had arranged for Woody to appear at his first important New York performance. On February 25, Woody sang at a benefit concert for the Spanish Refugees Relief Fund aimed at aiding those who had fled the Franco regime. Alan Lomax approached Woody after the concert, impressed by the performance.

But it would be Woody's appearance at a concert on March 3 that changed folk music history.

Geer was appearing at the Forrest Theater in a play titled *Tobacco Road* and had arranged the use of the theater for a midnight concert, a "Grapes of Wrath Evening" to benefit John Steinbeck's committee that helped agricultural workers. The movie version of Steinbeck's novel had just opened to great acclaim, especially on the Left.

The concert brought together the people who defined American folk music of the era. Leadbelly and Aunt Molly Jackson were widely known in left-wing circles. Guthrie's name was much less known, but his writings had gotten him some attention. Alan Lomax and his sister, Bess, were there.

Burl Ives also was on the bill. The name "Burl" meant a knot in a piece of wood; Ives appreciated the name. At 20, after two years of college, Ives and his banjo took to the road. He hopped boxcars and walked when he had to do so. He sang the song hoboes liked best, "The Big Rock Candy Mountain," as he begged food from tramps. He was arrested in Mona, Utah, for vagrancy and for singing "The Foggy, Foggy Dew," a tune the two police who arrested him considered obscene.

Making his way to New York with the aim of being an actor or a singer, one evening in 1937 he attended a performance of Marc Blitzstein's controversial musical, *The Cradle Will Rock*, which was directed by Orson Welles and was about the owner of a steel mill and much else who opposed efforts by workers to form a union. After the performance, Ives went to a bar next to the theater and spotted Will Geer, a performer in the play. Ives introduced himself. Geer, who was from Indiana, welcomed the young man from Illinois. When Geer heard that Ives played a guitar and sang, the actor quickly located a guitar and heard Ives's distinctive voice. A few days later Ives went to Geer's apartment for a party and met some of New York's left-wing activists. A woman at the party enlisted Ives to sing on behalf of the Abraham Lincoln Battalion. When Ives appeared, he was amazed at how well he was received; he saw in that audience the kind of people he liked. Alan Lomax had him on his radio show, and so it was natural for Ives to appear at the "Grapes of Wrath" evening. Six months after the concert CBS radio hired him to perform on the air, eventually leading to his own show *The Wayfarin' Stranger*.

There was also a 20 year old making his professional debut at the concert. Alan Lomax had invited Pete Seeger to appear.

Aunt Molly Jackson led off the evening. And then, Woody Guthrie, billed only as "Woody" and wearing his cowboy hat and boots, strolled onto the stage, scratched his head with a guitar pick, used his best Oklahoma twang to say "Howdy," and delivered his powerful Dust Bowl ballads. Like Will Rogers, he pushed his hand through his hair and filtered his experiences through humor: "There is one thing about New York, and that is the way you can get tomorrow's paper last night, that is ... tonight. The capitalist papers are so far ahead of the news that they know tonight what happened tomorrow, but they never do go to the trouble of informing their readers what they really knew yesterday."[2]

The crowd loved it. It was an act, but it was a great one. The singer seemed to come from some casting agent for a Hollywood movie about authentic folk singers — dirty, with an accent but not so thick he couldn't be understood, funny, radical, *real*. And the songs were hypnotic. Their pain seared in a way that the slick popular stuff never could. And, best of all, he had written them. Here was a man of the people who hadn't gone to a fancy college or grown up in intellectual circles in New York. Here was a man everyone in the crowd had been waiting to find, and a man many of them wanted to be.

For Pete Seeger, though, the evening was not so successful. Seeger had been in the wings throughout the concert, especially impressed by Woody. Finally, Seeger's name was announced. He ambled out and retuned his banjo although it was already tuned. He blinked; the stage was unfamiliar territory. He was surprised that the blazing stage lights would not let him see beyond the front row. He had not learned how to play his five-string banjo well. His fingers could not find the right strings. His mind failed him as he forgot one of the verses to "Ballad of John Hardy." It was a disaster.

But despite his shyness, the rawness of his talent, and the embarrassment of the performance, Pete Seeger would not quit. In a way, the evening's failure steeled his determination. He knew he belonged up there.

At a cocktail party after the "Grapes of Wrath" concert, Pete Seeger was determined to talk to Woody Guthrie. Alan Lomax did the introductions.

Lomax later dated the birth of renewed interest in folk songs to that meeting. Guthrie, Lomax, and Seeger were the heart of the new folk music movement. Guthrie wrote the songs using familiar folk tunes and substituting politically provocative lyrics for the regular ones. Lomax collected the folk songs, re-branded them as political songs, and found left-wing singers to sing them and the new songs that emerged. Lomax used his position on the radio and his connection to the Library of Congress to redefine what folk songs meant to the culture, and he did his best to make them understood as political statements. Pete Seeger popularized Woody's songs and many more traditional folk songs. And so that night a movement was born.

No movement was ever made up of more individualists. But they did see themselves as acting together in common cause. They didn't always find it easy to get along, but they were attracted to each other because they shared a great love of music and language, and a political ideology, and they had a powerful emotional affinity.

They were all idealists. They couldn't wait a single second before starting to make the world better. They dreamed in the day, not just in the night. They mocked the idea that a desperate society could leap across canyons in small jumps. They refused to see mere endurance, the strength to tire out a relentless fate, as the sign of a noble life.

Drawn together as though by some magnetic force, the three men began with a plan Alan Lomax had for Woody and a plan for Woody, Pete, and himself. He invited Woody to record for the Library of Congress and on March 21, 22, and 27, 1940, did the recording — which only became available decades later. He had a book in mind for the three of them. He noted that traditional collections of folk songs deliberately edited out political material and songs considered obscene for any reason. For two months starting in April the three worked on compiling a book of political songs. Woody provided information about the songs and Pete transcribed them. When the book was completed, Lomax unsuccessfully sought a publisher. The book, *Hard Hitting Songs for Hard Hit People*, appeared twenty-six years later.

Lomax didn't just envision one book; he had a vision and plan for an entire movement. He had a plan for everyone he admired who could promote and publicize the cause of left-wing music. Woody was his exciting new discovery, so he struggled to launch the young man's career. Victor Records had asked Lomax to record a folk song album, but, pleading time constraints, Lomax suggested that although he couldn't do the record there was an exciting singer who had lived the life of the Okies. Impressed by the publicity given the release of *The Grapes of Wrath*, Victor agreed provided Woody included a song about the movie's hero, Tom Joad. As Pete

Seeger tells the story, Woody asked Seeger where he could find a typewriter. Seeger took him to a friend's sixth-floor apartment. Woody sat at the typewriter, accompanied by a half gallon of wine, and his guitar. Using the melody from the song "John Hardy," Woody worked through the night. When Seeger arose the next morning, he found the wine bottle emptied, Woody sleeping on the floor, and the ballad "Tom Joad" still in the typewriter. Woody told the story in seventeen verses. John Steinbeck later expressed mock anger at Woody's accomplishment.

Woody recorded the album on May 3. It was his first commercial recording, and the most successful one he ever made — but fewer than a thousand copies were sold.

A few weeks later, Woody invited Pete to go on a trip west. Pete was then living in Arlington, Virginia, with Alan Lomax and Nicolas Ray, who went on to direct such movies as *Rebel Without a Cause*. Seeger, much more sheltered than Woody, agreed, and the two got into Woody's new Plymouth and headed toward Oklahoma.

They were a musical odd couple. Seeger was much taller, from a stabler family background. Woody could be mesmerizing when he talked. Seeger didn't have Woody's natural speech rhythms. But he was an eager pupil. Woody was warm and open with his emotions. Seeger was meager with emotional expression. Woody never passed an open bottle or a pretty woman. Seeger, as Woody noted, didn't look at the women, or drink, or smoke. Seeger's songs were his harem; the songs were always available to be called upon to please him.

And Seeger certainly did sing. He could follow Woody, not an easy task for other musicians. Everywhere they went the exuberant Woody and the restrained Pete wandered into bars, picked up hitchhikers, and heard story after story. They always sang. For Seeger, whose knowledge had come mostly from records and books, the trip was a revelation. Here he was, finally, with people who were characters, who lived the lives Seeger had only imagined, who lived the songs Seeger had learned.

In Oklahoma City they stayed with Communist Party organizers Bob and Ina Wood. They sang at a union gathering, and afterwards Ina Wood berated Woody and Pete for not singing about women in the union movement. Woody responded the next day by borrowing her typewriter and composing one of his most famous songs, "Union Maid." Still, though, the hero was an individual.

It is possible to consider Woody's songs of collective action as the third phase of his songwriting career, after describing the society and focusing on individual rebels doomed to failure because they acted alone. But Woody's greatest songs are about individuals or natural beauty.

After leaving Oklahoma City, Woody and Seeger drove to Pampa to see Woody's family. Seeger was shocked at the housing and embarrassed at Mary Guthrie's mother's request that he convince Woody to spend more nights with his family. Woody, ever restless, could stay only three days before the two travelers headed back to New York.

Meanwhile, Lomax continued through the year to promote folk music. In August, he and Nick Ray co-produced a significant new radio program titled *Back Where I Come From.* The show aired for fifteen minutes three times a week on CBS. Regular cast members included Woody, Leadbelly, Burl Ives, the Golden Gate Quartet, and a handsome, golden-voiced singer named Josh White.

White was born in 1915 in Greenville, South Carolina, and knew the burdens of being black from an early age. As a child, he saw his father, a poor preacher, beaten because of an unpaid bill. Dennis White eventually died in an institution, having never recovered.

At seven, Josh helped a blind man across the street. The blind man, a musician, asked if the young boy could lead him. For a decade, White went from city to city, leading a total of 66 blind musicians. Paid $4 a week, rarely fed, making his way without shoes, sleeping in open fields, Josh's job was to sing and dance, play the tambourine, and, most crucially, collect coins from the gathered audience. He saw a lynching and another black man who was burned at a stake. He learned that being black was a full-time job. The musicians would not teach him the guitar, so White had to learn himself, quietly at night while the musicians slept. He began recording at 13. White had a smooth, articulate voice.

Meanwhile, Woody and Pete had arrived back in New York in the spring, but Pete, having tasted the road, was hungry for more of its toughening lessons. Finally, the sheltered boy could be authentic, not by journeying to Harvard Yard but by hopping freight trains, eating a can of beans in some hobo jungle and meeting the real people, the ones whose culture was being ignored or mocked. He was back in New York in September 1940—arriving just in time to hear that Leon Trotsky had been assassinated in Mexico.

Seeger had started 1940 like a boy, but he was finishing it like a man. He was hardened, physically and emotionally. He now thought of himself as a musician; he had earned the right to sing American songs.

While Seeger traveled, Woody was becoming a radio attraction. And friends were coming to New York. Cisco Houston showed up, and he and Woody started to perform together. But while Woody liked the money from radio, he didn't like the rules. As he commented about broadcasting censorship: "The radio agent gave us friendly talks about not singing any song that took sides with anyone, anywhere, on any fight, argument, idea, or belief from a religious, scientific, political, legal or illegal point of view, nor from any point of thought that would cause anybody, anywhere to think, act, move or perform any motion in any direction, to agree or disagree with any single word of any one single song or conversation."[3] Woody was soon fired. He headed west.

Seeger was back again in New York in November. When he arrived, a friend named Pete Hawes told him someone else was compiling a book of pro-labor songs. Lee Hays was that someone else.

Hays was a tall, heavy man with a bass voice, a dry, cutting wit, a way with stories, and an ability to charm an audience. The son of an Arkansas preacher, he had gone to Commonwealth College, a place devoted to radical education. Drawn to left-wing causes, he headed to New York in October.

Millard Lampell, more a clever writer than a singer, was Hays's apartment mate. They had both written articles for the *New Republic*, liked each other's articles, and corresponded. Lampell couldn't resist joining in as Seeger came over. Hays was deeply impressed by Seeger's banjo, and Seeger liked Hays's manner. Hays immediately suggested they pair as a duet. Seeger was a bit hesitant, but he quickly realized he had not yet mastered the ability to sing and play the banjo simultaneously. Hays was the perfect complement to his voice and an antidote for his own performance weaknesses.

They made their first appearance in December at the Jade Mountain restaurant on behalf of Spanish loyalists. They got $2.50, but Seeger said, "You take it. I got five bucks for singing ten days ago, and still have most of it left. You need it more than I do."[4]

It wasn't long before Lampell started singing along with them and composing provocative lyrics. He wrote peace songs, protesting against potential American involvement in the European war.

As the trio began to get bookings, they searched around for a name and decided on the Almanac Singers. The name came from a letter written by Woody Guthrie. Hays later explained the name: "If you want to know what the weather is going to be, you have to look in your Almanac. And if you want to know when to plant your seeds or what side of the moon to dig 'em in, or when to go on strike, and if you want to know what's good for the itch, or unemployment, or fascism, you have to look in your Almanac."[5]

In early May 1941 Eric Bernay, who had sponsored John Hammond's "From Spiritual to Swing" concerts, and who ran Keynote Records, put out an album of their songs, though, in what turned out to be justifiable fear of political repercussions, he issued their album, *Songs for John Doe*, under the fictional name "Almanac Records." Bernay had received some financial support for the album from Hammond as well as Earl Robinson. At the time of the release, a Frank Capra movie titled *Meet John Doe* was creating a sensation on the Left because of the movie's political message, and so Nick Ray suggested that a variation on that title might help sales.

Seeger asked Josh White to join the group for the album, and White agreed.

Songs for John Doe was meant to be biting, sarcastic, and as bluntly opposed to America's entering the war as possible. It succeeded.

In "Plow Under" the Almanacs attacked the draft. In "Billy Boy," the wealthy war profiteers who made money on others' suffering were ridiculed. One way to interpret these songs is as simple parodies of popular songs put to use to promote a noninterventionist position. That is, the Almanacs did what Woody did: they took familiar tunes and provided new, political lyrics. But from a distant vantage point of history it is now clear that the songs on the album weren't just humorous songs. The songwriters misread history. For example, also in "Billy Boy" the character in the song says that he'll fight when England becomes democratic. That is, England was the moral equivalent of its enemies. President Franklin Roosevelt's efforts to provide assistance to England as it faced a formidable Nazi threat were hurt in the United States by labor strikes precisely at those factories producing war materiel that England could have used, so that such moral equivalence provided comfort and justification to those on strike.

Songs for John Doe had other clear targets: Franklin and Eleanor Roosevelt. "The Ballad of October 16" in particular electrified the Communist left. At one meeting of the League of American Writers, Theodore Drieser leaped up and kissed Lee Hays on the cheek. Positive stories about the group appeared regularly in *The Daily Worker* and other Communist publications. For example, a reporter named Don Russell wrote an article for *People's World* in which he caught the communal nature of the Almanacs' songwriting: "They all contributed — Woody a line, Pete a line, Lee a suggestion. Millard was at a portable typewriter, banging out the lines as they evolved. Occasionally they joined together to sing a completed verse or two. Then there were more rapid-fire suggestions, revisions.... New phrases came from the guitar or banjo.... Woody, leaning back on a couch, suddenly broke out with a brand new verse.... The verse went down on the typewriter — and then it was revised. At the end of about an hour's work, four verses were completed. They got together and sang the completed song."[6]

Woody did get into a lot of arguments about the songs, especially with Lampell. Woody hated songs with slogans. He was a balladeer, a songwriter who liked to tell a story about a real person and have any lessons emerge from the story. He thought too many of the folk songs the Left wrote and performed were about abstractions, not people.

The Almanacs produced songs that not only hewed to the party line but also were funny. The language was much more sophisticated than Aunt Molly Jackson's and so could more forcefully appeal to the intelligence of the music's still mostly urban audiences. Still, however clever the songs, they only stayed for a short while on history's stage. Because the songs were frequently tied to specific events in a specific era, they could not transcend the brief moment.

The songs, though, came at a useful time for the Communists. In a post–Cultural Front era, uneasily allied with corporate and isolationist right-wing forces in opposing American entry into the war, the Communists were dispirited. *Songs for John Doe* did what music does best. The album lifted their spirits, reinforced their sense of political identity, and offered much-appreciated laughter. For the first time union audiences heard songs about union members. "The only group that rehearses on stage,"[7] as Woody called them, was a hit.

The Almanacs moved to a loft on Twelfth Street. The loft became the central address for wandering singers. Pete Hawes joined the Almanacs. The group decided to host rent parties on Sunday afternoons. John Hammond had suggested the idea after seeing some of them in Harlem.

In May, the group recorded a second album called *Talkin' Union*. The Almanacs' pro-union songs were so popular that they planned to do a tour playing to selected Congress of Industrial Organization (CIO) audiences. The CIO organized workers into industrial unions and was more militant and assertive than their rival, the American Federation of Labor.

While the Almanacs were enjoying their success, Woody Guthrie was in Portland, Oregon. Alan Lomax had suggested his name to the Bonneville Power Administration. The BPA wanted to hire someone to write songs for a public information film. Woody immediately agreed. He was thrilled that the federal government was providing so many jobs and acting to help the farmers who got inexpensive electricity from the building of the Grand Coulee Dam on the Columbia River.

Woody had a chauffeur who liked to ramble as much as he did. The two spoke to workers and stared at the awesome power of the dam and the miraculous beauty all around them. Woody always took notes in his small notebook and sang in the back seat. Then he'd go to the Bonneville office and sit hunched over a typewriter working away. Of course, he was Woody so he'd stop from time to time to serenade the secretaries. Even by Woody's incredible standards of creativity, this was a remarkable period. He wrote twenty-six songs in the month of his employment, including some of his most memorable including "Roll On, Columbia" and "Pastures of Plenty."

In "Grand Coulee Dam," Woody's lyrics rose to poetry. The BPA had gotten a lot for the $266.66 it paid Woody for the month. The job ended on June 11, and Woody decided to return to New York. He was almost there when Hitler again shocked the world.

It was Sunday afternoon, June 22, 1941. A rent party was underway at the loft. Suddenly one of Lampell's friends charged inside and announced to the stunned group that the Nazis had invaded the Soviet Union. The people in the loft didn't know what to do. Since the Hitler-Stalin pact, they had argued vociferously for the United States not to get involved in the European war. But now the Soviet Union — that model society, that nation where the future was being hatched — was in trouble. How could the folk singers sit still? But how could they turn around and now urge U.S. intervention?

Two days after the invasion, the group stopped attacking the president in their songs. Ten days passed, and they decided that consistency was less important than defending the Soviet Union. They justified their change by citing British Prime Minister Winston Churchill's about-face and his urging immediate support for the Soviets. History itself had changed, they reasoned, and they had to change with it.

The peace songs were out. Roosevelt was an ally again. Pete Seeger didn't like any war. Now he had to support one. The internal struggle Seeger and many others had between their pacifism and their support for the Soviets or their struggle against the Fascists always remained even if it was sometimes submerged. But he did force himself to suppress any personal conflicts for larger issues. Seeger had joined the Party, and he was going to stick with it. It was a sign of Seeger's character. He did his duty.

Songs for John Doe albums were withdrawn from sale. By some accounts, Bernay destroyed the albums he still had left and tried to recall those sent out.

The CPUSA's change of position led to some unusual confrontations. A Philip Randolph, the prominent African American leader and President of the Sleeping Car Porters, wanted to march on Washington in 1941 seeking to end job discrimination in those industries focused on war production. But the Party was against all strikes, so even though the Party had a history of supporting the rights of African American workers, it nevertheless bitterly opposed Randolph's efforts.

Indeed, the CPUSA's position on blacks was complicated. People like John Hammond, who was absolutely devoted to providing blacks with equal rights and integrating blacks into the mainstream of society, felt stuck. The political right was hostile to integration, and parts of it were openly racist. The Communists were more tolerant, especially those involved in music as Hammond was.

The problem for Hammond and others like him was two-fold. The official Party position was segregationist; the Party wanted to carve a separate nation for African Americans in the American southwest. Additionally, the Party focused on overthrowing capitalism, believing that racial (and all other) problems would be solved once capitalism was gone. Hammond believed, with considerable justification, that the Party used racial tensions when they thought doing so advanced their agenda, as in the case of the Scottsboro boys. These problems were only exacerbated by the Party's reaction to the Nazi invasion of the Soviet Union.

Woody Guthrie returned to New York right after the Nazi invasion, headed straight to Pete Seeger, and declared that the two of them would no longer be singing about peace. Seeger immediately asked Woody to join them on their tour.

The Almanacs headed west in a limousine Millard Lampell had gotten from the family of a dead gangster. The tour was musically successful. Audiences joined in boisterous renditions of the songs. But a sick Hawes left the group in Philadelphia. Hays got very ill on the west coast and took a bus home. A lonely Lampell, who had realized that he wanted to be a writer not a singer, also departed. Seeger and Guthrie were left to carry on with it.

In Seattle, they went to a party called a "Hootenanny." The word was new to them, but they liked its sound. "Hootenanny" had been used from Appalachia to the Ozarks to mean "without a care" as in not giving a hootenanny about some matter. Elsewhere it referred to any gizmo. Terry Petrus, an editor of the *Washington New Dealer*, recalled the term from his Indiana youth where it referred to an unplanned party, and in Seattle Woody and Pete attended precisely such a party with the name.

Back home, the Almanacs were discouraged. Robbed of their anti-war identity, unsure of what they could write about other than unions, they talked of abandoning their efforts. But as they struggled, their sense of mission was renewed when Pete Hawes rented a three-story building at 130 West 10th Street. The group named the place Almanac House. The hall led on the left to a living room filled with decrepit furniture, some couches, and easy chairs. The dining room was behind the living room. There was also an office. The front hall led to the tiny, filthy kitchen. On the right as visitors entered they go up the stairs to front, middle, and back bedrooms. Woody lived on the third floor in what amounted to an attic.

New people came to join them, including Hawes's younger brother Baldwin, known as Butch; Alan Lomax's sister, Bess (who later married Butch Hawes); Arthur Stern; Agnes Cunningham, nicknamed "Sis"; and Gordon Friesen, her husband who arrived in New York in October 1941 and moved to Almanac House around the beginning of December. Others joined in irregularly so that the "Almanac Singers" could now perform in two places at once. Bess Lomax was the only Almanac House occupant to hold a regular job. Woody, perhaps on the principle of first you eat and then you can be honest, shoplifted some food from local stores, at least according to Sis Cunningham.

Lee Hays and Woody liked each other even when they argued the way brothers argue. They had been born near each other and shared similar senses of humor as well as religious and political sensibilities.

Hays and Woody also had their differences. Hays was a world-class kvetch, and Woody was always an optimist. But Hays didn't mind a drink or two. That pastime made them amiable companions. Seeger, always annoyed that the communal money needed for supplies seemed to vanish whenever Hays and Woody got thirsty, bristled at their behavior, as did most of the others. For many people, it was easy to see their drinking. Not so many could see their thirst. Eventually, the relationship between Seeger and Hays got so bad that Hays was forced to leave the Almanacs.

The Almanac House had regular hootenannies on Sunday afternoons in the basement to pay the $95 a month rent, but even people who didn't live there, like Mill Lampell, visited virtually daily. And when people came, they argued some and they sang. It was an endless hootenanny.

New people came along for the singing. One of them became Sonny Terry's musical partner. Brownie McGhee was from Knoxville. He had gotten infantile paralysis as a young child but an operation sponsored by the March of Dimes allowed him finally to walk without using crutches. McGhee began walking and playing his guitar, eventually meeting up with and serving as lead boy for Blind Boy Fuller. Because of Fuller, McGhee met Terry, but it was only after Fuller's death that the two first recorded together on October 22, 1941. In 1943 they moved into Almanac House.

Almanac House life, along with life in the rest of the nation, was completely disrupted on December 7, 1941, when the Japanese attacked Pearl Harbor. In certain ways, the war made the world a lot easier for Woody, Pete, and the rest of the Almanacs. Roosevelt and Stalin were allies, at war against the Fascists. The Almanacs were now indistinguishable from the fiercest American patriots. But as singers, the actual coming of war made their lives difficult. Hitler's invasion had robbed them of the peace songs in their repertoire; the war meant they couldn't sing the union-stirring songs because they didn't want to encourage any strikes.

Alan Lomax, always a clever strategist, urged Seeger to change the Almanac Singers' name, which was associated with peace and union songs. But for Seeger maintaining the name was a point of honor. He had used the name "Pete Bowers" as a member of the Almanacs, but that was not out of fear. He simply wanted to protect his father who was a government employee.

And Seeger found himself with another personal dilemma. He had fallen in love with Toshi Ohta, who was half Japanese. The Party supported the rounding up of Japanese in the country and putting them in internment camps. (It is one of the ironies of history that FBI director J. Edgar Hoover opposed the internment while the Communists supported it and Earl Warren, as Attorney General of California, led the state's efforts to implement the internment.) Seeger ultimately simply ignored outside influences and married the woman he loved on July 20, 1943.

But at the beginning of 1942, the Almanacs had to find a way to keep going. They had lost Almanac House because they couldn't pay the rent, and so they moved to an apartment on Sixth Avenue. They became newly born as pro-war and anti-strike. Woody used some blue paint to add a slogan to his guitar: "This Machine Kills Fascists." The Almanacs were still clever and talented musicians, so they looked for new material. In reaction to the death of ninety-five people on the first American ship torpedoed, the *Reuben James*, the Almanacs helped Woody finish a stirring song about the incident. Woody wanted the song to incorporate all the names, but Seeger and Lampell prevailed.

The patriotic Almanacs were suddenly hot. The talent agency William Morris signed them to do a national tour.

The problem was the Almanacs were not, by any definition, typical singers. Money and success were foreign ideas to them; they weren't sure if they wanted them or not. The Almanacs wanted to be purists. They thought that writing a song was like staring into a reflecting pool: A liar should not expect to see a prophet stare back.

Woody, in particular, scorned money and what he had to give up to get it. One famous incident, for example, involved a potential booking at the Rainbow Room, a famous nightclub on the top of Rockefeller Center. Even before they started, Woody hated the place for its wasteful elegance while his people starved. While Woody had lived in a piano box, the people doing the auditioning were the kinds of people who owned the piano.

The Almanacs sang their popular song "Round and Round Hitler's Grave," a rousing call to kill the dictators. Woody and Lampell, livid at the surroundings, stared at the three men facing them and improvised words slyly attacking the values of those listening to them.

The men listening, thinking the words simply clever and, not getting the message, laughed and applauded. They definitely wanted this group. But they had a few suggestions. They thought the group would work better if the men wore overalls and the women sunbonnets. And a few bales of hay for atmosphere would be great.

The group was shocked and humiliated as they left. They had mocked those wealthy people who had the great strength to endure the tragedies of the poor. Now the Almanacs were auditioning for them.[8]

Woody was determined that show business would not ruin the moral purity of the Almanacs. Woody stole silverware from a ritzy hotel where the William Morris Agency had organized a reception for the talent brokers needed to book the national tour. Several weeks later a William Morris agent, who had been forced to pay for the silverware, noticed it on the Almanacs' table.

But the Almanac fame continued to grow. On February 14 they appeared on the nationally broadcast "This Is War" and agreed to do a daily radio show. Decca offered them a contract to record.

The Almanacs' appearances in nightclubs and radio marked a new stage in the folk singers' movement. Rather than singing to unions, these radicals were now entertainers. Their songs could captivate the masses.

They had entered into the heart of American profit-seeking capitalism. Part of the reason for their appearing on radio at all had to do with competition in the music industry. The motion picture industry had controlled the music industry through ASCAP (the American Society of Composers, Authors, and Publishers). As radio competition reduced the size of movie audiences, the movie companies sought to make up for their losses by doubling the royalty rates paid to ASCAP. The radio stations, angered at this doubling of their fees for the music they played for their audiences, responded by forming their own organization, BMI (Broadcast Music Incorporated) on January 1, 1941. Having revolted, the radio stations now needed new music and that meant musicians who didn't have contracts with ASCAP. The Almanacs' timing, that is, couldn't have been better. The anti-capitalists got on radio in part because of capitalist competition.

Woody and Pete reacted to this new role in very different ways. Woody, while wanting recognition, could never see himself as a popular entertainer, as someone singing for someone else's pleasure rather than for their political education. Pete was much more conflicted. He shared

Woody's disdain for the corporate powers that put him in front of audiences. But he thought once he got the audiences, he could shape them. He thought he could beat the capitalists at their own game while Woody didn't like playing the game at all.

Seeger's analysis was crucial. It would later be the basis for another group he was in, the Weavers, and provide a justification for the folk singers of the 1960s. The Almanacs were the model for the folk song movement to cooperate with business without selling out. They let folk singers think of themselves not exclusively as radical activists but also as popular entertainers. Seeger himself could never quite resolve the inherent contradictions between the two identities, and some later folk singers could not either.

The Almanacs also did not see all the by-products of success. There was a natural tendency not to want to regress professionally or personally. Having tasted applause, money, and fame, it was not easy for the Almanacs to give them up for principles. And if an empty stomach does not always provide accurate political advice, neither does an overly full stomach. Every time they were in a nightclub, the Almanacs weren't playing to the workers and weren't hearing the stories they needed to hear to keep their material pertinent to their cause.

They didn't grasp that the American economic system — in front of their eyes and with them as an example — could absorb radical music by transforming rebellious songs into entertainment.

As quickly as fame had kissed them it slapped them. Three days after the "This Is War" show, the New York *World-Telegram* ran a story connecting the Almanacs to the Communists. The New York *Post* had a story the next day repeating the charges but with an emphasis on *Songs for John Doe*.

Bookings were canceled. So were future radio shows. The Morris agency dumped them. Decca told them there would be no record.

Once the Decca deal disappeared, the Almanacs released a new album, though one without Woody, on Keystone. Seeger had written "Dear Mr. President," which became the title song on the album. Seeger, speaking directly to a man he had politically opposed, urged a common effort to defeat Hitler. Any differences, he sang, could be put off until after that.

It was a conciliatory message, but it was not enough. The Almanacs were done.

Their role in folk music history, though, was enormous. They became the model for all future folk groups from the Weavers, in which Seeger and Hays took major roles, to such groups as Peter, Paul and Mary. Individually, Woody Guthrie and Pete Seeger had defined what it meant to be a professional folk singer.

Lomax, Guthrie, Seeger, and the others re-defined the whole idea of folk singer. Before them folk singers were anonymous people who sang for solace and family entertainment. The Carter Family and Jimmie Rodgers were professional singers, but they sang of personal not social issues.

Guthrie and Seeger created a new meaning for "folk singer" as someone who was concerned about the society as well as the song. Seeger especially worked tirelessly during his entire life to promote this idea.

After the Almanacs, Pete Seeger was fully formed as a folk singer. In many ways, he was an unusual person to become Woody Guthrie's heir. Woody needed a private self. Seeger needed a private world. The world within Seeger was kind, decent, friendly, humane, and idealistic. It did not, that is, very much cohere with the real world. Seeger wanted to believe the private world and the real world were the same, which made him not very knowledgeable about mundane matters in the real world. But he thought it was reality that was counterfeit, forged by the capitalist criminals in power. If facts were not in conformity with his ideology, he reasoned that something was wrong with the facts. He was an internationalist musically and politically. He sought to incorporate musical instruments and songs from around the world into his repertoire. And he saw a world undivided by nation, race, religion, or any other category he considered divisive and artificial.

Woody thought genuine prophets unmask the present to reveal its true nature and by doing so provide a guide to a brighter future. Seeger's prophet envisioned the future and lived in that vision, constantly acting so that society could conform to that vision. It was Seeger's political passion that allowed him to overcome his intense shyness and transform it into artistry.

But Seeger overcame it all on his way to embodying the very idea of folk singer. Such success was not apparent to the Almanacs as they broke up.

Seeger received his draft notice. Alan Lomax went into the army. Sis Cunningham and Gordon Friesen left New York for a while. Cisco Houston, who had joined the Merchant Marine early because his brother was killed in its service, eventually convinced Woody to join. Before he did, Woody's autobiography *Bound for Glory*, which is best read as a novel, appeared and received an appreciative review in the *New York Times*. Woody joined the Merchant Marine in June 1943 and served with great bravery.

Josh White meanwhile had become a favorite of Franklin and Eleanor Roosevelt. White played at the president's 1941 inauguration. His album *Southern Exposure* soon followed. There were a half-dozen attacks on segregation by the outspoken White. Roosevelt reacted to the controversy the album engendered by having White give a Command Performance at the White House, the first time that honor had been accorded an African American. Then White went to the First Couple's private quarters where they discussed White's songs and the nature of segregation and Jim Crow laws. White eventually frequently spent holidays with the Roosevelts, ultimately affecting the president's views on segregation, especially in the armed forces.

White also began to appear at Café Society in 1943 and by 1944 he was the club's most important act. This was more crucial than it might seem. Café Society attracted leaders of national culture. Josh White, that is, has the strongest claim to the title of the person most responsible for introducing the various types of black music, including gospel and blues as well as folk, to white audiences. And White had another breakthrough, not explicitly written about publicly at the time but in its own way just as important. Josh White intentionally and successfully exuded a highly erotic presence to the mostly white audience. This resulted in a few confrontations with white men who were unhappy that the women they accompanied were attracted to White.

He also had a weekly radio show. His most successful song, "One Meat Ball," was released in 1944.

Woody was back in New York in that same year. Alan Lomax (or perhaps Pete Seeger) told Woody about Moses Asch, who had a recording studio and a desire to promote folk music. Woody went there, introduced himself, and the irascible Asch eventually agreed. There were no formal sessions. Asch paid Woody about $25 a session and afterwards the two, often joined by others, had dinner.

Woody began to record on April 16, singing just two songs. He was back three days later, but this time Cisco Houston accompanied him on many songs. The next day, April 20, more songs were recorded. There were hundreds of songs on Asch's acetate discs.

At the last of those sessions, on April 25, Woody pulled out a song he had written four years earlier and included it nonchalantly in the middle of the session. The title was changed, and there was a new line at the end of each verse. *This Land Is Your Land* was recorded for the first time. The private property verse was included, but it was the only protest verse.

The song, still unknown to the public, continued to evolve. Starting in December 1944 and going to February 1945, Woody had a weekly radio show and used the song as his theme and included it within the songbook he offered his listeners. That version took out the two original protest verses but added a whole new one about freedom.

Asch didn't have the funds to release the recordings. (They remained unreleased until 1997 when Smithsonian Folkways Records issued them.)

Woody was never as vital a political songwriter again. In the postwar world, his health deteriorated because of Huntington's disease, and tragedy decided it was not done with Woody Guthrie. But Woody never lost his aura; he eventually couldn't sing, but at the end his face's lines were as true as a song's.

This is not to dismiss Woody's continuing musical contributions. He continued to write creative and moving songs. It is simply to note that the major political songs audiences associate with Woody had been completed.

Woody's contribution to political folk music was unique and enormous. He convinced political activists that they could take apolitical folk music, make it political and moving, and reach people. He proved that political folk music could be artistic, even poetic. He was unafraid to fuse his religious feelings to his political ones.

Woody transplanted the idea of mythic hero from stories to folk singers. Like the greatest of those mythic heroes, Woody had courage. He was resourceful. He had an enormous talent, and he used it in an extraordinary way. He lived, figuratively and sometimes literally, outside the law and wrote about others who did. He was wounded by fate, by fire, by poverty. His pain was profound. His story followed the story arc of a mythic hero. He came from common folks, but he heard a call. He went out into the world seeing its ruffians, criminals, cowards, victims, and heroes. He brought his message back to the people through his songs. Woody became the model of the singing hero.

But he was a hero with flaws. Woody's professional failures, his inability to reach a mass audience during his most creative years, stemmed in part from his unbending allegiance to doing what he thought right for the poor and his disdain for the commercial music world. His personal life was a shambles, hardly matching the soaring idealism of his lyrics.

The political folk singers tried to re-group as the Second World War ended, but they came under withering attack when the Cold War began. This ragtag, poor, radical group of musicians seemed headed for extinction. Josh White, Burl Ives, and many other folk singers were successful during the late 1940s.

The more explicitly political singers — Pete Seeger and Lee Hays, for example — survived because of their talent, evident in the emergence of an extraordinarily popular new group, the changing nature of music, and, most surprisingly, because of the vicious attacks and overreaction of their enemies.

Six

Are You Now or Have
You Ever Been...?
The Folk Singers Under Attack

The whole world changed. The Great Depression was over. In April 1945 three world leaders died. President Franklin Delano Roosevelt, far sicker than the electorate realized, died on April 12. Benito Mussolini was caught, executed on April 28, and placed upside down on a meat hook. On April 30, Adolf Hitler took poison and shot himself in the mouth. To avoid Mussolini's fate, he ordered that his body be burned. Within four months frighteningly powerful new bombs were dropped on two Japanese cities, and World War II ended.

After the war, buoyant young American soldiers wanted to return to get married, start families, and escape the cities by building homes in the wilds of suburbia.

But not everyone was happy with what they found. The spirit of cooperation that propelled America through a dark fifteen years of poverty and conflict eroded. The workers who had not struck during the war felt they deserved higher wages once the war ended, and they wanted the wages to be unaccompanied by a rise in prices.

In January 1946 two million workers went on strike. There were 5,000 strikes during the year. There were bread, meat, and housing shortages and a threat of inflation. It looked for a while like the labor unrest of old had returned.

But the American economy was not the same one of the 1930s. There was money to give to the strikers. The manufacturers paid for these union increases by raising prices, replacing some workers with machines, seeking help from the government, or — eventually — having goods manufactured by cheaper labor overseas.

Americans were desperate for peace, a chance to spend their new money, enjoy their children, and laugh. The Soviet Union, however, was not so obliging to those American dreams. While both Britain and the United States demobilized their troops, the Soviets didn't withdraw their troops from Eastern Europe after the war. They imposed Communism on the countries they controlled and built barriers made from barbed wire. They added mine fields and watchtowers to complement the guards at the border. (Winston Churchill made his "iron curtain" speech on March 5, 1946, because of such efforts to keep Eastern Europeans within the Soviet orbit.) Most Americans — particularly those of Eastern European origin, such as Poles — were shocked and outraged.

In July 1945 the hard-nosed William Z. Foster, who had opposed a ban on strikes during the war, was appointed to lead American Communists.

The folk singers, who had nobly and bravely served America during the war, came home expecting to build on what they had started. Pete Seeger and some friends had planned for a new post-war organization as early as 1944. After spending six months confined to a base in Biloxi, Mississippi, while Military Intelligence investigated his Leftist connections, Seeger had suddenly been sent to Saipan where he booked acts for soldiers wounded in hospitals. He had made his post-war plans there.

And a new tradition began in the summer of 1945. A printer named George Margolin had begun to sing on Sundays at the fountain in Washington Square Park. A crowd gathered the first time he had done so. The next week others brought guitars, and eventually everyone from a sick Woody Guthrie to Bob Dylan, who sang for quarters, showed up there.

Woody, in the army until January 1946, came home in November to marry Marjorie, the one person who, for a time, provided stability. Woody had divorced his wife Mary in March 1943. The eventual birth of Woody and Marjorie's first child together, Cathy Ann, brought him enormous joy.

On December 9, 1945, Oscar Brand began his Folksong Festival on radio station WNYC, a tradition that had lasted long enough to get Brand into *The Guinness Book of World Records* as the longest-running radio show with the same host.

On December 31, Pete Seeger called a meeting in the basement of his in-laws' Greenwich Village home. About thirty people gathered round to hear the ever-energetic, ever-visionary Seeger plot out the next steps. He wanted, he said, an organization — it was named People's Songs, Inc.— to spread the non-commercial songs that would make for a singing labor movement, that would reflect the joys and struggles of the lives of workers and their families. The group collected $150, rented an office on West 42nd Street (a tiny room with a library, desk, and file cabinet), and began the monthly publication *People's Songs Bulletin,* which was only available to People's Songsters, those who joined the group, as did, for example, George Margolin who sang the radical songs in Washington Square Park. A few months after the organizational meeting, in March 1946, a National Board of Directors was elected. Seeger was the national director.

People's Songs set up a booking agency called People's Artists. Woody Guthrie was often requested, but he didn't always show up or make much out of his performances. Even though Seeger spent hours on the phone trying to convince organizations that they pay actual money for the performers, People's Songs never charged more than fifteen dollars; five dollars for a half hour of singing was more common.

People's Songs also put on hootenannies and concerts, ran classes, and published song sheets and books, filmstrips, and records, in addition to their magazine. They made the word "hootenanny" popular as the name of folk music programs.

The folk singers were particularly fond of the hootenannies, which they began on May 9, 1946, at Town Hall. They thought the hootenannies, beyond entertainment, would serve a political recruiting function. The logic was clear. If the folk singers could sing the right songs well enough they would arouse the folk consciousness of the American working class. Then the workers would join arms and voices to rebel against the capitalists who were running their lives unfairly. The workers would awake and sing, as the title of a fervent 1935 Clifford Odets play put it. (The title was taken from Isaiah 26:19 in which it was the dead, not the workers, who awoke and sang.)

Instead, the hootenannies provide a good explanation about why People's Songs ended up without, as they so devoutly wished to do, changing the world. The folk singers misunderstood their audiences.

Some people in the audiences simply enjoyed the songs as entertainment. Some wanted a chance to feel rebellious without really rebelling. For the duration of a concert, these audience members could be in the company of noble, slightly dangerous singers and could feel as though they were genuinely taking part in some social movement — and then they could get in their Chevrolets and drive back to their suburban homes.

Even audience members who were genuinely capable of or actually had engaged in political activities were misunderstood. They were frequently audiences in transition. In the 1930s they were first- or second-generation immigrants who were using the folk movement as a way to assimilate into American society. (In the late 1930s, for example, there were about 20,000 American Communists. According to R. Serge Denisoff, an anti–Stalinist supporter of Leon Trotsky and a leading scholar in the folk music field, only one in seven of them spoke English.[1] Even if Denisoff's numbers are exaggerated, as they probably are, his fundamental point is valid: a large number of Communists had not yet assimilated into American life.) When they did assimilate, the music became either nostalgic or even an embarrassing reminder of their immigrant status. Relatively few retained their rebellious ways.

But the folk singers had problems bigger than the audiences, both on a personal and political level.

Woody Guthrie's Huntington's disease worsened, resulting in odd behavior, although even his friends ascribed what he did to heavy drinking. He wouldn't always show up for performances. When he did, he sometimes forgot the lyrics and stood swaying and strumming a guitar as his mind struggled to find its way back. His little daughter, Cathy Ann, provided his only refuge from the world inside his head that made less and less sense and his body over which he had less and less control. He loved to make up nicknames for her. He used her creative language to write songs.

A few days after Cathy Ann's fourth birthday, the girl was sitting on the couch in her pink birthday dress. Marjorie ran to the market across the street to get some oranges and milk; she was gone for under five minutes, but when she returned she saw smoke snaking its way out from under the front door. When she got inside, Marjorie saw her daughter burned and Arthur Young, a sixteen-year-old neighbor from upstairs, trying to smother the fire. The radio's electrical cord had short-circuited and ignited a fire in the folding bed. Firefighters concluded that Cathy Ann had gone to put the fire out. Arthur had heard the child screaming and come running to help.

Woody came back from a concert that night and found a note telling him to go to Coney Island Hospital. His neighbor, Mrs. Shapiro, answered his questions about what had happened.

Cathy Ann died the next morning, February 10, 1947, at 11:30.

In some ways, the death date that an indifferent artisan eventually carved upon Woody's tombstone was wrong. After Cathy Ann's death, Woody was never quite alive in the same way again. Only Marjorie's incredible dedication through unbearable times, and the joys offered by their new children, Arlo, Joady, and Nora, provided him with some relief, some moments when he wasn't overwhelmed by a sense of being bedeviled by fire and disease, of seeing the innocent in his family consumed by relentless flames or anguished illness.

Seeger and the others at People's Songs didn't face tragedies like that, but they had professional and political problems. Still profoundly believing they were making a difference or at least constantly concerned about whether or not they were, they did not back away from their politics and did not hesitate to adapt to the Soviet post-war line.

The United States, however, did fundamentally change its relationship with the Soviet Union. On March 12, 1947, President Harry Truman proclaimed that the United States would provide military and economic assistance to Greece and Turkey to aid their resistance to Soviet expansionist plans. This marked the first time that the United States articulated a goal to contain the Soviets and not stand by as they sought to expand their sphere of influence in Europe and Asia.

The enunciation of the Truman Doctrine was the beginning of the Cold War. On March 21, Truman signed an Executive Order instituting a loyalty program under which the FBI had the authority to investigate the political beliefs of all federal employees.

People's Songs was undeterred. They didn't care that the Soviets were now America's enemy, that Americans were angry at Soviet imperialism and fearful of Soviet power. They justified in their own minds the Soviet control over other countries.

The topical songs they had written in the 1930s and early '40s were so restrictive in content that they couldn't be transmitted to the current generation, and the generation of the late 1940s and early 1950s did not want any new songs glorifying Joseph Stalin and the great hope of Communism.

But the folk singers continued publishing their songs, trying to make a difference and come up with a way to adapt to the new American reality. In 1947, Seeger began singing "We Will Overcome," giving it new verses, part of the traditional "folk process," which is a euphemism for lifting or changing existing words and tunes. The Rev. Charles Tindley of Philadelphia had written the song in 1903. There was also a black spiritual titled "I'll Be All Right," which was similar to the Reverend Tindley's song. It remains unclear which song came first. Tindley's song spoke of the singer overcoming some day, and the spiritual spoke about the singers deep in their hearts believing they'll be all right some day. In 1946 at a strike, one of the striking workers, Lucille Simmons, sang "I'll Be All Right" very slowly, giving it its familiar sound. To arouse support among the strikers, she changed the word "I" in the lyrics to "we." Other strikers began to use it, and Zilphia Horton, a labor educator, learned it and passed it on to Seeger. He, in turn, passed it on to several people including Frank Hamilton who, in turn, taught it to Guy Carawan, who eventually played a major role in making the song part of the Civil Rights Movement.

But in 1947, People's Songs had very different problems. In May, Irwin Silber was appointed executive secretary of the organization. Silber's nasal voice rang with ideological purity and constant certainty. Through his thick glasses, his eyes saw a world in need of reform, and he intended to instigate that reform from the People's Songs office. But there was internal dissension. Lee Hays was still drinking when he could. Still cantankerous, still amusing with his rural stories, still heavy though even more than he had been, still spreading gossip, Hays was asked to leave. Once again it was Seeger who delivered the news.

But the biggest problem People's Songs faced was an external threat from government authorities. Ironically and unintentionally, in the very act of trying to destroy the folk song movement it was the overreaction of their enemies that would one day allow the movement to be revived.

The FBI was one of those enemies. In May 1947, the organization identified People's Songs as a Communist front and began its investigation in an attempt to stifle dissent. The FBI had already monitored the Almanacs' tour and had an undercover informant and files. The FBI began a file on People's Songs, sent infiltrators to their meetings, recorded phone calls, and stole documents. People's Songs' connection with unions diminished because the unions rooted out Communists, and many of the unions banned singers with Communist associations. The folk singers were losing their prime audience.

But J. Edgar Hoover made a fundamental mistake in failing to distinguish between dissenters and those who posed a genuine danger to the country. The dangerous spies and subversives were a direct threat to the United States government and the American people. Seeking out and stopping them was a vital task.

Dissent, however, is crucial in a democracy. It gives people a chance to air grievances. In that sense, without intending to do so, the political folk singers helped Americans in their struggle against Communism. It was another way in which the folk singers didn't understand audiences. They intended folk songs to rouse people to action. That may, indeed, have happened. But some audience members released their anger through song. Their emotions would be used up in the performance and not available for political action. In the very act of performing, the folk singers were sending a message that such musical activity was morally equivalent to political action. The folk singers, that is, gave unintended emotional permission to audiences to limit their own political activities to strumming a guitar and raising their voices.

Additionally, the dissent the folk singers offered and the reaction to it allowed those in power to take the political temperature of the electorate.

Finally, Hoover didn't understand that People's Songs could never be a true adjunct of the Communists. Some People's Songsters were Communists; the others were deeply sympathetic.

But while the *Daily Worker* wrote glowing articles and posted notices and ads for the political folk singers' concerts, the Communist bureaucrats and probably most people in the Party didn't think music was revolutionary; they thought revolution was revolutionary. They continued to prefer classical music, or even jazz, while they continued to identify folk music as being hillbilly music and therefore beneath them. Additionally, they didn't, with good reason, trust even the political folk singers to follow party dictates unquestioningly. Totalitarianism relies to a considerable extent on making people not think, on numbing their minds, on boring them. The folk singers were never boring. They made — and intended to make — people feel and think on their own. Surely their music stirred some ardent Party members, but as a significant part of Party discipline and activity, the music was as dangerous as it was helpful.

Hoover had a difficult time determining how much dissent should be tolerated during wartime; it was a struggle in American history that went back to the debate over the signing of the Alien and Sedition Acts. He knew that some members of the Party — including within the OSS — were also spies for the Soviet Union, spies who achieved considerable success in analyzing American industrial and military production, most crucially in developing atomic weapons. He knew that other spies deliberately avoided membership in the Party. Still, Hoover of all people knew that the entertainers weren't spies. At their worst, they were misguided. Hoover's error was crucial because his activities made some of the legitimate dissenters into heroes and made the public ignore their Communist past. Without his attacking them, their support for a totalitarian regime would have been much more harmful to their revival or their legacy.

Beyond the FBI's activities, there were other efforts to brand the folk singers as Communists, a term loaded with increasing menace as the Cold War progressed. Also in May 1947, the newsletter *Counterattack* began publication with the specific aim of keeping track of individuals and organizations the editors considered pro–Leftist or pro–Communist.

The folk singers faced a third enemy as well. In October, the House Committee on Un-American Activities (popularly known as HUAC) began to investigate supposed Communist influence in Hollywood.

In an earlier guise, the Committee had originally aroused public outrage about Nazi and Fascist threats in America, but its chairman, Rep. Samuel Dickstein, a liberal Democrat, would, as HUAC later did with the Communists it called to testify, exaggerate the threat from those investigated. It was Dickstein's successor, Martin Dies, who expanded the Committee's work to examine the Communist threat, an effort expanded further under John Rankin, an unapologetic racist and anti–Semite. He asserted that slavery had been beneficial for African Americans and believed the New Deal was part of a Communist plot hatched by Jews.

The Republicans gained control of the House in 1946, and HUAC's new chairman, J. Parnell Thomas, was almost inevitably more clear-eyed than Rankin and more serious. He turned his attention West to Hollywood, the American Dream Factory.

While there were certainly a considerable number of CPUSA members and sympathizers among Hollywood's actors and screenwriters, they hardly posed a genuine danger to the nation. With all their support, for example, there were few films ever produced that could be considered pro–Soviet. Some principal exceptions were *Mission to Moscow* (1943), which justified Stalin's political purges; *The North Star* (1943), which idealized Stalinist rule and displayed Nazi atrocities in a Ukrainian village during the 1941 invasion; and *Song of Russia* (1944), which romanticized the Soviet Union as virtually Edenic. But, as the films' production dates indicate, they were made during a time of co-operation and can be seen as part of a common war effort rather than anti–American propaganda. There were many other films that some suspicious viewers found redolent with left-wing propaganda — films like *Our Daily Bread* (1934), *The Grapes of Wrath* (1940), and *Meet John Doe* (1941). In one way or another all of these films do challenge the economic status quo and offer an alternative involving group cooperation. They may have been meant to be propaganda, but they, like the folk songs, also served as a much-needed safety valve to release pent-up frustrations of moviegoers who might otherwise have channeled their fury into radical politics. Simply judging by the failure of the Communists to gain electoral support or foment a revolution, it seems unlikely that the films or the folk songs were very effective propaganda tools.

The Hollywood hearings included a common question: "Are you now or have you ever been a member of the Communist Party of the United States?" On November 24, 1947, HUAC cited ten Hollywood writers and directors for contempt of Congress. The artists had declared that HUAC was "preparing a Fascist America"[2] and tried unsuccessfully to invoke the First Amendment as providing protection against their testifying. Two of the ten were sentenced to six months in prison, and the others to a year. Ironically, Ring Lardner, Jr., one of the Hollywood Ten, served his prison sentence at the same time as HUAC Chairman J. Parnell Thomas, who had been convicted of taking kickbacks from staffers and maintaining creative expense accounts.

For all the fireworks the HUAC Hollywood hearings caused, such hearings did not aid the anti–Communist effort; in fact, they did much to undermine it. Why was HUAC interested in the entertainers? HUAC's members were ambitious politicians. Interviewing famous celebrities created headlines, provided money from those with anti–Hollywood (in some circles that was a euphemism for anti–Semitic) feelings, and garnered votes.

The first "blacklist" began the day after the contempt citation; all of the Hollywood Ten were fired, a forerunner of the lists of supposed Communists or sympathizers that would haunt the entertainment industry for a decade, and in some cases even longer. It wouldn't be long before, with this precedent, Congress turned its attention to the folk singers.

Through it all, People's Songs continued to maintain that their songs could reach people in ways that endless speeches and dry prose could not, that they could provide a sense of being in a struggle together, of not being alone in their feelings.

But, as if they needed another failure, the 1948 presidential campaign was a low point for them, showing the whole world how weak they were. The pro–Communists supported Henry Wallace, a former vice president, running for president as the nominee of the Progressive Party. People's Songs was thrilled. Maybe the Soviet-American friendship during the war had been supplanted by mutual distrust, but in Wallace the folk singers found someone they could whole-heartedly support. Seeger saw the candidacy as a sure sign of a national movement; he thought Wallace would get ten million votes.

Wallace was adamantly opposed to the Truman Doctrine of confronting the Soviet Union. He had additional views to attract the Communists as well. He wanted to outlaw segregation and permit all African Americans to vote. He wanted the government to provide health insurance for all Americans. That is, he had a clear liberal, left but not far left, platform. The problem for his candidacy was not particularly Wallace or his views. The problem was that his organization outflanked him, letting radicals not liberals into key positions. Suddenly, campaign materials began sounding more and more like the views of the pro–Communist Left. Aware of the presence of Communists, Wallace defended their being part of the campaign because he said he didn't want to engage in the same sort of red-baiting as his opponents.

Alan Lomax arranged for People's Songs to provide the Progressive Party with music. Seeger traveled with Wallace.

The electoral results were a disaster for the Left. Harry Truman won with 49.6 percent of the vote. Thomas Dewey, the Republican candidate, had 45.1 percent. Strom Thurmond, the candidate of the segregationist

Dixiecrats, got 2.4 percent and Henry Wallace received 2.4 percent. That percentage represented 1,157,328 votes, almost half of which (509,559) came from New York State. And not all of Wallace's voters were Communists or pro–Communists. The Progressives had gotten 18,602 fewer votes than the Dixiecrats. Additionally, the Dixiecrats received 39 Electoral votes. The Progressives got zero.

There was to be no mass movement. The Left simply had very little support from the proletarians they sought to organize.

Even as People's Songs was in its death throes, though, a seed was planted that would allow the folk movement to survive. A few weeks after the election, People's Songs was preparing for a Thanksgiving hootenanny. A participating dance troupe requested that a singing group accompany them. Lee Hays saw his moment. He had been thinking that it would be a good idea to start a sophisticated version of the Almanac Singers. At the various hootenannies different singers had performed together, originally planning to put together a chorus, but one combination was special. Seeger and Hays were two members of the quartet. Fred Hellerman was a 21 year old who had learned to play guitar onboard a Coast Guard ship during the war. After finishing his degree at Brooklyn College, Hellerman drifted toward a musical career. As a teenager, he had wandered into Almanac House and frequently showed up at the People's Songs office. Ronnie Gilbert was the fourth member of the group. She and Hellerman knew each other from Camp Wo-Chi-Ca (*Wo*rkers' *Chi*ldren's *Ca*mp). Gilbert had sung on children's radio programs and had worked for the government during the war. The four met in Seeger's basement to prepare a medley of songs for the hootenanny.

As they sang, they heard an incredible harmony. Every part fit. They began to meet on Wednesday nights to continue playing even as the musical world they knew seemed to be imploding.

People's Songs couldn't survive. Because of economic and social pressures, it ceased its existence in March 1949. The whole movement seemed to fall apart. Seeger's connection to the Wallace campaign hindered his singing career; he considered working in a factory. He planned to move his family to upstate New York and build a log cabin. Woody was arrested on April 29 for sending obscene matter through the mail; he had written explicit letters to Lefty Lou's sister.

After People's Songs foundered, its idealistic, optimistic members could not face defeat. People's Artists was founded on July 8, 1949, to continue the efforts that People's Songs had begun. People's Songs had developed out of an era of Soviet-American cooperation with a palpable sense of Popular Front cooperation. But as the Soviet line changed, People's Artists hewed more closely to Communist dogma than had its predecessor.

People's Artists decided to begin its efforts with a concert on the Lakeland Picnic Grounds in Peekskill, New York. Paul Robeson was scheduled to be the major attraction. The Ku Klux Klan had a chapter there. But even without them, veterans and others were outraged that the pro–Soviet Robeson and others would come to their hometown.

On August 27, in the hours prior to the concert, workers arrived to set up the public address system and prepare in other ways. According to novelist Howard Fast, who was there, hundreds of angry opponents of the concert arrived, broke chairs, burned song sheets, and screamed racist and anti–Semitic taunts, including declaring their intention to finish what the Nazis had started. There was a standoff for three hours before police arrived. The police turned back people arriving for the concert, telling them the concert had been canceled.

People's Artists was not about to be deterred. Infuriated by the attack, they re-scheduled the concert for September 4 and added Pete Seeger to the program. They hired guards to protect the more than 20,000 people who attended the concert.

All seemed to be going well. The concert proceeded without interruption. But the protesters were there, waiting for their chance. According to Pete Seeger and others, the police directed people leaving the concert to an access road. Driving out involved running a gauntlet as screaming protesters lined the road and threw rocks at the departing cars. Pete Seeger's father-in-law had to hurl himself over his grandchild to provide protection from the flying glass. Toshi had been concerned about their 3-year-old son as well as the one year old. But Seeger, steeled by principle and softened by innocence, had decided to bring his children to let them see the concert.

The crowd yelled and taunted the concertgoers, telling them to go back to Russia and calling them racist names. Cars were overturned and, according to Fast, 160 bloody, beaten people had to be taken to the hospital.

Beyond these vicious attacks, world events made it harder and harder for People's Artists to maintain a pro–Soviet line. On August 29, between the original Peekskill concert date and the re-scheduled one, the Soviet Union conducted its first nuclear weapons test. On October 1, Mao Zedong and the Communists took control of Mainland China, declaring the existence of the People's Republic. Americans were getting more and more frightened as they envisioned a looming, and deadly, confrontation with international Communism.

Meanwhile, Mario "Boots" Casetta, the son of vaudeville dancers who had headed the People's Songs branch in California, uprooted and went to New York City along with the record label he had co-founded in December 1946 with a composer named Fred Warren.

Charter Records was an extremely distinguished label among folk singers, and in New York Boots Casetta asked Seeger, Hays, Gilbert, and Hellerman to put their songs on record. The group had settled on the name the Weavers, after an 1892 play with that title by Gerhart Hauptmann, a Nobel laureate in literature. The play was a shockingly realistic attempt to display the poverty of workers' lives.

The group recorded five songs for Charter. "The Hammer Song" (later known as "If I Had a Hammer") was by far the best known of those songs. Lee Hays had written the words, and Pete Seeger the music. Eleven Communists had recently been convicted under the 1940 Smith Act that legislated against advocating the overthrow of the U.S. government. Hays and Seeger wanted to show their support for those leaders and their sense that the freedom to dissent was endangered.

The song was a model of Popular Front theory. The most explicit public statement of Lee Hays's views was in a letter to *New Masses* he had written in 1933 in which he stated solidarity with "rank-and-file workers for a Soviet America."[3] He structured "The Hammer Song" by selecting a key symbol of the Soviet Union — the hammer from the hammer and sickle on the Soviet flag — and connected it to a classic American symbol — the bell as in the Liberty Bell. He tied the two together by song. It was through that song that united traditional American patriotism and Communism that the songwriters claimed freedom and justice would emerge. Seeger and Hays, of course, understood those ideas in ways vastly different from that of most Americans.

The Weavers didn't know it, but they were going to change folk music history. First, though, the whole community suffered a shock when Lead-belly died on December 6, 1949.

The Weavers were hired for a two-week holiday performance at the Village Vanguard. Toshi supervised their wardrobe; the men wore blue corduroy jackets. This was not to be a repeat of the casual nature of the Almanac Singers. But the argumentative aspect of that previous group continued. Seeger especially felt uneasy about playing in a nightclub, in essence singing to the enemy. The men were unhappy about dressing up though Ronnie Gilbert, who knew how much working people enjoyed putting on fine clothing, was irked by the others' discomfort. Their private quarrels, though, were not brought on stage. There they were magic. In tribute to the recently deceased Leadbelly, they closed each show with "Goodnight, Irene."

At first, the Weavers did well, but then customers stopped arriving. The ever-resourceful Alan Lomax was not about to let his friends down. He brought Carl Sandburg, by then a famous writer, to see the group. Sandburg's shower of generous praise brought in the customers.

Lee Hays and the others recognized a regular each night by his laughter. Hays told his country stories in his Arkansas voice, and the man just laughed night after night at the same jokes. The man, Gordon Jenkins, finally introduced himself. He worked for Decca Records, he said, and wanted to sign the Weavers. Jenkins had to fight for them though; others at the company were unsure how to market them, unconvinced they were marketable, concerned about their radical background, or just confused by them. Jenkins would not be moved.

All during the first few months of 1950, while the Weavers were preparing for their first recording, the fear of Communism was growing almost daily. In January Alger Hiss, a State Department official accused of espionage, was convicted of perjury, though the verdict was tantamount to a recognition of Hiss as a spy. Three weeks later, on February 9, Senator Joseph McCarthy, the Republican senator from Wisconsin, made a speech during which he held up a piece of paper claiming it listed Communists working for the State Department. There is no recording of the speech, and accounts vary of the number of people he claimed were on the list. Early reports said he had spoken of 205 names, though he himself cited a lower number in commenting on the speech.

On March 1, Klaus Fuchs, a German-born physicist who had worked at Los Alamos and moved to England, was convicted of spying. He had provided the Soviet Union with crucial American and British information about the construction of an atomic and hydrogen bomb. Americans were shocked as Soviet spies, especially atomic spies, began to be arrested. (Fuchs, Julius Rosenberg, and others were verified as spies only in 1995 with the release of the Soviet decoded messages known as the Venona intercepts.)

Despite the pervasive fear, McCarthy's tactics were immediately questioned. Herblock (Herbert Block), a *Washington Post* editorial cartoonist, coined the term "McCarthyism" only a month after the senator's speech, to describe what Block and many other Americans came to think of as bullying tactics and defaming people without adequate evidence simply to prevent dissent.

There is an incredible irony to McCarthy. Many Americans admired him; Jack Kennedy, then a young, handsome senator from Massachusetts, went around the Washington social circuit with McCarthy. Even some who thought McCarthy oafish were scared by what they perceived as the very real threats America faced from the Communists and if someone was looking for these enemies, well, then a little overreaction was better than a lot of underreaction.

The irony is not that Senator McCarthy never had a legitimate list. The real irony is that by the McCarthy era the three Communists who worked at important posts in the State Department were already gone, uncovered by the State Department Security investigations. Alger Hiss resigned in 1946. Lauchlin Currie's tenure as Franklin Roosevelt's administrative assistant had ended in 1945 when the president died. Through the mid– and late–1930s he had worked in the Treasury Department, rising to Assistant Director of Research and Statistics for the Federal Reserve System's Board of Governors. At Treasury he had worked with Harry Dexter White, who became an assistant secretary of the Department. Subsequently he worked at the International Monetary Fund. But White resigned his post in 1946.

With all the hearings, all the noise, the press, and the chest thumping, McCarthy's inability to name actual important Communists in the State Department was due to the simple fact that they were no longer there. But for the next few years, Senator McCarthy was to put the country and some of its citizens through enormous trauma.

It should be noted that while Senator McCarthy is useful as a symbol of the anti–Communism of the era, the attack on the Left was widespread. There were ongoing efforts by other congressional committees, state committees, the American Legion, various churches, columnists, and media figures among others determined to crush domestic Communism and undermine the Left's agenda to, for example, build labor unions or, in the South, argue for civil rights.

No doubt acutely aware of what they saw as a growing menace, the Weavers walked into their second recording session; the first session had included Christmas songs. The public didn't much respond to that.

But at this second session, on May 4, they made a single with "Tzena, Tzena, Tzena" on one side and "Goodnight, Irene" on the other. Decca insisted on using an orchestra with violins to provide back-up to the group. Certainly such orchestration fit the commercial music traditions of the era, but it nonetheless diluted the pure sound of the quartet.

The first was a popular Israeli soldier's song; "Tzena" in Hebrew is the feminine plural meaning "to go out." The song went to number two on the *Billboard* charts, while "Goodnight, Irene" went to number one. Beyond changing Leadbelly's erotic assertion that he would "get" Irene in his dreams to the polite hope that he would "see" her there, the Weavers also eliminated a line declaring that the singer, without Irene, would use morphine. As Seeger recalls, you couldn't have walked into a diner in the summer of 1950 and not heard the song on a jukebox. The record sold two million copies.

No one was more surprised than the Weavers by the record's success. Certainly they produced a very pleasing sound. The lyrics to "Goodnight, Irene" were clear and easy to remember. The cleaned-up song probed sensitive emotions concerning love and marriage more deeply than other contemporary love songs. Both the returning veterans who had returned, married, and started families and their new spouses received a shock of recognition from those lyrics. Americans clearly wanted what folk music did that other forms of popular music didn't do — provide some explanation about and guidance for the lives the audience members led. Also, Israel and the Holocaust that had preceded the nation's founding in 1948 had been in the news, and Americans were sympathetic to the new pioneers. Americans themselves felt re-born as a nation after the Great Depression and World War II, so the Israeli spirit in "Tzena, Tzena, Tzena" was refreshing and useful. Whatever the mysterious combination of factors that creates a hit might be, both songs found it.

But there was another reason for such success. The enterprising Howie Richmond, who would soon work hard to promote Woody Guthrie, mailed 1,500 copies of "Goodnight, Irene" to disc jockeys. As a press agent for Frank Sinatra and Dinah Shore, Richmond had gotten to know a lot of the people who played records on the air, and so they listened to the free copies, liked the music, and began playing it. Richmond not only sold records but also a quarter-million copies of the sheet music.

Seeger and Hays had deliberately decided to keep explicitly political material out of their repertoire. But that didn't mean they couldn't make subtler, coded statements. "Irene," after all, was written by a black convict, a statement in itself in a segregated country. And Stalin, although hostile to Jews, supported the birth of Israel. He was anxious to rid the Middle East of British imperialist power. Additionally, he had some hopes that the socialist Israeli pioneers, who had even established collective settlements, would be more attracted to the Communists than to the capitalists in America. In singing "Tzena," then, the Weavers, whether they meant to deliberately or not, were supporting Stalin as well as the United States.

Despite their quiet attempts to retain their radical vision, not everyone on the Left was satisfied with the Weavers. In May 1950, *Sing Out!*, the People's Artists magazine meant as a successor to *People's Songs Bulletin*, began publication and included songs that were mostly doctrinally strong and musically and artistically weak. The publication, though, took its title from "The Hammer Song," which it featured on the cover of its first issue. But *Sing Out!* only had 500 subscribers at the end of the first year. That didn't stop Irwin Silber from criticizing the Weavers for not having a black performer and for performing black songs in the first place.

But if the Weavers sang the perfectly right tunes, they sang them in what was a perfectly awful political time for them. On June 22, *Counterattack* issued a book titled *Red Channels: The Report of Communist Influence in Radio and Television*. In the book the editors named 151 musicians, writers, journalists, actors, and others in the entertainment industry whose affiliations and actions were suspect, and that the media should be alerted. With this careful language, the compilers of *Red Channels* were able to claim they were not supporting a blacklist.

The editors used both FBI files and had clearly been avid readers of

The Daily Worker. the Weavers were not listed, but Seeger was, along with such other people as Earl Robinson, Oscar Brand, Burl Ives, Millard Lampell, Will Geer, Josh White, and Alan Lomax.

Although the Weavers weren't mentioned, Pete Kameron, their manager, went to the *Counterattack* office and declared that the Weavers would not appear before any radical groups in the future. For the next two years, the Weavers did not play at any left-wing event, including protests about the Rosenbergs. Seeger was not happy about his acceptance of the arrangement. As he put it: "Our then manager would not let me sing for the hootenannies and workers' groups."[4]

Complimentary copies of *Red Channels* were sent to everyone involved in entertainment. The next phase of the blacklist — after the Hollywood Ten — had begun. Most of the people on the publication's list, and others deemed sympathetic to Communist causes, were no longer given employment in the entertainment industry. The only acceptable exit from the blacklist for most of those on it was to appear before HUAC, make clear they had been dupes or were no longer Communists, and in many cases name those they knew who were Communists.

Josh White voluntarily appeared before HUAC on September 1. Seeger recalls the decision to speak this way: "Josh got in debt.... Josh owed tens of thousands of dollars to his manager.... And they said, 'Mr. White you will say what they want you to say or your family really will have a problem.'"[5] Without a lawyer, White portrayed himself as a well-meaning innocent, an artist passionate about justice and therefore subject to manipulation. He said he didn't know the Communists were behind efforts to protest what he hated such as lynchings and poll taxes. He made it clear to the committee that he vehemently opposed these actions even though the Communists had taken similar positions as his own. He would not name people he knew who had belonged to the Communist party. The Committee especially wanted him to repudiate Paul Robeson's supposed statement that blacks in America would not fight in a war against the Soviets because they loved Russia so much. White expressed his admiration for Robeson's talent but added that Robeson's declaration was wrong. White declared that, of course, Robeson was entitled to his opinion.

White was trying, without success, to walk down the middle of a particularly angular road. The papers reported his testimony as an attack on Robeson. Even though his entire, nuanced testimony was made public

(*Billboard* printed it in full, for example), the Left felt betrayed. They believed that *Red Channels* had won, that White's case illustrated that it was incumbent upon those named to prove their innocence before continuing their careers and that, therefore, those who didn't testify didn't for a nefarious reason. And White was not done in attempting to clear his name. In the December 1950 issue of *Negro Digest* he wrote an article titled "I Was a Sucker for the Communists." In the article, White tried to take a common-sense, middle position — a view very much out of fashion. He wanted to stand against discrimination and Jim Crow laws, and he wanted to be seen as a good American.

After the appearance and article, White went on singing, becoming especially popular in England and on the European Continent. But White was not part of what would be the revival of folk music in the late '50s and '60s. And, although he arguably had the best voice of all the '40s folk singers, he failed to become part of the folk music pantheon. Perhaps as his son, Josh White, Jr., suggests, it was because he was frankly sexual in an age when black men were certainly not supposed to appeal to demure white women.[6] Perhaps it was because the Left that defined the canon of greats could never accept what they saw as White's betrayal and removed him. Whatever the reason, White's post–1960s fame faded; his enormous talent merits re-discovery.

Woody Guthrie's name was not on the *Red Channels* list. Maybe, given his views, he could have felt insulted. But Woody was no longer seen as much of a threat by any governmental or private anti–Communist group. He was just too sick, too incapable of making political appearances any more. If his body was fading, though, one part of his legend was growing.

Woody's 1947 recording of "This Land Is Your Land" for Moses Asch, a take without the political verses, appeared on a 1951 Folkways album and was the first commercial recording of the song. Pete Seeger remembers hearing the song for the first time from the Folkways recording. It was this non-political version that was repeated on lots of other albums. The song itself began to enter mainstream culture. It became part of the curriculum in many liberal private schools. But the big step in its becoming popular came in 1951 when Woody's music publisher, Howie Richmond, asked the increasingly sick folk singer to tape record songs. Woody sang several hundred for Richmond.

Richmond was immediately taken by "This Land." He had an idea. Richmond re-produced the song and distributed it for free to several scholastic publishers (such as Birchard, Ginn, and Silver Burdett) that published songbooks. They, in turn, sold the songbooks to schools. Within fifteen years, "This Land Is Your Land" would be sung in so many schools by so many baby boomers, that it became almost a substitute national anthem. Woody was not particularly happy with the fate of the de-fanged song, once teaching the missing verses to his son Arlo in hopes that they would not be forgotten.

Meanwhile, the confrontation with Communism kept growing. Just three days after the release of *Red Channels*, the Korean War began on June 25, On July 17, Julius and Ethel Rosenberg were arrested for spying.

The Weavers were forced to take the summer off. A promised television show ended because the sponsor grew concerned. But Americans knew the name of the group far more than the names of the performers, and they wanted to hear the Weavers sing their wonderful songs. So the Weavers started touring, playing in vaudeville houses, large hotel ballrooms, and everywhere else they could pack a crowd. They went to Reno and gambled, except for Seeger. Lee Hays quickly learned that, as a Weaver, room service would send up whatever he requested; he requested a lot.

Seeger especially enjoyed leading the crowd in singing the songs. Seeger may not have had his singing unions, but he had audiences. Finally, he heard America singing the right songs, confirming his deepest belief that American hearts beat to the same musical pulse as his own. Finally, he heard the pent-up energy he just knew Americans had released with boisterous if occasionally off-key gusto. When he was singing he wasn't in the real world, but the ideal one; the concerts were his vision of how all could be made perfect. If only those audiences had come from the right class, he would have been overjoyed; for now, his songs were bees spreading the pollen of folk music from one listener's mind to the next.

And so the Weavers kept going. In May 1951 they recorded "Kisses Sweeter Than Wine" and "When the Saints Go Marching In." But HUAC, now under Democratic control, was revived to take another shot at Hollywood, and on March 6 the trial against the Rosenbergs began.

On August 25, the *New York World-Telegram and Sun* published an article about the Weavers, describing their radical connections. The Senate's Internal Security Subcommittee began an investigation. The American Legion sought to prevent the Weavers' songs from being aired. There were no bookings in all of September.

And then on February 6 and 7, 1952, a former Communist named Harvey Matusow testified before HUAC. Matusow claimed that the CPUSA used the Weavers to recruit the young. He said Seeger, Hellerman, and Gilbert were members, and Hays was a former member though still sympathetic. (Three years later in his book *False Witness* Matusow said he had made up the story about the Weavers because he wanted publicity.) Matusow's tying the group's members directly to the Party proved too much. They continued to perform — much of the public still liked them and probably would have paid for performances — but the pressures on the nightclub owners and others in the field were immense.

On May 20, Burl Ives testified before the Senate's Internal Security Committee. Ives denied believing in Communism but noted that his early New York audiences had been on the Left. Unlike Josh White (who may not have been asked to name names because different rules applied to blacks than whites), Ives was asked to identify Communists, and he did name four people, including his former manager.

Irwin Silber, never shy in print or in person, accused Ives of singing a new song, "Ballad for Stoolpigeons." Even Seeger, always extremely charitable, attacked Ives for the testimony five years later.

The folk movement seemed to be falling apart. In September Woody Guthrie was diagnosed with Huntington's disease. In 1953, Joseph McCarthy was named to chair the Senate Committee on Government Operations, which had control of the Internal Security Subcommittee. The Weavers officially disbanded. On June 19 the Rosenbergs were executed.

On January 5, 1954, Woody was admitted to Brooklyn State Hospital. In April, without employment, Pete Seeger was forced to begin touring college campuses, schools, and summer camps. He introduced the students to Woody Guthrie songs. Seeger was planting the roots of the folk music revival that would sprout just a few years later. Had he not been banished from the nightclub circuit, it is unclear whether folk songs would have been known, much less popular, among so many of the young. By the end of 1954, Senator McCarthy was condemned by a majority of his colleagues; all of the Senate's Democrats voted for condemnation except for Jack Kennedy who was in the hospital for back surgery. Kennedy did not indicate how he would have voted.

117

The dark days for the folk singers, though, were not over. Alan Lomax had left the country. On August 16, 1955, Lee Hays appeared before HUAC. Hays took the Fifth Amendment and appeared only briefly. But that was only a preface to the real fireworks.

Pete Seeger appeared two days later, on August 18.

The U.S. Court House on Foley Square in New York, with its Corinthian columns, had a sobering effect on those who entered it. Seeger strolled into the hearing room to face three members from HUAC. As always, he seemed as innocent of danger as a cow might as it paused on railroad tracks. Toshi lugged his banjo behind her. Seeger, dressed in a plaid shirt with bright yellow tie and a checked suit jacket, sat down until his name was called. As he rose, the flash bulbs popped and the cameras clicked. Seeger took a seat under the hot lights.

Francis Walter, a Democrat from Pennsylvania, peered through his thick, black-framed glasses at the famous folk singer, known to the Committee as having had a long association with Communism. The Committee began by asking about Seeger's occupation. Seeger replied, "I make my living as a banjo picker — sort of damning in some people's opinion."

Seeger's veiled hostility continued with the first serious question when Seeger was asked if he sang for the Communist Party, as was suggested by an ad from the Communist paper, the *Daily Worker*. Bristling, Seeger responded: "I refuse to answer that question whether it was a quote from *The New York Times* or the *Vegetarian Journal*."

Clearly, Seeger was an "unfriendly witness," a legal designation that, Seeger's supporters noted, would deprive him of such rights as selling liquor or performing as a wrestler. If he moved to Washington, D.C., he would be unable to tune a piano legally.

Seeger continued with evasive responses until finally declaring, "I am not going to answer any questions as to my association, my philosophical or religious beliefs or my political beliefs, or how I voted in any election or any of these private affairs."

At one point, the discussion turned to a song, "Wasn't That a Time." The committee believed the tune subverted American values. Seeger was indignant and volunteered to perform the song to prove its patriotic nature. The offer was declined. Later, Seeger could not contain himself when asked to verify from a photograph that he had taken part in a May Day parade. He fumed, "It is like Jesus Christ when asked by Pontius Pilate, 'Are you king of the Jews?'" The Committee was deeply upset by the comment.[7]

Seeger spoke for almost an hour and then left. On July 26, 1956, he was cited for contempt of Congress. On March 26, 1957, he was indicted for contempt for his refusal to testify. In 1961, a jury convicted him, and Seeger was sentenced to jail. He did spend a few hours in a jail on April 3 while his lawyer desperately sought bail money. There were two other men in the cell with him. One of the men sang, "If that judge believes what I say, I'll be leaving for home today." The other man responded, "Not if he sees your record, you won't."[8]

It was only in May 1962 that an appeals court overturned the conviction.

Meanwhile, he never stopped singing. Just two months after his appearance before HUAC, Seeger was on a plane headed for a concert at Oberlin College in Ohio. Tired from the flight, he reached into his pocket and pulled out a paper on which he had written three lines in a translated copy of Mikhail Sholokhov's Russian novel *And Quiet Flows the Don*. The lines were from a song Cossacks sang as they head off to join the Russian army. Staring at the paper, Seeger suddenly recalled a phrase he liked that he had written down several years earlier. The words were "long time passing." Seeger added a lament wondering when people would learn that war was wrong and in twenty minutes, he had his song, "Where Have All the Flowers Gone?"

Seeger's song made an enormous leap. It was not a simple protest song tied to a particular grievance. Its language was allusive like a poem's but tied to the protest tradition by its anti-war subject matter and its accusatory question wondering when people would understand the horrors of war. Seeger had written an anthem, not a protest song, applicable to many situations and not tied to one. This song is the bridge between political folk music up to then and the new direction heralded by Bob Dylan's "Blowin' in the Wind," another anthem filled with questions.

Seeger ceased singing it, but Joe Hickerson, who led the Oberlin College Folksong Club, altered the rhythm and added some verses and, as music counselor, sang it the following summer at Camp Woodland. Peter, Paul, and Mary started singing the song using Hickerson's re-worked rhythm, and the Kingston Trio learned it from them and made it famous.

Seeger just kept singing. In the image he preferred, he was a musical

Johnny Appleseed planting political ideas and folk songs in the fertile soil of young minds at camps, schools, and campuses around the country. Pete Seeger kept the folk music movement alive during its Dark Ages. Virtually single-handedly he taught America the songs that Woody Guthrie had written and Alan Lomax had collected. Without Seeger, it is plausible that those songs would have disappeared. Without Seeger it is possible that all the folk singers who emerged in the 1960s would not have learned the songs. Most learned them directly or indirectly from Seeger himself. Seeger is quick to push credit away from himself and onto the tradition in which he worked, but in many ways he is its most important figure. Guthrie was its greatest songwriter — at least until Bob Dylan — and Lomax its greatest behind-the-scenes organizer. But Seeger was its greatest promoter, tirelessly exhorting audiences to sing along with him, patiently teaching the songs to the young, endlessly searching out new songs. It is no surprise that for some Pete Seeger is the folk song movement.

Seeger's successes were enormous. He lived his idealism. No hypocrisy ever attached itself to him. He had a clear political vision early, and he kept it — for too long, as he later admitted. He had more commercial success than Woody Guthrie, giving some moral permission to later artists to seek popular appeal. Seeger, unlike some of those who would follow him, remained ever-ambivalent about the success. He thought it useful to spread his message, but he recoiled at industry crassness and the general idea that profit trumped other considerations.

His failures were also enormous. He was rigid because of his Communist ideology, so he couldn't adapt to changing audience tastes and social change or, more significantly, understand that Communism was worse than the capitalism he mistrusted. He was politically naive in part.

American Communism was finished, and so, too, it appeared, were the folk singers who had provided its soundtrack.

Given the political environment, it would have been easy at that moment to compose an epitaph for the political folk music movement of people like Woody and Pete. They seemed to be false prophets. Beyond misunderstanding their audiences and the powerful opponents arrayed against them, the folk singers failed to change America. They failed for several crucial reasons.

They had unresolved internal struggles. Each singer had different struggles and tried to resolve them in different ways, but they all struggled between seeing themselves as musical entertainers or political radicals, as fierce individualists or dutiful supporters of a collective enterprise, as willing to present their real selves to the public or feeling the need to construct a persona.

They had a deep need to reject a vision of never-ending conflict between humans, and a concurrent need to envision a harmonic future. They saw that future threatened by capitalism as the snarling guard at the gates of the land of human bliss. It was as though they needed to believe that there had to be a perfect society somewhere on Earth, that if there weren't, life would be without hope.

As artists, in many cases as musical geniuses, they didn't understand that surrendering their art to a larger principle was a form of suicide. The ideology could either limit their overall subject matter or limit their views within the political subjects they wrote about. Their ideology stopped them from exploring other political views. They couldn't sing about personal freedom to dissent from supporting Stalin. The ideology made them listen to political ideas for lessons on art, not to the audiences to whom they were singing or wished to reach.

It can fairly be asked, though, if they would have written songs at all if not for their politics. That is, however much their ideology inhibited their art, that ideology may also have given it birth. But the greatest of the folk songwriters — Guthrie and Dylan — wrote about much more than politics and had artistic needs that required them to sing. Seeger's art was much more completely tied to his politics, but perhaps he wrote comparatively few songs because of that.

They were naive. Their songs were meant to be splinters under society's skin, causing pain and requiring attention. They were as young in thought as they were in years, readier to create than to evaluate. They wanted to build graveyards to encrypt the past. Their caution had been amputated. They were, to adapt T.S. Eliot's comment in another context, people "dreaming of systems so perfect no one will need to be good."9

The folk singers saw the horrors of the Great Depression, but they also saw the Roosevelt Administration using the federal government to fix economic problems. Woody Guthrie, for example, was an awed eyewitness to the use of federal funds for dams. Despite this, they continued to adhere to an ideology that was undemocratic and promised a more fundamental change. They didn't challenge the awkward psychological proposition that a change in economic systems would make competitive people cooperative.

They were far ahead of the rest of the country in the integrating of blacks and whites in summer camps, concerts, and singing events. They were ahead of the country in being outraged at the unbearable injustice of segregation and Jim Crow laws or in seeking to aid the many Americans still without adequate housing or health. But that prescience, that moral fierceness, did not lead them to seek simple reform.

To have sought reform within the American system would have required them to think differently. They would have had to start with the premise that America could adapt and improve itself within its current economic system, even if sometimes that improvement required radical tactics. The political folk singers, however, saw the United States government ultimately not as a protector of peace, justice, and democracy, but as a fundamental impediment to achieving such goals internationally. They were never able to see past their illusions.

The political folk singers like Woody and Pete genuinely believed they were patriotic Americans. They weren't lying or being misleading when they said they loved their country, its grand natural beauty and its promise of a future with happy, singing workers. The problem was one of definition. They were buoyed by such Popular Front–inspired beliefs and had America's founders and great leaders such as Tom Paine been alive in the 1930s they would have joined or sympathized with the Communist Party. But their understanding of what America should be was at variance with the overwhelming majority of Americans who didn't want a Socialist or Communist government with common ownership of goods and services and the abolishment of private property.

Despite their lapses of insight, none of the political folk singers were cynics. They weren't people who were aware of their own failures but continued with them anyway. They meant to do well. They weren't realists who could see in a clear-eyed fashion what was happening before them. They were idealists attempting to do good and believing with every fiber of their being that they were. They simply could not accept the death of their illusions and provide those illusions with the appropriate burial.

It is fair to ask: how is it possible to criticize an idealist? Certainly doing so requires more sympathy than criticizing a cynic, but everyone, with good intentions and bad, can be judged by their behavior.

And their behavior was judged. It is unsurprising that the folk singers in general, and Pete Seeger in particular, remain controversial in some circles. Given their full-throated support for the CPUSA, given Seeger's derisive nickname as "Stalin's Songbird," there were bound to be those who saw their actions as reprehensible.

For example, John Earl Haynes, a prominent historian of American Communism, argues: "Did the folk singers who assisted the CPUSA and its various causes and affiliated organization constitute a genuine danger to the U.S? In their purely individual actions one would not say so; it is hard to make a folk song into a genuine danger to the U.S. But they assisted, were part of, and used their talents to support a movement that in my view was a genuine danger to the U.S."[10] Despite this, there are many reasons why Pete Seeger and the other folk singers were not reviled as people who posed real dangers.

The folk singers' artistic output did not ultimately adversely affect the nation; ironically, the admiration they eventually acquired was gained in part because they failed to meet their political goals. Additionally, their talents were widely admired. They were genuinely decent, kind, good, and well-meaning people who were seen as having made a mistake.

One of the great reasons for their continuing to survive every seeming death, for the esteem in which they continue to be held, is that all of them without exception were deeply humane. They were neither cold nor calculating. They may have been deceived, but it was a deception that sought to help, not control, humanity.

Americans were prepared to forgive them especially because Communism did not triumph. The emerging anti–Communist movement through the late 1940s and 1950s was often crude and cruel. The anti–Communists frequently over-reacted and made the folk singers sympathetic even among many Americans who might otherwise have felt differently about them. In that sense, the anti–Communists deepened the later perception that the folk singing Leftists were part of an invaluable tradition of dissent at a time when dissent was stifled.

Finally, their ideas were given new life by various movements of the 1960s, a decade that turned Woody Guthrie and Pete Seeger into secular saints, not Communist sympathizers who sang for a few dollars in front of left-wing unions. But even before the baby boomers, the folk song movement stirred back to life in the form of a clean-cut trio.

Seven

The Great Folk Scare:
The Revival of Folk Music

In the middle of the American struggle against Communism a new generation arose, one much larger and very different from the previous generation. The parents, shocked, hardened, and deprived by depression and war, had wanted to return to a normal America. They believed in the country and themselves — they had, after all, triumphed over enormous adversities — and were optimistic that their sacrifices and hope would lead them to a prosperous and happy future. Conditioned to sigh and shrug at difficult conditions, the parents were used to following authority, conforming because of an unyielding social need, and exercising intense self-restraint in spending and expressing their emotions. They believed, at least in theory if not always in actual behavior, in honor, virtue, stability, monogamy, sacrifice for the family, community, nation, duty, self-discipline, and modesty. They were adults, but adults who deeply valued conformity as the road to success. And they stayed on that road.

There was no housing available in cities, so the young parents moved outside the city limits. The G.I. Bill made veterans able to afford mortgages. The suburbs were seen as perfect places by the parents. Jobs were near but city crime, crowds, smells, noise, and filth weren't. Families could live in a real home — with a yard — not in a cramped apartment. Parents believed their children would be safer and happier in this new lush Eden, with gleaming schools and dedicated teachers, with the gadgets that come with new homes, and with the refrigerators, stoves, furniture, and also cars to take workers to and from the office or factory.

And the greatest gadgets of all were the television sets, those magic boxes that provided them with pictures as well as sounds of the singers and comedians they had enjoyed on the radio and front-row seats to the daily distillation of history as presented on the news. Some of that history was unpleasant. Television brought Joseph McCarthy, the Cold War, and the looming presence of atomic and nuclear weapons into their living rooms.

Television became a required household item. In 1950, 9 percent of American homes had a television. Five years later, 64.5 percent of homes had at least one set. Television changed American lifestyles. Viewers stayed up later. They slept less. They ate pre-packaged "TV dinners" on small trays in front of the sets. They exercised less, read less, attended fewer movies, saw each other less. They viewed idealized visions of suburban family life on *Father Knows Best, Leave It to Beaver,* and *The Adventures of Ozzie and Harriet.* With only one television set in most homes, families had to struggle to find programs acceptable to everyone. They didn't talk during dinner; they watched shows. They knew less and cared less about each other's lives.

And the suburbs turned out to be more of a velvet trap than the paradise the parents had imagined. There was tremendous pressure on the breadwinners, and in 1950s America that mostly meant the husbands. A husband's commute to work jangled his nerves and separated him from his family for more time than his work hours. The new appliances everyone had to own could be bought cheaply enough on the installment plan, but all the installments needed to be paid. Women were also trapped. During the Second World War, many women had, by necessity, entered the workplace. After the War, women's roles reverted to what they had been prior to the War, although, by necessity or choice, an increasing number of women worked outside the home. In 1950, 21.6 percent did but by 1960 30.5 percent were employed. Most middle-class suburban women, though, were without jobs or cars and were confined to their homes or neighborhoods. Because their husbands worked so much to pay for the home, its furnishings, and the car, wives had enormous responsibilities in raising the children.

Those children were reared, on the advice of Dr. Spock, to be understood and indulged, not treated like miniature adults but as unformed youth whose individual needs should be met to shape them into contented, productive adults. Without the Great Depression or the War in their memory or their lives, the children didn't feel the need for self-discipline as much as their parents did. Eventually, their numbers, combined with common formative cultural, social, and historical experiences, forged them so that they developed a group social identity.

Both the older and younger generations were enchanted with the new consumer culture. Purchasing was the new form of happiness. When suburbanites didn't feel good they shopped to improve their mood. Both generations wanted to buy, but the younger generation didn't see the need to save money the way their parents did. They were indulged by parents with money and lured by ads on television. Especially as the Baby Boomers grew past childhood, teens became an identifiable, highly prized consumer market. Businesses and advertisers and cultural creators followed the money. Slowly at first, and then quickly as the boomers grew into youthful, eager consumers a certain authority in the culture was taken away from the adults and handed to the teenagers. Adolescence was transformed from an embarrassing hallway into adulthood to a highly prized state of mind. Manufacturers and advertisers much preferred working with young, inexperienced buyers operating with youthful impulses rather than adult considerations of whether a particular product was wanted, needed, or affordable. Adolescence suddenly wasn't a place to leave but a place to remain as long as possible. It was, after all, a place where responsibilities could be ignored or delayed, where the self could be constantly re-invented, where obligations to monogamy were not required, where boundaries could be crossed when desire wanted to make the journey. Many in the boomer generation were preparing themselves to grow into the sixties and search for a philosophy to justify their desire to remain in their adolescence.

And many started their search with a new form of music that spoke directly to them — rock and roll. In May 1954, Bill Haley recorded "Rock Around the Clock." The song did not become a major hit until the following year when it was used in the opening credits for the motion picture *Blackboard Jungle*. Whatever the real first rock and roll record was, "Rock Around the Clock" by Bill Haley was the first rock song to hit the number one spot on Billboard's main sales chart. In July 1954 Elvis Presley recorded "That's All Right (Mama)" at Sun Studios in Memphis. American teenagers were soon listening to Little Richard, or Jerry Lee Lewis, or Buddy Holly, or Chuck Berry, among many others. There was little radio airplay of folk songs.

Youthful rebellion was reflected in other art forms as well. On October 13, 1955, Allen Ginsberg read his landmark poem "Howl" in public for the first time. On October 26, *Rebel Without a Cause* was released, igniting anti-hero worship for the recently dead James Dean and for Jim, his character in the film.

Young intellectuals were influenced by existentialist philosophy, which stressed the personal responsibility of all individuals for their identity, the actions they took in life, and even for the society and world they inhabited. It was one more shift away from parental or social authority and onto individual autonomy.

For the folk singers, history was going to turn out to be far more complicated and far more interesting than the heyday of anti–Communism and the rise of rock and roll seemed to predict.

Some of J. Edgar Hoover's legacy as well as that of HUAC, McCarthyism, the blacklist, and those who physically attacked people on the Left eventually clustered as stains on American democracy rather than protectors of it. Inevitably, the people they went after were historically recast as victims or martyrs, not as subversives or un–American. Being blacklisted became a badge of honor, not shame. It was those who testified not those who resisted who came to be seen as shameful.

This distinction was crucial for the Guthrie and Seeger legacies. Their talent and drive were considerable, but their identity as heroes only arose because they had been able to defeat seemingly evil enemies. In one more exemplification of the law of unintended consequences, without persecution the folk singers would have seemed more like adherents of an old ideology than as rebels who had withstood rocks and hearings, the threat of jail and being blacklisted. Their influence and place in the society in the 1960s would have been far less potent. Instead they were the rebellious heroes and models for young singers.

The popular music business continued to work remarkably well in absorbing the radical music by re-branding it. "This Land Is Your Land" became a patriotic anthem. Its anti-private property message was simply erased. "If I Had a Hammer" became just a rousing song about justice; its Communist roots disappeared. Other songs let teenagers rebel safely. American business had seemingly beaten American radicalism. The folk songs became pure entertainment or safe and contained rebellion. Folk music was finally truly American, though not at all in the way Alan Lomax or Pete Seeger had hoped it would be.

The folk collectors like Lomax, and the folk writers and singers were rightly seen as heroic in collecting, preserving, and transmitting what would have been a forgotten American musical heritage. But their political influence looked finished.

It was not.

The younger generation, disdainful of suburbia, unable to connect to the moribund ideology of Communism, soon discovered that rock and roll freed their bodies, but their minds still hungered for idealistic direction. They needed heroes outside their families. They loved music. They were rebellious. They had the idealism of youth. Finding persecuted idealistic and rebellious singers was therefore profoundly resonant for them.

Folk singers could feed their hunger. But folk music itself, robbed of its Communist ideology, struggled in the 1950s to survive even without an overt political message. It would only be the arrival of the 1960s when the revival of folk music became complete.

During these hard times, though, there were still glimmers of a folk comeback. In 1956, the Tarriers became the first folk trio to have a hit single on Billboard's charts with "The Banana Boat Song." In that same year, Harry Belafonte released the album *Calypso*; the album was the first LP record to sell a million copies. "Banana Boat Song" was the major hit song on the album, and calypso music had a brief popularity. In July 1956 a folk club called the Gate of Horn opened in Chicago. Albert Grossman, later Bob Dylan's manager, was one of the owners.

In September 1956, Odetta recorded her first album, *Odetta Sings Ballads and Blues*. Born Odetta Holmes, she was trained in opera and musical theater, but in 1950 she began to devote herself particularly to folk music. The album had a mix of traditional songs and included "Alabama Bound" and "Take This Hammer," both by Leadbelly and "Muleskinner Blues," made popular by Jimmie Rodgers. She was widely regarded as the most important and influential African American folk singer of her era, but her influence extended well beyond the growing civil rights community. Bob Dylan recalled hearing Odetta's first album in a Hibbing record store, rushing out to get an acoustic guitar, and memorizing all the songs.

On April 6, 1957, Izzy Young opened the Folklore Center in Greenwich Village. Burl Ives and Harry Belafonte were his first customers. The Center, at the top of a flight of stairs, was about seven feet wide and twenty feet long. On the left wall there were instruments on top, and below that cases for records, and benches beneath the cases. There were flyers, business cards, and announcements for concerts. The wall on the right had books, magazines, and more instruments. There was a small room in back. It was not just the volume of materials Izzy had collected. He had unusual stuff, so that, by some miracle, he always seemed to stock the hard-to-find item a customer sought, the brand-new magazines or the foreign books. It was a place for people to meet, to test out new material, to leave a message on the bulletin board, to gather and pass on gossip. It became a post office for people with no fixed address. As Bob Dylan wrote in *Chronicles*, "It was like an ancient chapel, like a shoebox sized institute."[1]

The store was so needed that within a couple of weeks, Albert Grossman called Izzy and asked him to produce a concert for Peggy Seeger, Pete's half-sister. (Young eventually produced hundreds of concerts, including Bob Dylan's first one.) Izzy soon got a lesson in the real-life folk world when he organized a party for Alan Lomax, who had recently returned from overseas. Lomax left the party with the woman Izzy loved. Whatever romantic misadventures Izzy had there, the Folklore Center was the central meeting place for the beginning folk revival.

Meanwhile, folk's seeming successor was having a hard time. In 1957, Little Richard quit rock and roll. Elvis entered the Army on March 24, 1958. Scandal about Jerry Lee Lewis's personal life erupted during a 1958 British tour. His third wife was his thirteen-year-old distant cousin. Buddy Holly died in a plane crash on February 3, 1959. Chuck Berry had his own legal problems that December after a fourteen year old he had hired was arrested for prostitution. Berry was convicted under the Mann Act, fined, and sentenced to prison.

In the midst of all this, Americans looked for an alternative to rock and roll. Popular music turned to teen idols like Frankie Avalon, Bobby Rydell, and Fabian, pleasant music but music that didn't match folk's intelligent lyrics or rock's physically arousing sound.

Folk music's revival, what the folk singer Utah Phillips affectionately nicknamed the Great Folk Scare, got its giant boost from three young men on the West Coast. Dave Guard, Nick Reynolds, and Bob Shane had all been fans of the Weavers. Guard had learned to play banjo from Pete Seeger's self-published instruction book. The three were also influenced by the Calypso craze, and so they took their name from a port city in Jamaica. the Kingston Trio's first album was released in June 1958. "Tom

Dooley" was the crucial song on the album; as a single it sold three and a half million copies and was number one on Billboard's chart for the week of November 17.

The song concerned Tom Dula (pronounced Dooley), a Confederate veteran who was hanged in 1868 for stabbing to death his lover, Laura Foster. Some people think another of Dula's romantic partners killed Foster. Others believe Dula killed her when he discovered that Foster had given him syphilis. Dula always claimed his innocence. Thomas C. Land, a poet, wrote a song based on the murder and eventually that song made its way to the Kingston Trio. The song was deceptive. The Trio's harmony partly hid the carnal and homicidal urges presented in the song, feelings far darker than the then-current songs about puppy love and malt shops.

The song's popularity was ironically due, in part, to the public's knowledge of Dr. Thomas A. Dooley, an anti–Communist Navy doctor whose 1956 book *Deliver Us from Evil* told of the doctor's medical work and his Catholic faith, a faith he found at odds with Communism. The Trio eventually played benefits for Dr. Dooley.

The Trio had deceptively simple harmonies. They were funny. They meshed distinct personalities. Nick was huggable, a cute pixie. Bob was handsome, a rugged sex symbol. Dave was the intellectual. They were clean cut with their striped shirts and fraternity look. Their lyrics were smart, not dripping with the sap of teen love songs. The clubs loved them. The Trio replaced expensive touring bands. Here were three guys playing their own instruments and singing. They couldn't have made it easier for the clubs. They followed on the college circuit, a trail blazed by Pete Seeger in music and Mort Sahl in comedy. Their travels, along with Seeger's, created its own market. The older brothers and sisters of the Baby Boomers were in college, and if their young siblings were nice these seemingly worldly students would play the records.

The Kingston Trio was the group every parent could love. They provided much-needed reassurance after the appearance of rock and roll that the kids were all right.

The Trio also seemed to be erasing the political history of folk songs and going back to traditional folk songs. The startling realization that folk songs not originating from the political Left could attract a large mainstream audience must have pleased people in the music business and upset some of those committed to connecting folk music to radical politics. The

Lomax thesis that any folk song was inherently political seemed much weaker. Still, the idea that folk songs had widespread national popularity — the idea that the Weavers had explored — must have made Seeger feel vindicated. He could no doubt envision the possibility of following the apolitical songs with more explicitly political ones.

But even in 1958, the Trio was much more political than they first appeared. On their first album they already began to sing songs made popular by Woody Guthrie ("Hard, Ain't It Hard"), Pete Seeger ("Bay of Mexico"), and the Weavers ("Sloop John B"). At one point the Trio met with other folk singers at the Village Gate, a Greenwich Village club, and refused to play on the television show *Hootenanny!* because its network didn't allow Pete Seeger to appear on the show.

It's not certain how many of their fans realized the radical origins of some of the songs. The Trio was careful, in appearance and speech, not to be overtly political in a way that could endanger their career. Their politics was coded.

For example, in 1959 they decided to record a protest song titled "Charlie on the MTA," also known as "The MTA Song." Jacqueline Berman Steiner and Bess Lomax Hawes, adapting a tune made famous by the folk song "Wreck of the Old '97," had written the song in 1948 for Walter A. O'Brien, a Progressive Party candidate for mayor of Boston. Part of O'Brien's campaign was to lower the cost of traveling by subway and reduce a fare system so complicated that a nine-page booklet was required to explain it. O'Brien lost his race, but the song survived. Considering the song's radical origins — O'Brien was considered a Communist — the Trio decided to change the mayor's name to "George" so as to render the song amusing rather than political.

Using this coded approach allowed some songs to be popular without most in the audience fully understanding their implications, but it also prevented any artistic progress by the folk singers. They had to revert to pre-political folk songs or hide their message deeply enough so that it was virtually invisible.

But the renewed interest in folk music was political in other ways. It brought with it a revival of regional music. Young musicians went to record the banjo pickers on back porches in Appalachia. Bluegrass, Cajun, and various other types of music indigenous to particular regions of the United States were embraced with a resurgent enthusiasm. The energy unleashed by such music was not political in the precise way the old folk singers envisioned. But it did inspire a range of new activities that started in the 1960s and grew across the decades.

Additionally, the re-emergence of folk music brought with it hundreds if not thousands of new singers and songwriters, eager to find a place in the folk tradition. These musicians formed a core group to inspire the political traditions that later emerged, in some cases joining the traditional folk musicians in support of civil rights, opposing nuclear weapons and war, and later promoting the wide range of environmental movements.

This new political dimension of the revived folk movement wasn't immediately clear. the Kingston Trio, for example, seemed to spawn large numbers of clean-cut apolitical folk groups, eager to reach a young audience willing to pay for Kingston Trio–type music.

For all its obvious lyrical roots in folk music and for all its submerged or not yet directed political content, though, the sound produced by these groups for mass consumption was often a pop sound. It was very far from the rough-edged authentic hillbilly sound of the early, pre-political folk singers.

A bohemian collector named Harry Smith greatly aided those seeking the sounds of the original music. Smith gathered material from records released commercially between 1927, the beginning of such commercial music, and 1932, when the Great Depression profoundly decreased music sales. Smith compiled 87 of the songs into the *Anthology of American Folk Music* for Folkways Records in 1952. Suddenly such relatively obscure artists like Clarence Ashley, Furry Lewis, Blind Lemon Jefferson, Mississippi John Hurt, and numerous others were heard — and memorized — by the singers about to create a new folk movement.

Folk music's expansion from campuses and clubs was also spurred by the emergence of folk festivals. In 1958, the Berkeley Festival became the first major folk festival, but it would be overshadowed historically by a 1959 event in Newport, Rhode Island. On July 11 and 12, the Newport Folk Festival gathered an eclectic group of performers generally grouped as performing folk music. The first festival attracted about 12,000 people and the second one a year later was a similar financial failure. The producers discontinued it. But folk music was not going away, and the festival would be revived and become central to folk music's national identity.

Even in 1959, though, the festival had a major influence because of a young woman with an unforgettable voice. Joan Baez, though, had not even been officially invited. Her friend and mentor Bob Gibson had recognized her talent and asked her to appear with him.

He wasn't the first to be mesmerized. In Cambridge, Massachusetts, crowds gathered outside the huge plate-glass windows of Club 47 to see Baez, then a 17-year-old Boston University student, singing on stage. Her raven-haired, brown-eyed exoticism and her long, almond-shaped face unadorned by make-up along with a voice that was a chillingly pure soprano drew swooning fans.

It was 1958, and Baez sang weekly at Club 47, a block east of Harvard Square. The club's long, brown curtains and shiny black walls provided a perfect environment for Baez. She walked on, going straight to the microphone. There was not a whiff of self-promoting show business about her. She uttered no jokes, no fake-friendly patter with those seated in front of her. There was just a song and then another song. She almost always wore a simple sweater and skirt, sometimes with a plain dress as a variation. She sang English and Scottish ballads like "Barbara Allen." She was exotic, and her voice was beautiful. But there was also an emotion behind the songs, a sense of profound loneliness and despair that she could convey so that the crowd — or at least the men — wanted to protect and embrace her.

There was almost no advertising. The club owners distributed mimeographed flyers and managed to interest a few college newspapers to cover the emerging folk scene. Still, each week more and more people wanted to hear that voice and see that beauty.

Women had been part of folk music since its inception but had never achieved the kind of star status reserved for men. Baez appeared at the right time to overturn that tradition. She didn't just accompany some more forceful male; her voice gave her the control and with that control she ushered in a new era for women in folk music.

In July 1959 Albert Grossman approached Baez and invited her to perform at the Gate of Horn in Chicago for a couple of weeks. It was there that she worked with Bob Gibson before he invited her to go to Newport. She rode there with Gibson and Odetta. Once there, Gibson checked about including Baez in his act with Oscar Brand, serving as stage manager, and, after some misgiving, Brand agreed. Baez, wanting assurance that she'd get onstage one way or another, also checked with other performers seeing if they would let her on as well.

It was on Sunday, the second night of the festival. Gibson was on stage, telling stories, singing, and preparing to introduce a guest he wasn't supposed to include in his act. Baez was standing stage left, in the mud, wearing an orange, silk-lined Mexican rebozo and clutching her guitar. She heard her name and, with characteristic determination, climbed the stairs, and walked onto the stage. She joined Gibson in singing "Virgin Mary Had One Son." The crowd, absorbing her unforgettable voice, applauded wildly. Gibson and Baez — who sang with the rousing gusto made popular by Odetta — then burst into an upbeat version of "We Are Crossing Jordan's River." Baez's singing woke up Oscar Brand's sleeping son. No one at the festival knew it, but they had witnessed musical history.

Grossman wanted Baez to sign with John Hammond at Columbia. Baez recalls seeing Columbia's gold records and contrasting the company's commercial approach to the much smaller Vanguard label's approach, which she concluded was more concerned with the music than the money. In his memoir, Hammond recalls passing on signing Baez because Grossman was asking too much money. Whatever happened, Vanguard released her first album, simply titled *Joan Baez*, in November 1960. The album was filled with traditional ballads, such as "House of the Rising Sun," "Mary Hamilton," and "Silver Dagger." Similarly, her second album, released in October 1961, contained no overt political material. It was only in her album *Joan Baez in Concert*, released in September 1962, that she first introduced a political song — Woody Guthrie's "Pretty Boy Floyd." Her first album with any Bob Dylan material — *Joan Baez in Concert, Part 2* — appeared in November 1963. That is, despite her Quaker upbringing, her rebellious spirit, and her political beliefs, she didn't explicitly fuse her politics and her music until after the Civil Rights Movement began and after Dylan's searing political songs had been written.

As the Kingston Trio, Baez, and the other contributors to the nascent folk movement gained popularity, a main address for the movement began to be recognized as well. With Washington Square and the Folklore Center, Greenwich Village began to attract the folk singers. They were the new bohemians, entering the counter-cultural turf of the beatniks, the jazz-loving poets and writers who didn't think much of folk songs. The offbeat, the disenchanted, the artistic, the young, and the remnants of the Left found a safe world in Greenwich Village. Alan Lomax said it was "where people go to get away from America."[2]

Clubs began to spring up to accommodate the new movement. Gerdes Folk City was the first folk club. Gerdes was named after William Gerdes, who had opened a restaurant and sold it to Mike Porco, who eventually re-located at 11 West Fourth Street. The Gaslight Poetry Café, in the cockroach-infested basement of 116 MacDougal Street, next to the Folklore Center, had, as its name implies, originally opened in 1958 as a center for the beatnik poets to perform. It was eventually transformed into a folk club. The Gaslight was small — barely holding 110 people legally — and had an odd custom. The people who lived above the club were bothered by the applause; they voiced their disapproval by tossing various items down an airshaft. An agreement was reached: Gaslight audiences snapped their fingers instead of clapping to indicate their approval.

The folk singers gathered in a storeroom upstairs to play penny-ante poker. Hugh Romney (later known as Wavy Gravy) kept a portable typewriter there. Bob Dylan wrote at least part of "A Hard Rain's Gonna Fall" on the typewriter.

The Kettle of Fish, a bar, was upstairs and next to the Gaslight. Because it was so close, performers went there between their sets to relax. Soon the folk singers used it as a hangout, a place to swap songs, deepen or test friendships, and pass on the latest gossip. The first table as they entered became the folk singer table.

The Bitter End, at 147 Bleecker Street, was fancier than the other clubs, with a larger stage and brick walls behind the performer. Because of its reputation, it usually booked more well-known acts. The Village Gate (opened in early 1958 by Art D'Lugoff), The Commons (later re-named the Fat Black Pussycat), Cafe Figaro, and the Cafe Wha? were just some of the places where the folk singers performed.

Many of the clubs were "basket houses." Performers had to convince audiences to contribute as "kitty girls" passed a basket asking for coins. Idealistic college students made up much of the audience in the early days, before the tourists, gawkers, and those looking to make a buck off the folk movement arrived. There wasn't a lot of money in the audiences' pockets to put in the baskets.

Such a system did not provide any economic security; the folk singers went there because they had a deep need to perform, because they wanted to test out new songs, and because they could slowly build a group of followers.

The young folk singers making the trek to these clubs inevitably came across Dave Van Ronk, lovingly nicknamed "the Mayor of MacDougal Street." Van Ronk was large, talkative, able at any second to burst into laughter and rousing song, willing to drink, kibitz about leftist political theory, science fiction, jazz, or blues, or play chess while sitting in a window seat at the Café Figaro. Bob Dylan later played chess there for hours.

Van Ronk was a member of the Socialist Workers Party, a follower of Trotsky's Communism rather than Stalin's and thus at odds with some of the other folk singers. Despite his avid taste for politics, Van Ronk separated his music from his political fervor. He went to rallies but didn't sing about them, making the artistic choice — because of his voice and musical tastes — to avoid political songs.

Van Ronk was in the Village early and as the young folk singers began to arrive with the folk revival, Van Ronk was there as a coach, confidant, counselor, friend, and teacher. His couch was available for those who needed a place to sleep.

Tom Paxton met Van Ronk during the summer of 1960. Paxton was still in the army but came into New York on weekends. Van Ronk was playing at the Commons; he also hired and fired folk singers for the place.

Paxton had grown up in Oklahoma, developed a love for folk music generally and Woody Guthrie in particular because "he meant what he said. He wasn't kidding."[3] Paxton, unlike many of the folk singers, began writing songs in college. "I wrote my first song in back during a Shakespeare lecture."[4] It was an Elizabethan murder ballad. Whatever its merit as a song, it got Paxton composing. He began writing in a folk idiom, trying to write exactly the kind of songs he enjoyed hearing from the Weavers or Pete Seeger or Woody.

That Paxton performed his own songs sounds ordinary considering the history of the folk revival of the 1960s, but in fact most of the early musicians who came to the Village sang only traditional songs.

Dave Van Ronk credibly suggested that Tom Paxton was responsible for founding the movement for folk singers to write their own songs, though it is also plausible to credit Len Chandler, who went on to create numerous protest songs, especially in the area of civil rights. Both of them used familiar melodies and added their own lyrics. Paxton, like any great artist, listened to his audiences. They loved his original songs, so he wrote more.

Dylan eventually owned the title of the most famous of the singer-songwriters, but Paxton and Chandler among others first showed there was an audience for original material among those young, eager students, including political material.

Paxton wasn't the only young college graduate to fuse politics and folk music, but he was definitely in the minority. That would change.

The panic of the McCarthy era was over. Cultural ferment was bubbling much nearer the placid surface of American life than anyone realized. In such a new era, it was inevitable that some singers and some groups emerged to reach back across the 1950s to the traditions of Woody, Seeger, and the Weavers. Peter, Paul and Mary was the most important of the political groups to emerge.

Mary Travers had been raised in Greenwich Village by parents who were journalists deeply interested in folk music. Mary was there on the evening of December 24, 1955, when the Weavers re-united at Carnegie Hall. The holiday concert was a passing of the torch of sorts. The audience consisted of an enormous amount of young people who were about to come of musical age. Peter Yarrow was also in the audience that night, though he and Mary didn't meet until 1960.

In the late '50s, Mary was living in an apartment right above the Commons on MacDougal Street, across from the Gaslight. One evening at the Commons Mary met the tall, thin bearded M.C., a comedian and sometime musician named Noel Stookey who had arrived in Greenwich Village in 1959. Stookey had achieved some recognition for his sometimes unusual but always amazing sound effects, his ease in front of a crowd, and the ballads he sang as he strummed his guitar. Stookey invited Mary to sing with him first at the Commons and then at the Gaslight, where they sang such songs as "I Wish I Was a Single Girl." Mary was scared as she sang, almost to the point of being physically ill. Mary guided the young man from Michigan around the Village, introducing him, for instance, to zeppoli at an Italian street fair.[5] Stookey, meanwhile, was, under Dave Van Ronk's influence, focusing more and more on folk music.

Another young folk singer was trying to find his way. Peter Yarrow graduated from Cornell in 1959 and remained on campus to help teach a course on folk music. The class met three times a week, twice for regular classes and once on Saturday in the largest lecture hall at Cornell where Yarrow sang folk songs to the students. The effect on Yarrow was enormous.

Yarrow, made especially sensitive to a need for justice and fairness by a politically conscious mother, was infuriated that he lived in a land of separate drinking fountains for different races and where there was a lynching of a black man every three days.

As he sang in the class, the students seemed socially transformed by the music. As Yarrow remembered it, "The singing galvanized the spirit of the room.... Something was awakened.... It made me realize that if you create community by reaching the heart ... that another kind of sensibility could be reached.... Yearning for something like lost love or unrequited love is not terribly distinct from yearning for a world of greater justice."[6]

By the end of 1959, Yarrow had found his life's work. Realizing he couldn't reach people simply by logic, he decided that he would foster justice in the society through music. Armed with a mission, Yarrow moved to Greenwich Village and began singing in places like the Cafe Wha?

Folk singing as a business was just at its beginning. There weren't many folk entrepreneurs. Albert Grossman was the most important of those newcomers managing folk acts. Grossman was a man with a pitch-perfect ear for music, a rare vision that folk musicians could make money, a boundless energy to make that vision become real, an enigmatic, labyrinthine mind, a bear-like body, a sharp tongue that was able to wield silence along with praise or threat, and a psychological acuity that helped him shrewdly size up friend and foe alike.

Grossman had come to New York, and at the beginning of 1960 he wandered into the Cafe Wha? to watch Peter Yarrow perform, and strolled out midway through the show. But, characteristically, Grossman was observant. He no doubt noted that the women in the audience were moved by Yarrow, by his good looks and by the passion in his voice, a passion romantic but also high-minded. Yarrow performed "Buddy, Can You Spare a Dime?" and women cried.

Grossman saw Yarrow a few months later at a rehearsal for a CBS television show. Baez, a Grossman client, was also performing. Grossman, seeing Yarrow's progress, asked him to be a client, and Yarrow accepted. Grossman arranged for Yarrow to play at the next Newport Folk Festival where Yarrow sang, among other songs, "Puff, the Magic Dragon."

The song was based on a poem written by Leonard Lipton, Yarrow's friend at Cornell. Yarrow added to what Lipton had written and provided a melody so that he turned it into a song. Yarrow wrote the song as a memorial to the loss of childhood and the emergence into adult life when youthful beliefs, such as in dragons, need to be cast aside. Audiences in the 1960s saw marijuana references in the song, such as puffing a magic drag on, but the authors are adamant that such interpretations are completely misguided.

For a year, Yarrow traveled around to various clubs to perfect his act. At some point in 1961, Grossman made a decision about Yarrow's future. He approached the earnest young man with a suggestion: Become part of a folk group, the way the Weavers had been, and, Grossman promised, more success would follow.

Grossman had a whole plan. He wanted an updated Weavers, a group that would be attractive to the new audience of young college students who filled the Village folk clubs, a hipper version of the Kingston Trio. He thought the way vaudeville theater owners had. He wanted his group to provide for all audience tastes. So he started with a handsome and serious man with a social conscience and a sensitive soul. He knew he wanted a comedian and a woman in the group like the Weavers, a strong woman like Ronnie Gilbert, but with contemporary sex appeal, so he considered people to approach.

Yarrow knew of Noel Stookey's comedy performances at the Gaslight, and Grossman approached Stookey, who declined, saying, "No. I still have some things I want to do by myself."[7] But, Stookey notes, Grossman went right back to Yarrow and reported, "He said he doesn't want to do it, but I think he'll do it."[8]

Meanwhile, within the same week as Stookey had been approached, Grossman and Yarrow were in the Folklore Center when Yarrow spotted a picture of the blonde Travers.

"Who's that?"

Grossman responded, "That's Mary Travers. She'd be good if you could get her to work."[9] Despite any misgivings, Grossman surely saw in Travers's beauty exactly what he needed for his group. He urged her to stay out of the sun to maintain a pale attractiveness and to be silent on stage to create some mystery to her character.

Yarrow began to sing with Mary, liked the sound, but they both knew they needed a third voice. Mary knew Noel Stookey personally and recommended him, so Grossman went back to Stookey, who agreed to try. Still, he was a realist. He knew "there is a great gap between having the talent and having it publicly known."[10]

Travers and Yarrow went over to Stookey's apartment, but Stookey didn't know the folk songs that the others had grown up with. They had to settle on "Mary Had a Little Lamb," but, despite the song's simplicity, it was immediately clear to all of them that the sound was, in Yarrow's word, "magical." They agreed on material, rehearsed it, and then went to Grossman for an audition.

Grossman knew he had found his trio. He immediately sensed their financial possibility and heard their professionalism. The trio rehearsed every day for seven months. Grossman had originally suggested that the group be named "The Willows," but they liked a line from the song "I Was Born 10,000 Years Ago" with a reference to "Peter, Paul and Moses." Grossman suggested Noel Stookey take on the name "Paul" for the group; Stookey agreed. The change had an important effect. In a group name, the individual identities of the singers generally got lost, but with "Peter, Paul and Mary" each of the three singers could retain a crucial part of their selves. Their message was that individuals could join together to create communities without surrendering their own identities, so the group's name was insightful beyond the euphony of its sound.

After the rehearsals, Grossman arranged for them to play at Folk City and the Bitter End during the fall of 1961. Grossman was pleased with their progress and the reception from audiences, but he didn't want them to record for one of the folk labels because he thought folk music could make its way to the mainstream audience. Grossman reached a deal with Warner Brothers Records on January 29, 1962. Peter, Paul and Mary's first album, with its stark cover of the two bearded men and the blonde woman standing in front of the brick wall at the Bitter End and its distinctive script lettering of the group's name, was released in May 1962. By October the album reached the top of the Billboard charts and stayed there for seven weeks. It eventually sold more than two million copies. In July, "If I Had a Hammer" was released and reached tenth place on the Billboard charts in October. The single won the 1962 Grammy for Best Performance by a Vocal Group and Best Folk Recording.

Considering the song's radical origins and history, the choice of the song by Peter, Paul and Mary and its career as such a huge commercial and critical success provided the surest sign that the McCarthy era was over and that the radical folk singers of the 1930s could emerge from the cultural shadows to be welcomed as heroes and visionaries.

The Great Folk Scare had begun for real. It had revived the folk music movement, considered moribund after the decline of Communism in America.

To find its way, this new movement needed its own Woody Guthrie, a man who could produce blistering lyrics about the issues of the day, a poet with a guitar and the rough-hewn voice of the people. The audience went looking for such a man, and they found him just as he was looking for them.

Eight

The Runaway Prophet: Bob Dylan's Romance with Folk Music

The story of Bob Dylan's life for the decade before his 25th birthday was that of a young man exploring his artistic identity and an artist searching for God. On the way to God, he stopped to look, in despair, at his country.

Dylan searched for artistic heroes who could help him understand his own mind and provide guidance about how to live in a world not notably kind to the sensitive. He found Hank Williams, Woody Guthrie, Arthur Rimbaud, Jack Kerouac, Allen Ginsberg, and many others before settling on God.

In the way Dylan came to understand the divine, God had no restraints and no borders. God was the great Creator. No other being could be a better artist than God. And if you tried to be like God, you didn't have to be tied down to a single identity. You didn't have to be Jewish or Christian or any other religion. You were all, as Woody Guthrie had believed. You didn't have to be black or white, red, or yellow. You didn't, in Dylan's view, have to be male or female, on the political left or the political right, from the Midwest or from the coast. You didn't have to like folk or rock and roll or blues or country. God was all-embracing to Dylan and if God was your model, you could be as well.

Beyond heroes, Dylan also had the songs. When all else in his life evaporated or disappointed, shocked or angered, there were always the songs. They were the bedrock from which all sprang.

Dylan's artistic journey began under a different birth name in a frozen, remote town, seemingly a long way from Heaven. But Bobby Zimmerman from Hibbing, Minnesota, found in the town a setting that was good for him even as he outgrew it.

Had Dylan been raised in a noisy, lively city its lures and sounds might have distracted him or drowned out the lonely sounds of the blues or the jangling sounds of Little Richard that Hibbing's isolation allowed him to hear as he sat in bed and listened with a thirsty ear to the distant radio stations. He could close his eyes and in his mind be standing on the stage of Carnegie Hall.

He might not have met a teacher like B. J. Rolfzen. Dylan — Rolfzen continues to refer to him as "Robert" — sat in the front row third seat from the door during his junior year as he studied American literature. Rolfzen especially taught poetry, because he loved it and because he believed that poetry got at the truth. He never sat at his desk but in front of the class — in front of Robert Zimmerman — and recited the poetry he had memorized at home. "I used to read names on tombstones and repeat the names in class. I liked the sounds of the names," he recalls.[1] He still regrets giving Dylan a "B" on a paper about *The Grapes of Wrath.*

Dylan might not have dated a beautiful young woman named Echo Helstrom, whose father was a dirt farmer, and discovered that music brought him more than listening pleasure. Or met a friend like John Bucklen, whose father had died and whose mother took in sewing, and who shared and encouraged Dylan's musical passions.

Hibbing gave him a place from which he could run away. Dylan found it conformist, culturally oppressive, a place in which he couldn't be creative or spontaneous or emotionally unbridled enough. Having Hibbing was just as important as having a caring, kind, but traditional father in providing an emotional prison to escape. Misery is always a more interesting mystery than happiness, and Dylan wanted to find a solution. He knew he could not go forward unless he reacted vehemently against the past — a pattern that endured in his life. As a content young man, he would have driven through life. As an angry, confused rebel he ran society's stop signs to find his way, to figure out why he was born and what he was supposed to do with his life.

There in the North Country he needed to step out, to get on the road, even if it was just to Minneapolis. Hibbing was the place that prompted him to change. It is no mystery, then, that when Robert Zimmerman legally became Bob Dylan on August 9, 1962, he didn't go through a ceremony in New York City but journeyed back to Hibbing's court house to appear before the presiding judge with the arresting name of Christ Holm.

Dylan did learn in Hibbing that he was going to be a musician. Music could take away the confusion he felt. Music could make him into a whole new person.

He was in a series of bands in Hibbing and learned about performing, about audiences, but most of all he became an explorer searching all the realms of musical geography. He learned where one song stood in relation to others. It was music that taught him how to live, and music that was a refuge from the thwarted hopes and shattered loves that he encountered.

Despite all this, it must have provided him unrelieved joy to see Hibbing in the rear-view mirror when he left after graduating high school. He didn't know where he was going, but he wanted to get there fast.

Dylan stayed in Minneapolis for fifteen months. He tried at first to attend classes at the University of Minnesota, but his mind was enraptured by music. Robert Zimmerman gave himself a new name, drawn from Dylan Thomas. He discovered folk music, a harsher voice, a leaner look, and, evidently, drugs.

Alcohol and drugs had long been connected with the artistic imagination. Many writers, especially, drew a connection between alcohol and drugs and the freeing and fueling of what would otherwise be hidden thoughts and visions. They were in search of a discontinuity of consciousness to interrupt received knowledge that blocked visions of the real. The stimulants were also a way of escaping pressures and the endless droning on of normal consciousness. In the music world, drugs became a way to maintain a grueling touring schedule. Eventually, they were a signal distinction of the counterculture. Already in 1959 and 1960 they were part of the Beat movement's way of exploring life and at least at the edges of the folk of leftist movements. For some combination of these reasons, Dylan was drawn to mind-altering substances.

He also found a role model in Woody Guthrie.

Woody showed him that words mattered. Dylan had been writing poetry since he had been a young child. He loved rhymes the way Woody did. Woody showed him, as Hank Williams and others had, that there was a place to combine words and music. Song lyrics could be poetry. Dylan hungrily learned and performed Woody's songs. Like his model, it turned out that Bob Dylan, too, was bound for glory.

Dylan's first journey to New York to visit Woody and become a star started in December 1960. There are conflicting reports about the trip. Here is one interpretation.

Dylan journeyed first to Madison, Wisconsin. Dylan returned to Madison a year later and some events on that trip have been reported as being on the first one. Therefore, it is hard to separate the trips.

Dylan arrived in Madison and approached Ron Radosh, whose name he had been given from a mutual friend, for a place to stay. Radosh, now a well-known scholar and then a campus radical, made a suggestion. Radosh saw Dylan frequently, sitting out on the lawn, commenting on passing females. Dylan once told Radosh, "I'm going to be bigger than Elvis." Radosh recalls, "He said it with total certainty. It wasn't adolescent bravado or bragging. He was very nice, friendly, and warm."[2]

Dylan's certain sense of his own musical future was in many ways odd. It's not unusual for a teenager to be convinced that greatness lies around the next corner. It was as though he felt begotten by Destiny, that God and Greatness were his parents. And however strongly Dylan may have felt the cosmic gears clicking into place for him, he still had chosen an odd way to cooperate with fate. Elvis was a pop singer, disliked by the very folk musicians Dylan idolized. Woody Guthrie was unknown outside of a relatively small circle of friends and admirers. There was, of course, a folk revival going on, but its successes had smooth voices and clean-cut looks. Pete Seeger was still fighting legal battles. There didn't seem to be a reasonable chance to being very popular at all in the Woody Guthrie tradition of folk music. Still, there was Dylan in Madison, ready to change the world.

Paul Breines recalls Dylan playing with Danny Kalb, already an extraordinary blues guitarist. "Danny and Dylan played a bunch at a place on State Street." Once at a party at Kalb's, Breines saw Dylan "a little drunk and imploring me ... to listen very closely to a 45 rpm he was playing by Gene Vincent ... focusing on a couple of bars here and there where you could hear his [Dylan's] guitar notes. I remember being, on the one hand, impressed that this guy had played with so cool a group, and, on the other, struck by how remarkably self-absorbed he seemed to be. My impression was that he was a musical phenom, clearly some sort of weird genius."[3]

As he had done in Hibbing, Dylan was inventing his own fame, so hungry was he for it. His association with people like Kalb was important. Dylan was playing Woody Guthrie songs and so needed to know a couple of chords. If he was to play more sophisticated music he needed to learn more from guitar players who were better than he was. As he would be in New York, therefore, he was drawn to people like Kalb.

On one of his trips to Madison, Dylan stayed at an apartment in a room that belonged to Jennifer Warren, now a professor and actor. She recalls Dylan taking over her room. "Girls would come visit. He was fascinated with what he could learn."[4] She recalls a very boyish Dylan endlessly playing Woody Guthrie songs and rambling on about his travels.

Dylan was also drawn to someone else in the apartment, Fred Underhill. Underhill was tall and lanky with straight, dark hair. He was funny. He could draw pictures (later in New York, Dylan's girlfriend Suze Rotolo drew a portrait of Underhill).

Ann Lauterbach, currently a poet, professor, and recipient of a Mac-Arthur Fellowship, was Underhill's girlfriend at the time. She recalls Underhill as talkative and compelling, with a sophistication and a mystique and remembers walking with both men and noting a hole in Dylan's shoe; Underhill gave him money for a new sole.

Underhill gave Dylan lessons in charisma. Jennifer Warren notes, "Dylan was a little boy very into himself. People came up and talked to Fred."[5]

Dylan evidently stayed for several weeks in Madison before heading east. In the standard re-telling of this first trip Dylan first went to Chicago, headed west instead of east and came to Madison and got a ride to New York from a Madison student named Dave Berger.

There are several problems with the story. The driving distance between the two cities is almost 150 miles. It wouldn't make sense to go first to Chicago. Secondly, Berger recalls the trip vividly as having taken place in January 1962, when Dylan returned to Madison, not January 1961. Berger lived around the corner from the apartment where Dylan was staying with Underhill and the others. Berger notes that Dylan mentioned already having a contract with Columbia Records. Berger drove straight through for 17 to 20 hours and remembers Dylan "didn't have any money to pay for the ride. He was singing and playing guitar in the back."[6] Berger kept calling him "Marshal Dillon" from the *Gunsmoke* character and at one point was so annoyed with Dylan's singing interfering with the jazz on the radio that Berger told Dylan to shut up. "He didn't have a nickel or if he did he wasn't willing to spend it. Every time we stopped ... he would hover over you. I remember him eating whatever anybody left over. Somebody left french fries over. Dylan would eat 'em. He really did not spend a penny."[7]

Finally, Dylan himself notes in his autobiography *Chronicles* that he came to New York "across the country from the Midwest in a four-door sedan, '57 Impala — straight out of Chicago."[8] Dylan's memory may be off here. The Impala was not introduced until 1958, although it is possible that it was bought in late '57 or that Dylan meant a '58 version.

So, either driving with Underhill or by himself, Dylan left Madison and headed to Chicago. Once there, Dylan headed immediately to see Kevin Krown. The two had met in the summer of 1960 in Central City, Colorado, and Krown had told Dylan to stop by if he was ever in Chicago. Krown, very much like Fred Underhill, was a character. Ed Blum, a friend of Krown's, recalls him as a charmer, someone who admired con men, who even visited the notorious con man Joseph "Yellow Kid" Weil in a Chicago hospital.

The late Mark Eastman was another friend of Krown's. The two frequently hitchhiked to New York and strolled through the Village; Krown had connections in the city. Eastman recalled that Dylan arrived at a dorm in Chicago, looking like a "lost soul carrying a guitar."[9] He was very shy, Eastman noted. "He seemed like a little lost boy, with a frail quality, like he couldn't cook a cup of soup. He was in constant motion."[10] But he was playing the Guthrie tunes Eastman and Krown loved. Eastman said, "His peculiar emphasis on words was really compelling."[11] Blum agrees, "He sang through his teeth so you had to listen to him and what he was saying was worth listening to."[12]

Blum and Eastman had caught the Dylan secret. His singing was better than it sounded. He had the timing of a gifted actor or comedian, though in singing the timing came in the way Dylan phrased his songs. He didn't just play a song. He haunted it. He jumped into its center, found its emotional appeal, and delivered that emotion. The songs he picked were emotionally informative. Listeners could learn from hearing him. The voice was a distraction for some, an appeal to others, but he was always more than a voice, a guitar, and a harmonica. As Blum notes, "He was playing the music and also playing the character."[13]

Indeed, the hobo orphan, the child of the carnivals, the re-born Woody Guthrie that Bobby Zimmerman had created was absorbing bits and pieces, re-inventing himself as he went along.

At some point, Dylan, Krown, and Eastman determined to head east to meet Woody Guthrie, and several weeks later they did so. Eastman and Krown hitchhiked to New York, and Dylan got a ride in the "'57 Impala." Krown had a friend who had a vacant apartment in midtown. The three — and a fourth person whose name Eastman didn't recall — met at the apartment. Dylan probably arrived sometime after the snowstorm on January 20, 1961. Eastman recalled there was snow on the ground when he got there and that he would have only gone to New York on Fridays and weekends. Therefore, Dylan probably arrived in New York on Friday, January 27.

On the day after they got to New York, Dylan, Krown, Eastman, and the mysterious fourth person took a bus trip of about an hour and a half to Greystone Hospital to visit Woody Guthrie. Eastman remembered, "We walked into the floor where someone asked for Woody. There were chairs along the wall, attendants in green mopping the floor."[14] Eastman looked at the patients wandering around and felt depressed. "We sat down on some chairs in the corner of the room. Finally an attendant walked out with Woody, whose body was bent in strange angles. He almost looked like a prisoner from Auschwitz. However, he seemed happy and excited to have company. He did not recognize Bob Dylan. My feeling was that it was the first time Dylan and Woody met. It was hard to understand Woody. Dylan played him some songs. Woody was very interested. He really bonded with Dylan. It seemed as if everyone present paid attention and felt that something significant was happening. The mopping of the floor stopped. I remember Woody asking the attendant to bring out his own guitar. Somehow even under the terrible weight of the crippling effects of Huntington's disease, Woody hammered out some chords to "This Land Is Your Land," and Bob and he sang the song together. It was a very powerful moment.

"As we were getting ready to leave, Woody wrote a few words for each of us. For me it was on the back of the University of Chicago Folklore Society membership card." Eastman could only recall the first words that Woody wrote, "I wrote the best seeds of my life for those who...."[15]

On Dylan's card, Woody wrote, "I ain't dead yet."[16]

Eastman continued the story. "That evening we went to a party in Greenwich Village near NYU. Dylan played a couple of songs, but he wanted to leave. So he and I left and walked down the street [MacDougal] and went into the Commons or some other club. Dylan convinced the guy to let him play and a basket was passed around."[17] The Commons, later named the Fat Black Pussycat, is the most likely place they went. As Robert Shelton reported, "Dylan first performed in the Village at the Commons coffeehouse."[18]

Kevin Krown helped Dylan in many ways. Krown introduced him to people such as the singer Mark Spoelstra and, crucially, to Howard (Mac) and Eve McKenzie, who had a tiny apartment, but who let Dylan stay there. "They treated him like their own kid."[19]

Dylan came to the Village a few days after John F. Kennedy was inaugurated as president on January 20, 1961. The new president brought in his wake the freshness of a new generation, one filled with hope and idealism, a sense that the world needed to be changed and could be. Much of that idealism found its expression in the support of civil rights for African Americans, people whose ancestors had been kidnapped and brought to America as slaves, who had endured unending physical, psychological, and emotional torment in trying to come to terms with that legacy, and who, in the South and elsewhere in 1961, continued to be deprived of many basic rights. This was the cause that first drew Dylan and many others to political songwriting. As Tom Paxton notes, "I loved the music, but I also felt that the music could change the world, and in the case of the civil rights movement it did. I felt impelled to comment. I felt deeply about these issues, and I tried to express it in song."[20]

The Greenwich Village Dylan reached was not always attractive. As Tom Paxton notes, "The smell wouldn't be that aromatic. The Village was not a tidy place at all. It was pretty dirty and buildings were old. You go into the hall of one of the tenements and it would stink. It was loud. People weren't necessarily polite."[21]

Dylan went everywhere, but he never confused activity with achievement. He moved, but he was headed in a direction. Feeling exiled from Eden, he sought to find its gates.

He went to Gerdes Folk City for the Monday night hootenannies. He went to Washington Square Park and played, hoping for some spare change.

And he went regularly to Izzy Young's Folklore Center. Young played records for him, gave him materials to read. Young saw a quiet, intense young man. Dylan kept asking to play songs for him, and when Young saw the text of one song (he doesn't recall which), he asked to interview Dylan. Young kept a voluminous diary, but Dylan's responses — many of which he entered himself — were those of his created character Bob Dylan, not Bobby Zimmerman.

Young fell for Dylan's tales and, extremely rare for Young, he sent Dylan up to meet Moe Asch at Folkways. Asch turned Dylan down. Young then sent him to Maynard Solomon at Vanguard Records, a company that had recorded the Weavers. According to Young, Solomon had a strongly negative reaction to Dylan: "I don't record freaks."[22]

Why did Young do all this, putting his own reputation on the line for a decidedly unusual kid? "I didn't think of Dylan as an investment. I just enjoyed him."[23]

Dylan spent much of his time meeting and learning from other performers. He went to regular gatherings with Woody Guthrie and his friends at the East Orange, New Jersey, home of Bob and Sidsel (universally known as Sid) Gleason. The Gleasons lived near Greystone Hospital, and started to visit Woody. They then began to bring him back to their home on weekends. Many in the folk community came to the Gleason home on Sunday afternoons, especially the young folk singers who profoundly admired Woody.

Dylan played for Woody, and Woody enjoyed his singing. Dylan stayed with the Gleasons for a few weeks poring over the tapes made at the Gleason house and listening to old records.

Dylan became friends with Ramblin' Jack Elliott as well when the two met while visiting Woody. Dylan absorbed (some of Elliott's supporters used a stronger word) Ramblin' Jack's style. He listened to Liam Clancy's Irish songs and sayings.

Dave Van Ronk was perhaps the most influential of those early singers Dylan met. Van Ronk knew everybody. He was well-read. He could talk gruffly and sharply, but he was warm-hearted. He played chess with Dylan, taught him songs, and was one more charismatic figure for Dylan to depend upon and learn from.

Eventually, Van Ronk provided Dylan with a place to stay and books to read as well. Van Ronk first met him at the Cafe Wha? and became a friend and mentor, helping him get stage appearances. His wife, Terri, tried to book spots for Dylan.

In his autobiography, Van Ronk reaches the plausible conclusion that Dylan wrote "Song to Woody" (on February 14) to sing to Woody at Greystone. Dylan the child poet had written songs before, but not a serious one, none that could genuinely be sung in public. Dylan needed the song, and he wrote it.

Terri Van Ronk, Liam Clancy, and others convinced Mike Porco, the owner of Gerdes Folk City, to give the new kid a chance, and so on April 11, Dylan opened for John Lee Hooker during a two-week engagement. For the occasion, Sid Gleason provided Dylan with one of Woody Guthrie's suits. It was an extraordinary gesture, a real sense that Woody was passing himself on to the next generation.

Dylan came across many other people trying to succeed in the Village. On June 19, for example, Noel Stookey was in the Gaslight reading the *Herald Tribune* and came across a story involving a doomed cruise up the Hudson to Bear Mountain. Stookey showed the story to Dylan and was surprised when, overnight, the newcomer came up with a song about the incident. Stookey had assumed that like most of the other young kids with guitars slung over their backs, Dylan just played traditional songs. As he listened, Stookey sensed the talent. Dylan could grasp "the skeleton that held pieces of information together."[24] Stookey told Albert Grossman to watch this young man.

While Bob Dylan was focused on music, he was, intentionally or not, surrounded by people on the political Left. Ever since Dylan had first become attracted to folk music in Minneapolis, he had heard political arguments, been dragged to events, listened without necessarily agreeing. In New York, Van Ronk was a superlative political educator. In the film *No Direction Home*, Mark Spoelstra claimed of Dylan, "He had a great desire to change the world. We even talked about it. We thought that segregation wasn't going to last, and that we were going to have something to do with ending it. We really believed we were going to have a part as songwriters in changing the world."

However affected Dylan was by all this, he didn't write his first explicitly political song until after he met Suze Rotolo on July 29, 1961, after a hootenanny in support of Riverside Church's new radio station.

Suze's sister, Carla, who introduced the two, was Alan Lomax's secretary, so Dylan ended up frequently at the Lomax apartment at 121 West 3rd, learning directly from the major living folk collector what records he should know. The Rotolo family and the Lomax collection guided Dylan into leftist politics. Suze herself was a member of SANE, an anti-nuclear organization. She picketed on behalf of southern blacks.

Dylan had heard the language of the Left before, sometimes intensely delivered, but now he began to absorb it. His love for Suze became intertwined with a political viewpoint. As they had for Woody, women could, consciously or not, control the buttons on Dylan's emotional elevator.

But Suze did much more than that. "I read poetry by Rimbaud, and it piqued his curiosity. When you are intrigued by a poem, a song, or a painting, the tendency is to search out more poems, songs, paintings by that person. It went back and forth. We fed each other's curiosity. Allen Ginsberg took it further with his great spontaneous knowledge."[25]

Dylan's new animated attachment to the political Left was perfectly timed. A rave review from Robert Shelton in the *New York Times* on September 29, accentuated by its prominent placement on the page and an intriguing photo, coincided with Dylan's schedule to be at a recording session playing harmonica for the beautiful young singer Carolyn Hester. She was recording for Columbia Records, and John Hammond was her producer.

Hammond and Dylan had met a couple of weeks earlier, on the 14th, at a rehearsal and Hammond had been intrigued by Dylan then, asking him to come to Columbia for an audition. Shelton's review, the explicit imprimatur of the *Times*, provided cover for what Hammond wanted to do, which was to sign the still baby-faced and raw young singer.

There are various explanations for Hammond's decision. He had recently signed Pete Seeger and was looking for people in Seeger's tradition. At the rehearsal, Hammond heard as Dylan taught Hester a blues song called "Come Back, Baby." Hammond must have been impressed by the young man's knowledge, especially of the black music Hammond revered. With his emotional empathy for black music and his great ability to absorb the music he loved, Dylan even sounded black. It must have been irresistible for a man like Hammond — watching someone who could channel black music and Woody Guthrie at the same time. Hammond asked if Dylan wrote songs himself. Here was a clear indication of what Hammond wanted. He was not looking for a Guthrie imitator; he wanted a new Guthrie, someone who could write as well as perform. In Dylan's Huck Finn hat, harmonica playing (and using a holder to play it while he also played harmonica), and foreign accent — that is, not a New York accent — Hammond saw an original character. This wasn't a kid who just listened to Guthrie records. Of course, that's exactly what Dylan was, but the ability of Bob Dylan to take over Bobby Zimmerman was such that Hammond was entranced, whether or not he knew the truth, as he might have from his son, John Hammond, Jr., who knew Dylan's Minnesota roots.

There was another appealing element. Hammond ignored Dylan's questionable guitar and harmonica skills, in part because, as he told Shelton about Dylan, "He was very disenchanted with our social system. I encouraged him to put all his hostility on tape because I figured this was the way, really, to get to the true Bob Dylan."[26] Here was the real appeal. Hammond didn't just want a musician; he wanted a new Guthrie and Seeger. Hammond was trying to find a singer who could carry on the tradition that Hammond so admired. It wasn't that Dylan was the most gifted musician. It was that he was angry at the country, and he could write. That was it. Hammond had found his man. Dylan's new embrace of politics after meeting Suze Rotolo led him to speak Hammond's language.

It's possible for a cynic to conclude that Dylan — brilliant reader of people that he was — sensed what Hammond (and much of his audience) wanted, and so Dylan invented such a persona for the legendary producer and his listeners. Dylan surely realized that it was virtually impossible to survive being in the folk movement and not be part of the Left. And he certainly worked to develop an image. He once told folk singer Bob Cohen that he'd gone to the supermarket but he didn't want anyone to know that. Evidently, Dylan was concerned that had he been seen in a supermarket people would think him bourgeois and middle class.[27]

But that's not completely fair to Dylan. His romantic fervor gave him a genuine, if relatively short-lived, political fervor that coincided with his meeting Hammond. He believed in the Left. Later, he feared that it wanted to control his music.

In his autobiography, Hammond wrote that it was after the rehearsal and before the Shelton review that he learned that Dylan could indeed write his own songs. Hammond heard "Talkin' New York" and, he claimed, offered a contract to Dylan right away. It is also possible, as Shelton reports, that the contract was offered the day of the review and the recording session.

Either way, Dylan was suddenly the center of Village attention. He had already met Joan Baez, who overlooked his appearance to be entranced by "Song to Woody." And Albert Grossman was asking people if he should be Dylan's manager. Grossman got lots of advice. Peter Yarrow, Noel Stookey, and Judy Collins all liked Dylan. Others were less complimentary. But a Columbia contract could stifle a lot of a businessman's doubts.

Still, Grossman was cautious. He encouraged Izzy Young to produce a concert for Dylan on November 4. Only 53 people attended. Dylan surely must have been upset. Young gave him ten or twenty dollars of his own money.

On November 20 and 22 Dylan recorded his first album, went back home, and returned at the beginning of the year, still with little recognition.

In January 1962, Dylan performed in the San Remo Café in Schenectady, New York. Peter Lefcourt, now a producer, screenwriter, and novelist, was then a senior at Union College who waited on tables in the café. He recalls that "the owner would bring up folk singers from the city, pay them $75 plus a round trip on Greyhound and a night at the YMCA.

"One night I went to pick up the folk singer at the Greyhound bus terminal. Funny looking little guy gets off the bus with a guitar over his back and a bunch of harmonicas. Doesn't talk a whole lot. Has a head cold and keeps blowing his nose on his sleeve.

"There wasn't a big crowd that night, maybe a dozen people. When he played his first set, we all thought he wasn't going to go far. [The owner] thought that $75 was too high for this guy. High-pitched nasal voice, retro Woody Guthrie repertoire, lots of wheezing harmonica.

"I remember dropping him off after the last set, for the three people left in the place. When we pulled up to the Y, he asked me if I had a joint. I didn't, but I would have given him one if I had it because you don't want to face a room in the YMCA in Schenectady without a little help."[28]

Such were the challenges even a Columbia recording artist faced.

At the end of January, in preparation for a benefit for CORE (the Congress of Racial Equality), Dylan wrote "The Death of Emmett Till," about the 1955 murder of a young black man. It was his first explicitly political song. He followed it up with other songs, including "The Ballad of Donald White" and what was then called "Talking John Birch Paranoid Blues."

Pete Seeger, as impressed as everyone else that Dylan could write songs, introduced him to Sis Cunningham who, with her husband, was publishing a new magazine. *Broadside* offered its first issue in February and included the Birch song. The influential publication would go on to publish many more of Bob Dylan's songs.

Dylan's first album was released on March 19. It could not find a large enough audience. Hammond came under pressure from Columbia executives to let Dylan go.

But one song changed Dylan's fortunes. It convinced Albert Grossman of Dylan's incredible talent and the opportunities such talent offered the person who could manage Dylan. It was a sign to John Hammond that Dylan's future was open-ended. "Blowin' in the Wind" was the real opening shot of the Dylan revolution. Its origins began when Dylan heard an old spiritual.

The New World Singers was one of the young folk groups trying to be the new Weavers. Bob Cohen, Delores Dixon, Happy Traum, and Gil Turner played at Gerdes and invited Dylan up to play with them sometimes. In the middle of their set, Dixon, an African American woman, sang "No More Auction Block for Me," a profoundly moving howl from the heart sung from the point of view of a slave.

Dylan and Dixon were sometime lovers. According to Bob Cohen, Dixon was astonished when she heard Dylan using the spiritual's melody and creating new words for it.[29] Dylan famously did this with words as well as songs, borrowing but reconstructing, filtering it through his imagination and, at least in terms of lyrics, always improving the words. Dylan worked best when he worked off existing material, grabbing a word or phrase here and there and letting his mind go with it, undoubtedly often astonished himself at what that mind produced. Dylan didn't create from nothing; he wasn't God, but he was an incredibly imaginative artist.

A few days later, on April 9, Dylan asked the folk singer David Blue to play the chords while he finished the lines of the song he had started. When its then two verses were completed, they went to Gerdes. Between sets, as Turner rested from his chores as host of the Monday night hootenanny, Dylan performed the new song as the other New World Singers listened. Turner immediately asked if he could sing the song, and he did. The New World Singers were the first to record the song.

Dylan's song is the child of "Where Have All the Flowers Gone?" Indeed, the Kingston Trio had released their version of the Seeger song in March, signaling the acceptance of political material by popular music. But Dylan's questions were not Seeger's. They were still allusive, but the social problems they asked about were more recognizable. Peter Yarrow suggests that the song "perfectly expressed the yearning of the time."[30] Mary Travers thought it was "the perfect issue song because it's got a line for everything."[31] Seeger had taught Dylan that the protest songs were too tied to a specific event. But, in evading that error, anthemic songs could overreact and be too general. Dylan walked the fine line between the two perfectly.

His song had no clear answers. The wind sweeps away the old and brings in the new, so that some force will change the current society, but the force is natural, not controlled by humans. The inherent political images in the verses are betrayed by the anti-politics of the chorus.

If "Blowin' in the Wind" established Dylan as a folk artist, "A Hard Rain's A-Gonna Fall," a song he wrote in September — *Broadside* published it that month — was a herald that Dylan had artistic yearnings that could not be contained by even the urgent political reality of the day, a reality that seemed eerily and tightly tethered to the arresting images, startling phrases, and moving sounds he created. It is the first of Dylan's songs that allows for complex interpretations.

Dylan's fame was accelerating, spreading quickly beyond the small Village folk scene. Dylan was still extremely young, though people like Rimbaud and many of the Romantic poets also wrote their most startling work while young. But Rimbaud or Keats didn't have to face modern media or impatient reporters anxious to get a story on deadline. Dylan, the quiet Minnesota kid who wanted to be a star, suddenly had to deal with the pressures of fame: produce great art seemingly on demand; respond to the insatiable public taste for the most private bits of information; watch as friends began to act differently or people he didn't know assume they knew him; be unable to go to public places without people pointing him out, yelling that Bob Dylan was here, demanding autographs or explanations of songs or help with their careers; lead a personal life without intrusion; find people to trust; and all the while search for a private space away from the intrusive noise and endless pull of public life. To paraphrase Joan Didion's observation about Joan Baez in *Slouching Towards Bethlehem*, Dylan was a personality before he was a person.

Evidently, part of his way to cope was to consume alcohol and drugs. Another part was mocking people, among them women, friends, and competitors. But it was how he dealt with pressure that was remarkable. He went on to produce the most startling body of songs certainly in the second half of the 20th century and, perhaps, in all of American history.

"A Hard Rain's A-Gonna Fall" is often considered Dylan's response to the Cuban missile crisis. Since President Kennedy gave his national television talk on October 22, that is clearly inaccurate. "Hard Rain" is a warning to the society. Instead of telling a story, Dylan offers a flashing chain of apocalyptic images that foretell doom — the hard rain — if the society doesn't change. This is, therefore, Dylan's first clearly utopian song. For if the rain will fall if we continue our ways, we can change the society to prevent it. Indeed, taking on the mantle of prophet, Dylan says he can change the society. He will examine the depths of the society's depravity before the disaster, learn what's wrong, and then, standing on a mountain like a prophet speaking to the people, sing songs that point the way forward.

Dylan differs from Guthrie and Seeger in that Dylan's visions of a doomed society are not matched by a social vision of an alternative. He just promises to sing out a warning. Without the belief in Communism or at least some variant of socialism, Dylan is left filled with rage at the current system but unable to describe what the new society would look like, other than it won't be like this one.

The poetic imagery of the song is important because it indicated that the folk music tradition had a competitor for Dylan's artistic attention. The song vastly increased the temptation — impossible to suppress — to interpret Dylan's songs. Dylan wrote it before meeting Allen Ginsberg. That meeting — which would not take place until December 26, 1963 — would complement Dylan's personal study and lead to the even more explicitly poetic content of *Bringing It All Back Home, Highway 61 Revisited*, and *Blonde on Blonde*.

Dylan had always been attracted to poetry. Certain poetic movements shaped his vision, particularly the Beat movement, and, working ever further back in literary history, the Surrealist, Symbolist, and Romantic movements.

The Beats offered apocalyptic visions, but of the conformity of the 1950s, not the upheaval of the 1960s. They found American culture oppressive. They believed in experiences from life not the academy. This anti-intellectuality in favor of instinct was matched by a disdain for politics and the championing of individual liberation. They got involved in criminal activities, drug use, and hedonistic behavior, especially of a sexual kind, and — in some of their writings — celebrated homosexual sex. They wanted their emotions to escape the prison imposed by society and their creativity to emerge in artistic form as in poems ("Howl" by Ginsberg) or novels (such as *On the Road* by Jack Kerouac or *Naked Lunch* by William Burroughs).

The Surrealist poets, believing dreams and the imagination contained realities that were available only in limited form in the real world, explored these as a source of material. These experiences were super-real ("surrealism" is a fusion of those two words), and so the subconscious and the dream world were seen as the truer containers of insight into reality.

The Symbolists like Baudelaire and Verlaine didn't look to the society to give them symbols to represent their lives. Rather they looked inward, preferring private symbology to stand for personal emotional reactions to the realities of their lives. A poem was a concatenation of those private symbols.

A poem for the Symbolists (and their modernist heirs such as Eliot) was not a puzzle to be solved. It does not have a meaning. "Meaning" for them was a diversion to keep a reader paying attention while the poem stealthily insinuates itself into a person's consciousness.

The critic Terry Eagleton described this in writing about Eliot: "Eliot was interested in what a poem did, not in what it said — in the resonance of the signifier, the echoes of its archetypes, the ghostly associations haunting its grains and textures, the stealthy, subliminal workings of its unconscious.... Eliot was ... a writer who made guerrilla raids on the collective unconscious."[32]

The exact words could be written about some of Dylan's work. That is why he mocks those who look for a single meaning in his songs. Although his songs cannot be definitively deciphered, interpretive suggestions about them might still offer illumination for listeners as a supplement to the way a listener already experiences the song.

All three of these literary movements were preceded by what was, in many ways, the most important influence on Dylan. The Romantics who flourished in the first half of the 19th century developed the model of artistic hero that in almost every way reflects Dylan. The Romantics challenged the Enlightenment ideas that reason was the surest path to knowledge (though they borrowed Enlightenment ideas that stressed the importance of freedom and the need to challenge social traditions). The Romantics focused on artistic heroes, creative geniuses who unashamedly expressed their emotions. These heroes could not lead practical lives. They were alienated from society, constantly in rebellion against it. Introspection was their path to knowledge. Ignoring schooling, they focused on experiences mediated through their feelings to examine their selves. It was that self-examination that would lead to knowledge. Their emphasis on the extremities of feelings incapable of being captured by reason led many to an interest in spirituality. Their separation from others and a feeling of superiority to others inevitably led to despair, to skepticism that ordinary social life could progress, to rebellion against the existing and accepted forms of art, indeed to defiance of all kinds of existing conventions, and to an acceptance that they would be misunderstood. But all that was the necessary admission price to enter realms of insight where ordinary people dared not and could not go.

The Romantic heroes lived their lives as though they were works of art. Many died young, still a characteristic of Romantic heroes and one explanation of why Dylan's flirtation with early death in what was probably a minor motorcycle accident on July 29, 1966, at the age of twenty-five looms so large in the Dylan myth, in part because of his extended seclusion mimicking death after it.

These four artistic movements, along with the Guthrie tradition of poets and singers of common people, a tradition that included Walt Whitman and Carl Sandburg, were important for Dylan in many ways. They, as Guthrie did, provided him with some artistic ancestors and models. It was not mass movements, but loners and outsiders, rebels without causes and wild ones who shaped Dylan. He was interested in how individuals reacted to society not how large social movements had shaped individuals. He wanted to understand how music and artistic lyrics could combine to help audiences find in themselves what would have remained undiscovered without the songs.

But history would not let him leave social reality to explore himself, at least for a while. He could not ignore the Civil Rights revolution. Additionally, the New Left was emerging looking for the vision of a new society. A war in faraway jungles was creeping around the edges of the news.

Dylan continued to write and perform the protest songs that made him the darling of the folk movement. In February 1963 *Broadside* published "Masters of War." The songs came pouring out.

On May 12 he solidified his credentials as a serious non-commercial artist by refusing to change songs to appear on Ed Sullivan's career-making television program. On May 27, his second album was released. It had an interesting hint of his future. In "Girl from the North Country," he noted that he prayed frequently.

On July 6, Dylan appeared in Greenwood, Mississippi, at a voter rights rally and first performed "Only a Pawn in Their Game," about the murder of civil rights organizer Medgar Evers. The song is remarkable in Dylan's seeming understanding of, if not sympathy for, the killer as simply a pawn of southern society's racism.

Alan Rinzler, an editor and cousin of Ralph Rinzler, an important folk singer and scholar, included Dylan, despite concern expressed by others, in Dylan's first inclusion in a book, the *Young Folk Song Book*. Rinzler remembers Dylan as "guarded, eager, ambitious.... He had an authentic voice."[33]

On July 26 Dylan made his first appearance at Newport singing "With God on Our Side" in a duet with Joan Baez. Baez had been performing "We Shall Overcome" at rallies and marches, making the song even more widely identified with the Civil Rights Movement, and she found in Dylan's song another powerful anthem, though on a different subject. "With God on Our Side" is an attack on those who use God's name to go to war. He performed four songs by himself that evening and returned to accompany Baez, Seeger, Peter, Paul & Mary, the Freedom Singers, and Theodore Bikel. They joined arms and offered a rousing "Blowin' in the Wind." In retrospect, that performance was the apex of the folk music revival.

Even at this moment of its greatest triumph, the folk music movement couldn't see what was in front of it. The older folk singers assumed a new generation of 1940s left-wingers had emerged, and they were delighted especially because they had thought the McCarthy era destroyed the movement. But they didn't see the key difference between themselves and the new singers. The Almanac Singers, by their very name and in the interchangeability of group members for performances, had suppressed their individuality. All of the new folk singers, even the most political ones, relished their individual identities. They were writing about their feelings, their sense of political problems. In this sense, the old guard never really had a chance to revive the political song-writing movement as they understood it.

Soon after the triumph at Newport, beginning on August 3, Dylan began to record his third album, *The Times They Are A-Changin'*. In "North Country Blues," Dylan began experimenting with point of view, using the first person point of view to tell this tale of miners from a woman's perspective. Such experimentation continued in later albums. In "Boots of Spanish Leather," he uses dialogue between a male and female, an approach he returned to in "Visions of Johanna."

Most of *Times* was filled with protest material including, besides "With God on Our Side" and "Only a Pawn in Their Game," the title song promising a generational change; "The Ballad of Hollis Brown," a haunting story of despair on a farm leading to homicide and suicide; "The Lonesome Death of Hattie Carroll," about the inequities of justice when a white man kills a poor black woman; and "When the Ship Comes In," a companion song to the title song about the triumph of the new.

"Times" is a battle cry proclaiming that a better society is on the way, one in which the social hierarchy is turned upside down, so that those at the bottom of the social order will be at the top, that those who lose in the current system will win in the new one. But in such a new system, there will still be losers, evidently punished for their previous misdeeds by seeing what it's like to be crushed by those above them.

Some of Dylan's lines seemed to have a precise perception of the future. That led to Dylan being labeled with the burdensome title of prophet. It was as though he knew all the secrets of life but was allowed to reveal them only cryptically.

Maybe such skills came from his Jewish heritage. After all, Jewish survival often depended on an acute sense of how changes in their society would affect them. Jews developed an early warning system, constantly on the lookout for danger, often finding it, and preparing to face it or escape it.

Maybe his emotional antennae were so acute they could pick up feelings that others were slower to apprehend, but once they did, they could act on them. Dylan's emotional acuity, that is, may have allowed him to sense future actions before they occurred.

Whatever the explanation, these skills when combined with his linguistic and musical skills and his belief in himself and drive produced the great artist that he became. His growing audience was overwhelmed by his lyrics, enchanted by the rhymes and the sense that his lines had a galloping inevitability. His voice delivered raging emotions that seemed their own. The songs connected listeners' thoughts and feelings to the English language, and in so doing connected listeners themselves to the world. It was as though Dylan could single-handedly help young people overcome adolescent loneliness and provide emotional permission for them to see their individual selves as authentic. He took them on a bone-chilling but exhilarating journey to the center of their beings.

In "When the Ship Comes In," nature itself changes when the new social order arrives. The sun shows its respect. Fish laugh. Seagulls smile. Rocks are proud. And the oppressors will be drowned just like the biblical Egyptians chasing the escaping Israelites.

The album concludes with "Restless Farewell," a sign that Dylan was nearing the end of his songs written in the idiom of the Left. He would continue to protest in his own way, not theirs. He's angry at the movement that tries to control him. He believes that on his own he can see what's ahead, but he won't be able to see if he remains chained to the preconceptions of a received political ideology. Boldly, he asserts that on his own he can see the new day coming while they stay staring at the old night.

For a long while, no one noticed such apostasy. Dylan was the new Guthrie, the replacement for Seeger. Dylan was the radical folk song movement's future. Of course, Dylan was not the only protest songwriter. Others were anguished about society and looking for a better way. The problem for the other songwriters was that Dylan was so spectacular. It was as though he stole all the dazzling language of the age, leaving little for others. Joan Baez relied on him for many of her songs. Peter, Paul and Mary continued to have enormous success both in concert and with record sales singing many of his songs. Peter Yarrow also wrote an affecting anti-draft song titled "The Great Mandala," but the original efforts of the group, though of high quality, were less common than the borrowed material. Buffy Sainte-Marie broke through with a protest about the draft in "Universal Soldier"; Tom Paxton had some wonderful songs as well. Judy Collins interpreted many of the folk songs movingly, as did Richie Havens. Joan Baez reigned as the Queen of Folk, though she never became a prolific songwriter. And there were many others who thought they would be successful. But no one produced a body of work comparable to Dylan's.

Phil Ochs tried his hardest to compete with the Master. With a driving determination, Ochs tossed off clever, passionate lyrics decrying the draft ("Draft Dodger Rag" and "I Ain't Marching Anymore") and challenging the liberal, rather than radical, inclinations of some on the Left ("Love Me, I'm a Liberal"). In an age without Dylan, Ochs, Paxton, and others would have been greater superstars than they were. In an age with Dylan, Ochs in particular simultaneously admired Dylan's work and was frustrated by its brilliance. Dylan liked to tease Ochs, to taunt his skills. Ochs, like so many others, eventually could not compete and found that difficult to accept. As Tom Paxton says, "Phil was jealous of Bob and he loved Bob as well. That was a theme that ran through the whole village. We were, after all, competing in a way, but we were also supporting each other. Phil really envied Bob."[34]

Meanwhile, Dylan's political efforts continued. On August 28 he participated in the March on Washington, performed "Only a Pawn in Their Game," and was standing not far from Dr. Martin Luther King, Jr., as the civil rights leader gave his "I Have a Dream" speech. Mary Travers, who also sang, recalls the event this way: "I had an epiphany that day, that people could change history."[35] But, according to Anthony Scaduto, his first major biographer, Dylan had a more cynical reaction to how much the March would affect American politics: "'Think they're listening?' he asked, glancing toward the Capitol. 'No, they ain't listening at all.'"[36]

In its November 4 edition, *Newsweek* punctured the Dylan myth by revealing that the singer was a middle-class Jewish kid from Minnesota. Given his intense sense of privacy, Dylan was understandably outraged by the story. It is unclear about what he did for the next several weeks as he retreated into a private world. He evidently took solace from the Van Ronks and others. He may have sought refuge back home.

David Miller, then a graduate student in Theater at the University of Minnesota, went, sometime in the fall of 1963, with friends to a particularly seedy place in Minneapolis called the Triangle Bar, known for its cheap beer. Miller says, "I was seated at the bar with my friends when we noticed some guy at a table behind us being loud, rude, obnoxious, and 'putting down' people around him and anyone who looked his way. The bartender, who we knew well, told us that the guy disturbing everyone was 'one of those folk singer types.' The guy looked like he had slept in his clothes ... three day growth of beard, messed up hair. The bartender said he was going to ask the guy to leave and would we back him. So, when the bartender went over to the table we followed. I don't know if the guy was drunk or not, but he was ... maybe stoned. He began to argue and then realized that the odds were against him. He got up and we escorted him to the door as he continued arguing. He left without any physical pushing. I learned the next evening that the guy's name was Bob Dylan."[37]

However personally intrusive and hurtful the revelations in the article were, they were overtaken quickly in the public mind on November 22 when President John Kennedy was assassinated.

It is difficult to gauge the boundless effects of that murder. It was a personal tragedy for the family and a public one for the nation. But it was also a major historical event. Sometimes the 1960s is listed as a single decade, but President Kennedy's death was a division within the decade. From his inauguration to his death there was promise and hope for a new society. Idealism seemed justified by history. Folk music's own idealism therefore perfectly fit the historical moment as well as the youthful idealism of most of its listeners. The civil rights struggle combined with a glittering national leader to promise a new world. After Kennedy's death, there was a reaction of shock and confusion. There were, under Lyndon Johnson, determined efforts to pass civil rights legislation but also to escalate sending troops to Viet Nam. Among the young there was a slow change from wide-eyed youthful idealism to more knowing drug and sexual experimentation and a change in musical tastes from the more staid, idea-driven folk music to an emotional feeling-driven rock generation. Folk songs, it turned out, could not stop tragedy or steer history.

The confusion that followed Kennedy's death and the changes that emerged took place slowly. It is always difficult to point out precisely when history changed, but it is possible to suggest that the confusion ended and the wilder rebellion of the 1960s began on June 1, 1967, when the Beatles released *Sgt. Pepper's Lonely Hearts Club Band*. This wilder rebellion ended either when the Manson Family murdered Sharon Tate and others early in the morning of August 9, 1969, or when there were shootings at Kent State on May 4, 1970.

But none of this was immediately obvious after the presidential assassination. Dylan reacted to Kennedy's death, but not in the way anyone expected. On December 13 at the Tom Paine Award Dinner, Dylan, used to performing not speaking, amused or annoyed members of the audience by making fun of their bald heads and pot bellies. Then he angered virtually everyone present by expressing some understanding of Lee Harvey Oswald. He was evidently referring to a profound alienation from the society, but such sentiments spoken so soon after the assassination tarnished Dylan's reputation as the Crown Prince of Folk.

Given the final song on *The Times They Are A-Changin'* (which was released on January 13, 1964) and Dylan's speech at the Paine dinner, it might be concluded that he was done with politics. But a few weeks after the dinner, in late December, Dylan attended a National Council meeting of the Students for a Democratic Society. SDS was part of the "New Left." Like the Old Left of the Socialists and Communists, it saw American society as deeply flawed, but instead of turning to the Soviet Union as a model, it found models in other anti–American nations such as Cuba. SDS focused on creating what it called a "participatory democracy" in the United States. Its tactics involved mostly non-violent protests, but one more radical faction later separated from SDS and, borrowing from Dylan, called itself the Weathermen and advocated violence. SDS was small (there were only 50 people at the meeting Dylan attended) though anti–Viet Nam sentiment helped it grow until its dissolution in 1969. That is, there never grew a complete New Left ideology to rival Communism, one shared by millions of Americans. Instead the Left could only organize based on particular issues: Viet Nam, the draft, civil rights, and then rights for others such as women's rights or gay rights. Absent an overarching ideology, Dylan really had nowhere to go except backwards to the Old Left, the generation his was trying to escape.

Todd Gitlin, one-time president of SDS and currently a professor at Columbia, remembered Dylan's visit: "A recess came, and Dylan told a group of us he'd be interested in working in one of our incipient ... projects.... Dylan said he would sing some benefit concerts for SDS. (But afterward he didn't answer our letters or phone calls.)"[38] Dylan evidently changed his mind.

On February 3, Dylan began a three-week road trip. On February 9 the Beatles appeared on the Ed Sullivan show. The arrival of the Beatles was, like Kennedy's assassination, another stop on the road of folk music's demise. Rock music was back to reclaim its place as the music of American youth after the interregnum by folk artists had replaced the vacuum left by the drafting, voluntary departure, scandal or arrest of the original rock artists. To the folk establishment, the Beatles meant that the real sign of the times was not the protest sign but the dollar sign. The music-buying public, though, wanted the Beatles, not Pete Seeger, to hold their hands.

Unlike the folk establishment, Dylan embraced the new sound despite its popularity and lack of explicit social comment. He first heard the Beatles on the radio. Having no political home to go back to, discovering a new musical sound, breaking up with Suze Rotolo, and enamored by Beat, symbolist, and romantic poetry's emphasis on the self, Dylan was about to abandon the folk ship captained by Seeger.

The folk movement was about to fail again for some of the same reasons it had failed before. Many in the movement supported anti–American dictators such as in Cuba and, later, anti–American fighters, such as those in North Viet Nam. They didn't understand that blacks couldn't be truly liberated until they themselves controlled the civil rights movement, not well-meaning whites on the Left. They couldn't adapt to the new audience's musical tastes. They couldn't see that Bob Dylan was not Woody Guthrie, that the new generation ultimately believed in exploring the self more than in fixing society.

Dylan began to see politics as a symptom not a solution. He could not listen to political discussions where people could talk for hours without discharging an idea. Dylan looked for an alternative to politics within himself, seeing the artist as a radical individualist. The inner world was more under his own control. It allowed for ambiguities not permitted by physical laws or fundamentalist political ideologies. If folk music made Dylan speak in the name of others, doing so had provided permission for others to presume they could speak in his name. Other people carved him up for their own use. They had betrayed his most precious possession, his unfettered artistic soul. He wanted to speak in his own name, to reclaim that soul.

Dylan's formal separation from folk music began on June 9 with the recording of *Another Side of Bob Dylan*. "Chimes of Freedom" — taken from

"The Chimes of Trinity," a song Dylan heard from Dave Van Ronk, who had learned it from his grandmother — was the only song that might be considered as social protest.

But in songs like "My Back Pages," Dylan raged against the leaders of the folk community who preached dead ideas and fought new ones that challenged their own.

In "To Ramona," Dylan goes beyond attacking the folk establishment and attacks the idea that politics can make a difference, asserting that politics won't let the activist Ramona win any battles or lose any.

In November 1964, Irwin Silber wrote an open letter to Dylan, decrying his purported betrayal. For his part, Dylan continued to listen to the emerging rock sounds; met his future wife, Sara; and went on exploring the inner artistic world, the only place where there was peace. His artistic journey was one that demanded he cross the boundaries set up by rulers of all kinds. If being Jewish meant he couldn't explore Christianity, then he had to abandon the usual Jewish identity. If being a folk singer meant he couldn't demean himself by crossing into popular rock music's land, then he had to let go of folk singing.

His explorations exploded into the first of a trilogy of albums that are unarguably among the best produced by any artist ever. Dylan recorded *Bringing It All Back Home* on January 13–15, 1965.

Some of the songs on the album are political, but not in the direct way of a typical protest song. Their protests are more poetic or at least abstract. In "Subterranean Homesick Blues," Dylan sings of a society with corrupt cops, authorities that wiretap beds, a society that stresses staying in school and obeying all the rules but one that only offers a lifetime of drudgery at work. It is a society whose leaders shouldn't be followed. In "Bob Dylan's 115th Dream," Dylan offers a cautionary, nightmarish myth about America's founding. In "It's Alright Ma (I'm Only Bleeding)," Dylan more explicitly portrays what he sees as the moral bankruptcy of the nation. But these lingering elements of protest are only part of the album. There were songs of a much more personal nature.

"Mr. Tambourine Man" has frequently been interpreted as a hymn to drugs and their abilities to induce visions. But the real visions in the song are artistic. The Tambourine Man is Dylan's own musical imagination or a male muse or even God, some higher power that fuels his creativity. This hymn to artistic creation envisions escape from the stifling limits of the real world into a world where the imagination can create what the real world doesn't contain. Language is stripped of all but the sensual.

Dylan, using self-mockery, realizes that his songs can never really approach the perfection of the Tambourine Man's, but he'd like to try to be at least a reflected image of that center of creativity.

In "Gates of Eden," Dylan contrasts this utopian place, here called after the biblical setting of paradise, and American life. Eden is the place of ultimate truth. Silence is the only language necessary. There are no leaders and no trials because there are no sins.

The real world is a nightmare of war, struggles over ownership, and a meaningless search for goods because the way to search for real meaning has been forsaken. In this horror-filled reality, there are those, like in the political folk community, who promise people that they own a magic lamp that only has to be rubbed to produce a better world, who promise that altering social and political conditions according to their designs, will make the world perfect. Dylan mocks their political utopianism.

Dylan praises uninterpreted dreams as the access point to this new utopia, this world of the imagination.

At the end of April through May 10, Dylan toured England, a trip captured in D.A. Pennebaker's remarkable documentary *Don't Look Back*. Allen Ginsberg came along as did Joan Baez, though Dylan was already involved with Sara and in a few months would marry her. Pennebaker has an interesting exclamation of Dylan's attraction to Ginsberg beyond the enormous literary talent: "Allen was naive in a certain way, and Dylan really dug that."[39] Ginsberg was authentic; he loved Dylan on many levels, but he didn't seek to use him. Additionally, Dylan "was looking for people that were outside of the system, which is how he always saw himself. He wanted to empathize with them."[40] But Pennebaker knows, even after working closely with Dylan, that it was not easy to understand him. "In everybody's life he was like a shadow. He just sort of went through their lives and out the front door.... He just was hardly there."[41]

There are many scenes of an overwrought, spoiled, or petty Dylan overwhelmed with responsibilities. But the film's outtakes, eventually released as *Bob Dylan 65 Revisited*, show a warmer Dylan talking kindly, for instance, to British children and teenagers.

The recording of his next album, *Highway 61 Revisited*, was interrupted by Dylan's appearance at Newport. There are many accounts of the events on July 25, of Dylan appearing on stage with a band and breaking into a loud electric three-song set before leaving the stage, of Pete Seeger sitting in a car and covering his ears after being unable to stop the noise, of Alan Lomax and others being infuriated with Dylan.

But Dylan meant to confront the folk purists. He knew the '30s and '40s still loitered in their minds, and he wanted to sing his declaration of independence. He sang it with full-throated heresy. As Mary Travers put it, "He just hit you with the express train."[42]

There has been much dispute over whether there was booing and, if so, how much. Murray Lerner, who filmed the event and examined the footage and soundtrack repeatedly for its release as part of his documentary *Bob Dylan: Live in Newport 1963–1965*, prudently concluded, "It was no more than a third booing, and probably a third applause, and a third confusion."[43]

The audience knew they were eyewitnesses to music history. After all, even though there had been electric music at Newport, Dylan was the pure protest song's future. The prophet was running away, toward the enemy: commercial popular music. The folk purists were horrified. Folk provided an intellectual and emotional experience, not a physical one like rock. And, the folk purists claimed, in rock music you couldn't even hear the lyrics, much less let them inform you about political actions to take. Its insipid subject matter was frequently about the overpowering waves of love's feelings or the emptiness caused by love's departure. That was no way to build a new society. And the folk purists knew painfully well that Dylan's leaving wasn't the loss of one singer. No one else had his lyrical abilities or his capacity to inspire.

Those who rejected the emergence of rock were, at least in part, unfair. They dismissed the profound influences of the blues artists like Muddy Waters or the blues and folk artists like Leadbelly, on the rock musicians, especially those from England. The British singers had listened to Alan Lomax's folk programs in England. Additionally, some of the blues singers themselves were going electric. Dylan saw the connection between traditional music and rock in a way some of his listeners didn't. He understood its beauty and its power, as he had in Hibbing, and he would not let what he saw as the pompous and unimaginative reluctance of the folk movement to embrace rock and roll stand in his way. He knew rock was the future, and he was unafraid to let everyone else know.

Peter Yarrow and others implored Dylan to return to the stage with his acoustic guitar. He did and sang "Mr. Tambourine Man" and his song of departure "It's All Over Now, Baby Blue." The audience cheered, thinking they had won, clearly not understanding the words or sentiment of his closing song.

The folk movement, left for dead in the mid-fifties, had been revived in the late fifties and early sixties. That July night the re-born movement symbolically drowned in a sea of noise.

Dylan's relationship with folk music was similar to a romance. He met it, fell passionately in love, embraced it to his heart, cheated on it with rock music, became disenchanted with it, and by his own actions at Newport in 1965 induced it to get angry at him and leave him. Then he felt surprised, upset, hurt, and betrayed by that anger and that departure.

Dylan's departure from folk music coincided with the start of enormous social changes. The integrated, non-violent, struggle of Martin Luther King, Jr., became the sometimes violent struggle for Black Power. Malcolm X denounced King's working with white people. As if in a direct rebuke to the whole folk song movement, in 1966 Julius Lester wrote a letter to *Sing Out!* noting the existence of a new era: "Now it is over: the days of singing freedom songs and the days of combating bullets and billy clubs with love. 'We Shall Overcome' (and we have overcome our blindness) sounds old, outdated, and can enter the pantheon of the greats along with IWW songs and the union songs."[44]

There were many other changes as well. Lyndon Johnson's decisions to increase the number of American troops in Viet Nam led to widespread discontent among the young about drafting men to fight in a faraway land for what seemed to many to be unclear, unjustified, or immoral reasons. Folk music gave way to rock. The artists' experimental use of drugs gave way to overdoses and the embrace of drugs by large numbers of people as a badge of generational membership. Peaceful musical concerts gave way to Altamont. Living together communally gave way to Charles Manson. Student protest gave way to the Democratic convention in Chicago and Kent State. The decade began with the election of John Kennedy and ended with the election of Richard Nixon.

The disintegration of society was matched by Dylan's personal disintegration. On August 4, soon after Newport, Dylan finished recording

Highway 61 Revisited, his first all-electric album of what was called "folk rock" music.

Once again, Dylan mixed various kinds of songs. There were political messages embedded in the cascading imagery of the lyrics. For example, in "Tombstone Blues" he makes an allusion to President Johnson, the king of oblivious, uncultured Americans. In this parable, Johnson praises the dead and in so doing thinks he is saving them, imprisons those who would lead the young away from the society's rules, and prepares more soldiers to be killed in the jungles of Viet Nam.

But the most prominent distinctive characteristic of the album is the exploration of Dylan's gender identity. Those songs can be seen as a dialogue between different parts of Dylan's self.

Many interpreters understandably consider "Like a Rolling Stone" as a mockery of some woman. Candidates have included the pop actress Edie Sedgwick, Joan Baez, and others. But, especially in the context of other songs on the album, it is also possible to view the song in another way completely.

This alternative interpretation is that a new creative part of Dylan, formed by a reaction to maddening internal confusion and the roar of demands from the world, is angrily snarling and singing to the old Dylan, the one who was sure of himself and clear about his identity as king of the folk singers.

What makes the song particularly intriguing is that the new Dylan refers to the old Dylan as a lonely woman. Why a woman? One interpretation is that this newer creative self sees itself as fragmented and is allowing one part of the self to explore another. Additionally, within a self are all sorts of "others" that the uncreative self suppresses. So the new self notes the existence of a feminine side.

In one verse, the new Dylan sings to the old Dylan about Albert Grossman, calling him a diplomatic representative. The concluding line is about Grossman's supposed taking of Dylan's money. At the end of the song, Dylan pleads with his former self to go see someone who used to amuse him with language.

In 1970, Nora Ephron and Susan Edmiston interviewed Dylan and asked about the identity of Queen Jane in the song "Queen Jane Approximately." Dylan answered in what must have appeared to be one of his whimsical and nonsensical responses. He said: "Queen Jane is a man."[45]

But he was having fun with them by sneaking in the truth in a barrage of evasive responses.

In the song, the new Dylan is speaking to the old Dylan, again represented as a woman. In this case the king of folk music is appropriately a Queen. The "approximately" in the song's title is there because such a feminine representation is not precisely his former self. The speaker mentions the exhaustion Dylan must feel about his self and his songs and the anguished folk crowds angry that he is not singing protest songs. The speaker then invites "Queen Jane" to see him, to get away from the commercial world in which "Queen Jane" lives out a musical life. The speaker is Dylan's untainted creative self urging the successful Dylan to return.

Dylan's dialogues with his self continue in another way on the album in "Ballad of a Thin Man." Most critics see the song as an attack on journalists, who don't understand Dylan at all but continue to write about him. This is certainly plausible — especially considering the mention of a pencil in the first verse — but the song seen in its entirety leads to a very different interpretation. In this interpretation, the new genuine and creative Dylan uses the common name Jones to represent the old, confused Dylan. That old Dylan is someone who doesn't understand the homosexuality around him and is confounded by it. The language of the song is filled with very explicit gay imagery.

The new Dylan is angry at the old Dylan for not understanding what is happening to him, for not comprehending the warping of his own creative core, the part of himself that was genuinely thrilled by the creative possibilities of combining language and music. The song is a cry from within mourning for what has happened to that part of Dylan's self. These songs can be interpreted as Dylan exploring the "other." He was white, Jewish, male, and heterosexual. To be all-embracing, to understand, he needed to explore in his mind and songs what it meant to be black, Christian, female, and gay.

The songs can also be understood as signs of a self fragmenting, unsure of its center, living among desolate grotesqueries. Others noted Dylan's dissolution. As Robert Shelton wrote, "In the winter of 1965-66, [prominent music critic] Ralph Gleason agreed that Dylan looked close to death.... 'I was astounded he was still working, because I figured he would have had a breakdown. I thought he was having some severe abdominal pains, or a brain tumor.'"[46] This "breakdown," this intense inner chaos, could not be expressed if he sang alone with a guitar and a harmonica. It needed a gang, and the band had to produce a clanging, raucous, and especially very loud sound playing a variety of electric instruments.

Dylan kept struggling and eventually came to a possible answer. The feminine subject matter would soon return as part of that answer in a very different form on *Blonde on Blonde*.

After completing *Highway 61 Revisited*, Dylan went on tour, where he continued, in most cases, to be booed. Some of his band members couldn't take it and quit. Dylan claimed that he enjoyed the booing, but he had to feel wounded. The folk God was being rejected.

On November 22, he married Sara. His ongoing tour continued, but he took time out when he could to work on songs for his new album.

Under enormous pressure, with his identity under attack, scorned by some of his most ardent fans, Dylan could no longer rely on music or poetry to save him.

He found another path, a spiritual one, but as always with Dylan this path was not one walked by others. He was interviewed in Austin, Texas, on September 24 before a concert and he was asked about his belief in God. Dylan answered: "Well, first of all, God is a woman. We all know that. Well, you take it from there."[47]

Once again, Dylan provided some insight that sounded like a throwaway piece of nonsense. But it wasn't nonsense. He was working on material that emerged on the new album. The author Michael Gray quotes Bill Aikins, who played keyboard on *Blonde on Blonde* as saying: "Dylan would sit there at the piano for hours with the Bible, and then he'd come and say 'OK, I'm ready.'"[48] (However, Charlie McCoy, a guitarist on the same album says, "I did not see Dylan with a bible."[49]) In April 1966, after the album's completion, Dylan played an acetate of "Sad-Eyed Lady of the Lowlands" for writer Jules Siegel and said, "Now that is religious music!"[50] A month later in Australia he was asked about the subject of his new songs. His biographer Clinton Heylin notes he responded "in deadly earnest." His response was: "The Second Coming."[51] Nat Hentoff interviewed Dylan in *Playboy* that March. When Hentoff asked him what he looked forward to in life, Dylan responded: "Salvation. Just plain salvation."[52]

At the time, even such a series of similar responses might have been dismissed as Dylan being his evasive self. But given the later public turning to religion, such comments are useful in understanding *Blonde on*

Blonde. Bob Dylan was always trying to calculate how far he was from Heaven.

His approach to religion separated him from Woody Guthrie and Pete Seeger. Woody identified with Jesus as a rabble-rouser. Seeger was secular. Dylan's religious approach was mystical and dialogical. He could speak with God, not just worship God. He had discovered a sacred reality far more real to him than worldly reality, and he oriented his self and his creations toward the sacred.

Blonde on Blonde is about two women, both blondes. The first woman is earthly, attractive but incapable of providing adequate meaning. The second woman is a religious symbol, specifically a Christian one. The tension in the album is Dylan longing for the religious woman, or a combination of the religious and earthly woman in one person, while living with the earthly one.

It is unclear when exactly Dylan fused his sexual interests, interests in the feminine as made evident on *Highway 61 Revisited*, and his spiritual interests. He did read *The White Goddess* by Robert Graves in the beginning of 1963 while visiting Britain. The book is about how poems construct myth and posits a "White Goddess" as a deity who has a son and who is intimately connected to the creation of poetry.

Maybe he drew on experiences of Christianity from his past. Perhaps he became enticed by reading the Bible or having a personal spiritual experience. Perhaps his repeated rejection by crowds made him identify with Jesus. Perhaps he saw himself as Jesus during a dream, vision, or drug experience, or read a press account comparing him to Jesus heading toward an untimely death. However the ideas arrived, he struggled to formulate them and put them into songs on *Blonde on Blonde*. These efforts can be seen in some of the album's major songs.

"Visions of Johanna" opens with the singer seeking retreat from a noisy, confusing world by making love to a woman named Louise. She doesn't ease his anguish by providing emotional shelter from the violent storm outside their loft (the night is playing tricks, providing thunder and lightning, the lights flicker, the rain comes inside).

But if Louise is not capable of providing such much-needed solace, the singer has visions of a woman who can. He longs for Johanna, who can save him.

In the third verse, Louise speaks about Dylan, mocking him, angry with him for talking to her about Johanna. But Dylan's hopes for Johanna, for some religious release, are not realized because Johanna has not arrived. Indeed, his feelings were expressed in the less poetic original title of the song, "Seems Like a Freeze Out." That is, he felt Johanna had exluded him from her company by her unfriendly treatment. Johanna is not a sexual substitute for Louise; she is a spiritual rival for his feelings because she can provide peace, calmness, and meaning that the earthly Louise cannot.

The rejection of the earthly woman continued on other songs. "Just Like a Woman" is a break-up song with the earthly woman. Here speculation about the woman is more appropriate. Joan Baez is one candidate, in part because of her place as the reigning Queen of folk music when he tried to enter the realm. In the middle of the song, he sings about his need to return to the visions that sustain him.

His longing and waiting continue in other songs, including the appropriately titled "I Want You." In "Absolutely Sweet Marie," with its titled woman having a name that is derived from Mary, Dylan is angry that his Mary, the woman who can save him, has not arrived. He wants to embrace God.

The final song on this double album (the symbolism of having two records becomes obvious considering the subject matter) is the one on which Dylan comes closest to resolution. Part of the brilliance of "Sad-Eyed Lady of the Lowlands" is that the title refers to multiple earthly women as well as the religious woman praised earlier in the album, but this time in all her aspects. Her physical aspect is presented in the form of a church, with a silver cross and chimes that sound like a voice. But the Sad-Eyed Lady is more than a building. She is real spirituality, a kind abandoned by people. As Dylan envisions her, he asks the repeated question of the song about whether he should embrace her now or delay that embrace.

He doesn't seem to care about his rejecting his Jewish past. In "I Want You" he expresses indifference that his forefathers didn't accept Christianity. Despite this rejection, Dylan remains unsure not about whether to put himself in the hands of the Sad-Eyed Lady, the Christian church, but about when. He wonders whether to do so now or to wait. He ultimately decides to wait.

"Sad-Eyed Lady" is also about earthly women. Certainly, the song is in part a hymn to his new wife. Her father had been a scrap metal dealer, and her first husband, Hans Lownds, was a photographer for magazines. In a later song, "Sara," Dylan explicitly mentions writing the song for her.

But there are also allusions to Joan Baez, including her father's Spanish heritage. Baez's mother was born in Edinburgh, which is on the east coast of Scotland's central lowlands.

Dylan mixes the imagery between the earthly women and the religious Sad-Eyed Lady, but it is to the latter that he directs his poignant question about embracing. That Lady is surrounded by supposed friends who just want to manipulate her for their own good. He ends the song talking directly to the Sad-Eyed Lady about these people who speak falsely in her name.

Dylan's dialogue with the Sad-Eyed Lady, or the later, more masculine, God he will accept was a crucial turning point in his career. *Blonde on Blonde* was the crossroads Dylan played at before eventually turning to the path towards God as a heroic role model. The artists who preceded God as role models became incapable of helping Dylan confront the enormity of the world. While Dylan's spiritual quest saved him in some way, he — arguably — never again reached the artistic heights of the three albums culminating in *Blonde on Blonde*. The saddest of the sad-eyed prophets, the poet of personal freedom, could take the sadness no more.

While Dylan has, to one extent or another, in one form or another, maintained a spiritual dialogue, there is another way of looking at his life. In a way, Bob Dylan has had two dialogues in that life, one with desire — for love, fame, money, recognition, experience, and much more — and one with God. Or perhaps they have both been dialogues with death.

Nine

The Very Sound of Hope: The Legacy of the Sad-Eyed Prophets

In the more than forty years after Bob Dylan appeared at Newport in 1965, folk music never fully recovered its once powerful status in American life. Woody Guthrie died of Huntington's disease at age 55 on October 3, 1967. Woody's dwindling powers and death unfairly robbed him of the ability to appreciate the enormity or depth of his fame and influence.

Lee Hays, after earlier having had both legs amputated, died at age 67 on August 26, 1981. He and the other Weavers did have a Carnegie Hall reunion in November 1980. John Hammond died at age 76 on July 10, 1987. Earl Robinson died at age 81 on July 20, 1991. Alan Lomax died at age 87 on July 19, 2002.

Some of the folk singers who became popular in the 1960s also have died. Perhaps most tragically, Phil Ochs, having suffered a severe deterioration in his mental abilities, took his life at age 35 on April 9, 1976. Dave Guard died at age 56 on March 22, 1991. Dave Van Ronk died at age 65 on February 10, 2002. Nick Reynolds died at age 75 on October 1, 2008. Odetta died at age 77 on December 2, 2008. Mary Travers died at age 72 on September 16, 2009. Bess Lomx Hawes died at age 88 on November 27, 2009. William "Liam" Clancy died at age 74 on December 4, 2009.

As of July 2009, Ronnie Gilbert and Fred Hellerman of the Weavers were still alive, as was Pete Seeger. Joan Baez, Tom Paxton, and others continue to perform regularly to large and adoring crowds.

Seeger lived to triumph over all his detractors. He became an American icon. His Communism either wasn't mentioned or any criticism because of it was muted; his politics were, with more compassion than historical accuracy, transformed into a sort of eccentricity of a beloved uncle. And he did, after all, play a crucial role in the fight for civil rights, a defining role in the preservation of American folk music, a pioneering role in environmental preservation with his efforts on behalf of the Hudson River, and in convincing many young people that they needed to do more in society than be selfish consumers.

He won a Grammy Lifetime Achievement Award in 1993 and a Kennedy Center Lifetime Achievement Award in 1994. Seeger sang with Burl Ives and Josh White, Jr., the man and son of a man he had earlier fought with over appearing before the House Committee on Un-American Activities. In 2007, Seeger, in a principled act of reconciliation with his detractors, wrote "The Big Joe Blues," a song that finally recognized Stalin's failures. As he told the Associated Press, he had left the Party in 1950 and had previously apologized for not recognizing Stalin's cruelty. But there was a poignancy to putting his feelings into a folk song, the medium he most cherished to express his feelings.[1]

Seeger also sent the song to the historian Ronald Radosh, who had once been a student of Seeger's but had become increasingly hostile to his former allies on the Left. Seeger wrote to Radosh, noting he should have seen the camps on his various visits to the Soviet Union.

There is continued widespread audience interest in folk music. Part of that can be ascribed to the immense talents of folk musicians. But part is also due to nostalgia. Nostalgia is a deeper emotion than memory, locating a time, often a youthful period filled with pleasure and pain and the promise of what would surely be a million tomorrows. Audiences remember the sweet sense of hope in the air when the folk singers first sang. They remember their own youth and can re-capture it again for the duration of a concert. The folk singers let them be young again.

And there is a revival of the political tradition. There is a resurgence of political activism on the Left, a return to motivating audiences politically through music. In 2003, for example, Texas-born Natalie Maines of the country music group Dixie Chicks told a London concert audience that the group was ashamed that President Bush came from Texas. Radio stations, especially country stations, began to drop their music, and fans boycotted their concerts. Rock Against Bush was an effort to organize punk rock musicians against George W. Bush's 2004 campaign for re-election. The project organized concerts and albums, featuring various bands including Green Day. These and other politically motivated singers are the direct heirs of the folk singer tradition of mixing music and the politics of the Left.

Many singers have, unfairly to them, been branded as Bob Dylan's successor. They either sang like him or wrote lyrics that could be compared to his (such comparisons always favored Dylan) or had political content within their songs or lives. Some of the singers compared to Dylan include, in order of their birth, Neil Young, Bruce Springsteen, Tom Petty, John Mellencamp, Steve Earle, Billy Bragg, and Ani DiFranco, among many others.

What stands out, beyond the startling fact that Dylan's artistic achievements have remained unmatched, is that these singers did not create a new political vision. Dylan had ultimately rejected the socialism of the Left for an artistic and religious individualism. His songs had catalogued social ills but could not provide a solution. Those who followed in the tradition of political folk songs generally have not followed Dylan by focusing on their intense inner spheres. They have, though, followed in the tradition of defining problems, in some cases calling for an unprecisely defined revolution but not clarifying what a new political world would look like. They generally focused on individual causes — such as opposition to the war in Iraq, or concern about what they perceived as an erosion of civil liberties, or opposition to the death penalty — as well as routine electoral politics — such as supporting left-leaning Democrats in presidential elections and opposing presidential policies they found unpalatable. Indeed, they have gone backward, bypassing Dylan and instead calling on the spirits of Woody Guthrie and Pete Seeger, as though the radical politics of the 1930s fit seamlessly into the twenty-first century. That is, they never found a replacement for Communism, some all-embracing political theory.

Bruce Springsteen's central concerns spring directly from Woody Guthrie: the intense identification with workers struggling to find dignity in their daily chores, to survive in a world that seems constructed to make their lives unendurable. It is no surprise, therefore, that it was John Hammond, faithful to the end to his 1940s self, who signed the highly talented New Jersey singer. In 1984, Springsteen sang "Born in the USA" which was, in contradiction to its seemingly patriotic title, an attack on a society that could find no better use for its youth than to transform them into soldiers. As the culture had done to Guthrie's "This Land Is My Land," so, too, Ronald Reagan and others transformed Springsteen's anguished lament into a pro–American anthem.

In 1995, Springsteen explicitly found a voice from the 1930s when he recorded *The Ghost of Tom Joad,* an album in which the title song compared the plight of contemporary Mexican immigrants to the Okies in Steinbeck's novel. The new immigrants and the old, Springsteen suggested, were common victims, seeking fair wages but cheated by the powerful who sought cheap workers. He continued his songs of social conscience in 2000 with "American Skin (Forty-One Shots)," protesting the police shooting of Amadou Diallo, an African immigrant from Guinea. The lyrics are not simply an indictment of the police, but an attempt to understand the event. Similarly, the album *The Rising* is sympathetic to America, especially after the September 11, 2001, attacks. The title track tells the story in the first person of a firefighter struggling up a tower through the darkness. Springsteen also took part in "America: A Tribute to Heroes," a benefit concert to help families of the victims, especially families of firefighters. In 2004, he took part in the Vote for Change Tour to elect John Kerry. By 2006 this working-class identity had become so powerful that he offered an album of fifteen songs that Pete Seeger had made popular. *We Shall Overcome: The Seeger Sessions* paid homage to the last of the surviving old-time folk singers but also offered the power and urgency of the songs as guideposts changing contemporary America. In 2008 he endorsed Barack Obama.

Springsteen's ultimate faith in an America that still needs to improve is far less radical than the vision Guthrie and Seeger offered in the 1930s, a vision in which American capitalism had to be replaced in order for the country to survive. Springsteen's vision is more liberal than radical. He does not follow Guthrie and Seeger's utopian visions even as he identifies with their core humane values. Springsteen is not asking, "Which side are you on?" but rather "How can we find a connection between the sides?" Here he also parts with Dylan, whose separation was first political and then between his consciousness and the rest of the world. Springsteen wants connections; he wants the roads he's wandering to meet, not diverge.

Billy Bragg is a British singer and political Leftist. In 1995, Nora Guthrie, Woody's daughter and director of the Woody Guthrie Archives, approached him with a project. Woody had left behind hundreds of lyrics without accompanying music. Bragg's task was to write the music. Bragg wanted to distinguish Woody's songs from his own and so approached the American band Wilco to work with him on the project. *Mermaid Avenue* was released in 1998 and was a critical and commercial success. A second collection was released in 2000.

Nora Guthrie's vision of giving the songs a contemporary sound and sung by a man who still followed her father's politics showed the ongoing vitality of Woody's work.

But Billy Bragg was caught in a trap. By recording the extraordinary Guthrie lyrics, he was simultaneously emphasizing the failures of his own generation in advancing on those visions. They were conservators in their efforts. They were musical but not political innovators.

No one, that is, has yet emerged from the shadows of the giants.

It is unclear exactly why that is, but one possible reason is that no one can get by Bob Dylan. His presence and his legacy continue to present a looming challenge to new folk singers.

No individual person had more influence than Dylan on audiences in the 1960s. In a 1979 book titled *Woodstock Census: The Nationwide Survey of the Sixties Generation*, authors Rex Weiner and Deanne Stillman organized an unscientific but telling survey of such influence.

Dylan's presence in the 1960s was enormous; 72 percent of the respondents asserted their admiration for and his influence on them. (Only the Beatles at 79 percent had more influence on the respondents. John F. Kennedy and Martin Luther King, Jr., were both cited by 62 percent.) Of the respondents, 69 percent used to quote Dylan's songs. The authors note the reasons for Dylan's influence: "Those who say they admired and were influenced by Dylan are quick to mention either the political aspects of his songs or his open expression of personal sensitivity. It may be that his great power was in transforming the process of self-discovery and growing up into a political adventure; Dylan's songs equated the normal confusion of adolescence with the problems of society as a whole."[2]

When Dylan seemed to leave the problems of society to focus on the self, done earlier but most symbolically at the 1965 Newport Festival, people continued to fuse the political and personal from him onto themselves for a few years until the sixties came to a crashing end. By the 1970s, politics had been replaced for many by the attention to self and Dylan's fusion of the two became less important, and so his influence began to wane.

That is, it will take a songwriter with comparable talent to Dylan's to advance the legacy of the songwriters. But the absence of radical songwriters capable of competing with him gives rise to a question: Why have there been no famous conservative folk singers? After all, conservatives gathered increasing energy from the late 1960s on from parts of the electorate recoiling at a society whose young seemed to them to embrace drugs, sexual experimentation of all types, a loud, rhythmic music that made people lose their moral inhibitions, a tolerance for violence to accomplish political goals that were anti–American, a belief in the primacy of newer and wilder experiences over reason, a belief in images and sounds over words and ideas, and a seeming irresponsibility to the task of growing up. Why, then, weren't there singers to give voice to these conservative sentiments the way, say, Ronald Reagan did in electoral politics?

There are many possible answers. Perhaps people who become conservatives are more drawn to business, politics, and other "real world" enterprises than they are to the arts. That is, they are less likely to have a utopian temperament, less likely to live for an explicitly internationalist political ideology, and more likely to live for themselves, their family, their communities, and their nation. Perhaps the music industry generally and the folk music world specifically are left-wing and strained out those who do not agree with their positions early on and monitored the ideological purity of those who were admitted. The careers of Burl Ives, Josh White, and even Bob Dylan are telling here. Perhaps those singers who were politically conservative found a home not in folk music but in country or bluegrass music. There, conservative values were expressed through religious music, patriotic songs, and songs about family.

And what of the future? Folk singers to come can draw on Woody Guthrie, Pete Seeger, Bob Dylan, and all the rest to learn lessons about songwriting, drive, dedication, idealism, and much else. But armed with knowledge about the political shortcomings of these folk singers, they will have to tread carefully as they create their own visions of what an ideal community — as ideal as humans are capable of, at least — would look like. They will have to sift through, analyze, and evaluate the complex legacy of the folk singers.

The folk singers were sad-eyed prophets. They were sad-eyed because when they looked at their country, they saw greedy bosses controlling workers or powerful bigots controlling blacks, or the establishment trying to make young people conform. They were self-proclaimed prophets believing they could envision a new world and would fight for it through their songs.

But these sad-eyed prophets could not foresee the future. There was no One Big Union as Joe Hill wanted, no end to capitalism in America as Woody and Pete wanted, no land filled with everyone having an individual artistic vision as Dylan wanted. Their predictions were wrong, but their warnings that we need to find a humane way to live together or otherwise perish remain powerful and resonant.

The sheer honesty of their music and their concern for suffering people remain extraordinarily attractive and admirable. Their music raised moral issues when other music didn't. Their songs made listeners think, letting them agree or disagree with serious ideas about important issues put in a work of enticing art. Independent of anyone's view of their politics, that is, their songs are artistic treasures.

Perhaps as a new generation emerges in America, there will be a new vision, a new revival of folk music to nurse the alienated and mistreated and point a finger at injustices. Perhaps a new political folk song movement, inspired by its ancestors' undeniably moving music and admirably humane impulses but chastened by some of their misguided political embraces, will emerge having found what is the best of the folk singers' legacy: the very sound of hope and the unshakeable belief in a triumphant humanity.

Chapter Notes

Chapter Two

1. "I believe he was a crook": July 17, 1947, letter from McClintock to Wallace Stegner as quoted in Smith, *Labor Martyr*, 59.
2. "Self-preservation": Foner, *Letters of Joe Hill*, 18.
3. "Animal instinct": *Ibid.*, 13.
4. "Underdog": *Ibid.*, 22.
5. "Pamphlet": *Ibid.*, 16.
6. "Social feeling": *Ibid.*, 16–17.
7. "I'll take shooting": Foner, *Case of Joe Hill*, 49.
8. Telegram: Foner, *Letters of Joe Hill*, 84.
9. "Aim!": Foner, *Case of Joe Hill*, 97.

Chapter Three

1. "Don't you cry": Mary Jo Guthrie Edgmon interview with author.
2. "I've never seen him cry": *Ibid.*
3. "He never did want": *Ibid.*
4. "I told him I had intelligence": Guthrie, *Woody Guthrie: Library of Congress Recordings.*
5. "If you use more than two chords": *A Vision Shared: A Tribute to Woody Guthrie and Leadbelly.*
6. "Woody wasn't ever easy to live with": Cray, *Ramblin' Man*, 67.
7. "And the farmer owes": Cray, *Ramblin' Man*, 70.
8. "Why don't we go out": Robbin, *Woody Guthrie and Me*, 27–32.
9. "Some of them I wrote": *Ibid.*
10. "Left wing": *Ibid.*

Chapter Four

1. Draper, *American Communism and Soviet Russia*, 171.
2. Henrietta Yurchenco: Interview with author.
3. "One morning": John Lomax, *Adventures of a Ballad Hunter*, 107–109.
4. He "would have found friendship": Wolfe and Lornell, *Life and Legend of Leadbelly*, 210.

5. "We don't realize": Interview with author.
6. Shaw's visit: Johnson, *Modern Times*, 276.
7. Chaplin "horrified": Robinson, *Chaplin*, 489.
8. "His curiosity": Interview with author.
9. Diane Kovacs explanation: Ed Cray interview with author.
10. "Great tendency": *Woody Guthrie: Ain't Got No Home.*
11. "I have always said in my songs": Woody Guthrie Archives.
12. "He put aside his judgment": Interview with author.
13. "They were so well organized": Interview with author.
14. "When three Communists meet": Guthrie, *Pastures of Plenty*, 89.

Chapter Five

1. First draft of "God Blessed America": Cray, *Ramblin' Man*, 165.
2. "There is one thing about New York": Klein, *Woody Guthrie*, 154–55.
3. "The radio agent": Yurchenco, *Around the World in 80 Years*, 41.
4. "You take it": Willens, *Lonesome Traveler*, 66.
5. "If you want to know": Hays, "On Almanacs," 9.
6. "They all contributed": Russell, "They Sing the Hard Hitting Songs," 5.
7. "Only group that rehearses on stage": Dunaway, *How Can I Keep from Singing*, 80.
8. Rainbow Room: *Ibid.*, 100.

Chapter Six

1. Denisoff, *Great Day Coming*, 9.
2. "Preparing a Fascist America": Haynes, *Red Scare or Red Menace?* 72.
3. "Rank-and-file workers": Hays, *New Masses*, January 11, 1933, 21.
4. "Our then manager": Seeger, *Incompleat Folksinger*, 22. The original story about Kameron's visit was in *Counterattack*, June 1, 1951, 1. Kameron himself verified the story in the *Columbus Evening Dispatch*, August 25, 1951, 1. A full account of the Weavers' experience with blacklisting can be found in Spector, "The Weavers."
5. "Josh got in debt": Interview with author.
6. Josh White, Jr.: Interview with author.
7. "It is like Jesus Christ": Dunaway, *How Can I Keep from Singing*, 174–82.
8. "If that judge believes": Interview with author.
9. "Dreaming of systems": T.S. Eliot, Choruses from *The Rock*, VI.<AU: Please add to references.>
10. "Did the folk singers": E-mail to author.

Chapter Seven

1. "It was like an ancient chapel": Dylan, *Chronicles*, 18.
2. "Where people go": *Lomax the Songhunter.*
3. "He meant what he said": Interview with author.
4. "I wrote my first song": Interview with author.
5. Mary Travers: Interview with author.

186

6. "The singing galvanized": Interview with author.
7. "No. I still have some things": Interview with author.
8. "He said he doesn't want to do it": *Ibid.*
9. "Who's that?": Yarrow and Travers interviews with author.
10. "There is a great gap": Interview with author.

Chapter Eight

1. "I used to read names": Interview with author.
2. "I'm going to be bigger than Elvis": Interview with author.
3. "A little drunk": E-mail to author.
4. "Girls would come visit": Interview with author.
5. "Dylan was a little boy": *Ibid.*
6. "Didn't have any money": Interview with and e-mails to author.
7. "He didn't have a nickel": *Ibid.*
8. "Across the country": Dylan, *Chronicles*, 8.
9. "Lost soul": Interviews with and e-mails to author.
10. "He seemed like a little lost boy": *Ibid.*
11. "His peculiar emphasis": *Ibid.*
12. "He sang through his teeth": Interview with author.
13. "He was playing the music": *Ibid.*
14. "We walked into the floor": Interviews with author.
15. "As we were getting ready": *Ibid.*
16. "I ain't dead yet": Spitz, *Bob Dylan*, 114.
17. "That evening": Interview with author.
18. "Dylan first performed": *No Direction Home*, 92
19. "The treated him": Interview with author.
20. "I loved the music": Interview with author. Additional material is in Paxton, *Honor of Your Company*.
21. "The smell": *Ibid.*
22. "I don't record freaks": Interview with author.
23. "I didn't think of Dylan": *Ibid.*
24. "The skeleton": Interview with author.
25. "I read poetry": E-mail to author.
26. "He was very disenchanted": Shelton, *No Direction Home*, 115.
27. Dylan and the supermarket: Bob Cohen interview with author.
28. "On night I went to pick up the folk singer": E-mail to author.
29. Lyrics for "Blowin' in the Wind": Interview with author.
30. "Perfectly expressed": Interview with author.
31. "The perfect issue song": Interview with author.
32. "Eliot was interested": Eagleton, "Raine's Sterile Thunder."
33. "Guarded, eager": Interview with author.
34. "Phil was jealous": Interview with author.
35. "I had an epiphany": Interview with author.
36. "No, they ain't listening": Scaduto, *Bob Dylan*, 151.
37. "I was seated at the bar": Interview with and e-mail to author.
38. "A recess came": Gitlin, *Sixties*, 198.
39. "Allen was naive": Interview with author.
40. "Looking for people": *Ibid.*

41. "In everybody's life": *Ibid.*
42. "He just hit you": Interview with author.
43. "It was no more than a third booing": Murray Lerner interview, WNET, 12/4/07.
44. "Now it is over": Dunaway, *How Can I Keep from Singing?* 301.
45. "Queen Jane is a man": McGregor, *Bob Dylan*, 88.
46. "In the winter": *No Direction Home*, 332.
47. "Well, first of all": McGregor, *Bob Dylan*, 163.
48. "Dylan would sit there": Gray, *Bob Dylan Encyclopedia,* 2.
49. "I did not see Dylan with a bible": E-mail to author.
50. "Now that is religious music!": Siegel, Australian interview in Heylin, *Behind the Shades Revisited.*
51. "In deadly earnest": Heylin, *Behind the Shades Revisited,* 243.
52. "Salvation": Hentoff, *Playboy* interview in Heylin, *Behind the Shades Revisited.*

Chapter Nine

1. Associated Press, "Seeger Protests Stalin in Song."
2. "Those who say they admired": Weiner and Stillman, *Woodstock Census.* Dylan influence, asserted effect, 79; Beatles, Kennedy, and King, 242–243; quoted Dylan's songs, 239; reasons for Dylan influence, 69.

References

The references included here represent only a fractional part of the enormous literature and music of the folk song movement. Space limitations prevent me from listing all the materials I consulted and that are worthy of appreciation and study.

Books and Articles

Associated Press. "Seeger Protests Stalin in Song." *Chicago Tribune*, September 2, 2007, 29.

Baez, Joan. *And a Voice to Sing With*. New York: Summit, 1987.

_____. *Daybreak*. New York: Dial, 1968.

Benson, Carl. *The Bob Dylan Companion: Four Decades of Commentary*. New York: Schirmer Books, 1998.

Boucher, David, and Gary Browning. *The Political Art of Bob Dylan*. London: Palgrave Macmillan, 2004.

Bowden, Betsy, ed. *Performed Literature: Words and Music by Bob Dylan*. Bloomington: Indiana University Press, 1982.

Brand, Oscar. *The Ballad Mongers: The Rise of the Modern Folk Song*. New York: Funk and Wagnalls, 1962.

Brazier, Richard. "The Story of the I.W.W.'s 'Little Red Songbook.'" *Labor History* 9, Winter 1968: 91–105.

Buhle, Mari Jo, Paul Buhle, and Dan Georgakas, eds. *Encyclopedia of the American Left*. Urbana: University of Illinois Press, 1992.

Cantwell, Robert. *When We Were Good: The Folk Revival*. Cambridge, MA: Harvard University Press, 1996.

Cohen, John. "Conversations with Bob Dylan." *Sing Out!* October/November 1968.

Cohen, Norm. *Folk Song America: A 20th Century Revival* [book and cassettes]. Washington, DC: Smithsonian Collection of Recordings, 1990.

Cohen, Robby. *When the Old Left Was Young: Student Radicals and America's First Mass Student Movement, 1929–1941*. New York: Oxford University Press, 1993.

Cohen, Ronald D. *Folk Music: The Basics*. New York: Routledge, 2006.

_____. *Rainbow Quest: Folk Music and American Society, 1940–1970*. Amherst: University of Massachusetts Press, 2002.

_____, ed. *"Wasn't That a Time!" Firsthand Accounts of the Folk Music Revival*. Metuchen, NJ: Scarecrow, 1995.

_____, and Dave Samuelson. *Songs for Political Action: Folk Music, Topical Songs and the American Left, 1926–1953* [book accompanying the 10-CD set with the same title issued by Bear Family Records, 1996].

Cott, Jonathan, ed. *Bob Dylan: The Essential Interviews.* New York: Wenner Books, 2006.

Cray, Ed. *Ramblin' Man: The Life and Times of Woody Guthrie.* New York: W.W. Norton, 2004.

Cunningham, Agnes "Sis," and Gordon Freisen. *Red Dust and Broadsides: A Joint Autobiography,* ed. Ronald D. Cohen. Amherst: University of Massachusetts Press, 1999.

Day, Aidan. *Jokerman: Reading the Lyrics of Bob Dylan.* New York: Blackwell, 1988.

Denisoff, R. Serge. *Great Day Coming: Folk Music and the American Left.* Urbana: University of Illinois Press, 1971.

_____. *Sing a Song of Social Significance.* Bowling Green, OH: Bowling Green University Press, 1972.

Denisoff, R. Serge, and David Fandray. "'Hey, Hey Woody Guthrie I Wrote You a Song': The Political Side of Bob Dylan." *Popular Music and Society* 5.1, 1977: 31–42.

DeTurk, David, and A. Poulin, eds. *The American Folk Scene: Dimensions of the Folksong Revival.* New York: Dell, 1967.

Dickstein, Morris. *Gates of Eden: American Culture in the Sixties.* New York: Basic, 1977.

Dietz, Roger. "Peter, Paul & Mary: Harmony from an Era of Protest." *Sing Out!* 44:2, Winter 2000: 34–40, 43.

Draper, Theodore. *American Communism and Soviet Russia.* New York: Vintage, 1986.

_____. *The Roots of American Communism.* New York: Viking, 1957.

Dunaway, David King. "Folk Protest and Political Music in the United States." *Journal of American Folklore* 105, no. 417, Summer 1992: 374–379.

_____. *How Can I Keep from Singing: Pete Seeger.* New York: McGraw-Hill, 1981. Revised Edition, *How Can I Keep from Singing? The Ballad of Pete Seeger.* New York: Villard, 2008.

Dunning, Michael. *The Cultural Front: The Laboring of American Culture in the Twentieth Century.* New York: Verso, 1996.

Dunson, Josh. *Freedom in the Air: Song Movements of the Sixties.* New York: International, 1965.

Dylan, Bob. *Chronicles: Volume 1.* New York: Simon & Schuster, 2004.

_____. *Writings and Drawings by Bob Dylan.* New York: Knopf, 1973.

Eagleton, Terry. "Raine's Sterile Thunder." *Prospect Magazine,* March 2007, http://www.prospect-magazine.co.uk/article_details.php?id=8312.

Eliot, Marc. *Death of a Rebel: A Biography of Phil Ochs.* Secaucus, NJ: Carol Publishing, 1995.

Eliot, T.S. *The Rock.* London: Faber & Faber, 1934.

Fast, Howard. *Peekskill, USA.* New York: Civil Rights Congress, 1951.

Filene, Benjamin. *Romancing the Folk: Public Memory & American Roots Music.* Chapel Hill: University of North Carolina Press, 2000.

Foner, Philip S. *The Case of Joe Hill.* New York: International, 1965.

_____. *The Letters of Joe Hill.* New York: Oak, 1965.

Garman, Bryan K. *Race of Singers: Whitman's Working Class Hero from Guthrie to Springsteen.* Chapel Hill: University of North Carolina Press, 2000.

Gill, Andy. *Don't Think Twice, It's All Right: Bob Dylan, the Early Years.* New York: Thunder Mouth Press, 1998.

Gitlin, Todd. *The Sixties: Years of Hope, Days of Rage*. New York: Bantam, 1987.

Gleason, Ralph J. "'The Times They Are A-Changin'": The Changing Message of America's Young Folksingers." *Ramparts*, April 1967: 36–48.

Goldsmith, Peter D. *Making People's Music: Moe Asch and Folkways Records*. Washington DC: Smithsonian Institution Press, 1998.

Goodman, Fred. *The Mansion on the Hill: Dylan, Young, Geffen, Springsteen, and the Head-On Collision of Rock and Commerce*. New York: Times Books, 1997.

Gray, Michael. *The Bob Dylan Encyclopedia*. New York: Continuum, 2006.

_____. *Song and Dance Man III: The Art of Bob Dylan*. London: Continuum, 2000.

Green, Archie. "Charles Louis Seeger (1886–1979)." *The Journal of American Folklore* 92, no. 366, October 1979: 391–399.

Greenwald, Matt. "Billy Bragg Carries On for Woody." *Sing Out!* 43:3, Winter 1999: 34–48.

Greenway, John. *American Folksongs of Protest*. Philadelphia: University of Pennsylvania Press, 1953.

Guthrie, Woody. *Bound for Glory*. New York: Dutton, 1943.

_____. *Born to Win*. New York: Macmillan, 1965.

_____. *Pastures of Plenty: A Self-Portrait*, ed. Dave Marsh and Harold Leventhal. New York: HarperCollins, 1990.

Hajdu, David. "Folk Hero." *New Yorker*, March 29, 2004: 92–97.

_____. *Positively 4th Street: The Life and Times of Joan Baez, Bob Dylan, Mimi Baez Farina, and Richard Farina*. New York: North Point Press, 2001.

Hammond, John. *John Hammond on Record: An Autobiography*. New York: Ridge, 1977.

Hampton, Wayne. *Guerrilla Minstrels: John Lennon, Joe Hill, Woody Guthrie, and Bob Dylan*. Knoxville: University of Tennessee Press, 1986.

Haynes, John E. *Red Scare or Red Menace? American Communism and Anticommunism in the Cold War Era*. Chicago: Ivan R. Dee, 1996.

Hays, Lee. Letter. *New Masses*. January 11, 1933: 21.

_____. "On Almanacs" (Part II). *People's Songs Bulletin* 3, no. 10, November 1948: 9.

Herdman, John. *Voice without Restraint: Bob Dylan's Lyrics and Their Background*. New York: Delilah, 1981.

Heylin, Clinton. *Behind the Shades Revisited: Bob Dylan*. New York: William Morrow, 2001.

_____. *Bob Dylan: A Life in Stolen Moments: Day by Day, 1941–1995*. New York: Schirmer Books, 1996.

_____. *The Recording Sessions, 1960–1994*. New York: St. Martin's, 1995.

Hinton, Sam. "The Singer of Folk Songs and His Conscience." *Western Folklore XIV* 1955: 170–73.

Holzman, Jac, and Gavan Daws. *Follow the Music: The Life and High Times of Elektra Records in the Great Years of American Pop Culture*. Santa Monica, CA: First Media Books, 1998.

Irwin, Colin. *Bob Dylan Highway 61 Revisited*. New York: Billboard Books, 2008.

Isserman, Maurice. *If I Had a Hammer: The Death of the Old Left and the Birth of the New Left*. New York: Basic, 1987.

Ives, Burl. *Wayfaring Stranger*. New York: McGraw-Hill, 1948.

I.W.W. Songs: Songs of the Workers: To Fan the Flames of Discontent. Chicago: IWW, various editions.

Jackson, Mark Allan. *Prophet Singer: The Voice and Vision of Woody Guthrie*. Jackson: University Press of Mississippi, 2007.

191

Johnson, Paul. *Modern Times*. New York: Harper Colophon, 1985.

Kisseloff, Jeff. *Generation on Fire: Voices of Protest from the 1960s: An Oral History*. Lexington: University Press of Kentucky. 2006.

Klein, Joe. *Woody Guthrie: A Life*. New York: Knopf, 1980.

Koppelman, Robert S. *Sing Out, Warning! Sing Out, Love!: The Writings of Lee Hays*. Amherst: University of Massachusetts Press, 2004.

Kornbluth, Joyce, ed. *Rebel Voices: An I.W.W. Anthology*. Ann Arbor: University of Michigan Press, 1964.

Lawless, Roy M. *Folksingers and Folksongs in America*. New York: Duell, Sloan, and Pearce, 1960.

Lieberman, Robbie. *"My Song Is My Weapon": People's Songs, American Communism, and the Politics of Culture, 1930–1950*. Urbana: University of Illinois Press, 1989.

Lomax, Alan. *Folksong Style and Culture*. Washington, DC: American Association for the Advancement of Science, 1968.

Lomax, Alan, Pete Seeger, and Woody Guthrie, comps. *Hard Hitting Songs for Hard-Hit People: American Folk Songs of the Depression and the Labor Movement of the 1930s*. New York: Oak, 1967.

Lomax, John A. *Adventures of a Ballad Hunter*. New York: Macmillan, 1947.

_____, and Alan Lomax. *American Ballads & Folk Songs*. New York: Macmillan, 1934.

Lornell, Christopher, and Kip Lornell. *Introducing American Folk Music: Grassroots and Ethnic Traditions in the United States*. 2nd ed. New York: McGraw-Hill, 2002.

Marcus, Greil. *Mystery Train: Images of America in Rock 'n' Roll Music*. New York: Dutton, 1975.

Marqusee, Mike. *Chimes of Freedom: The Politics of Bob Dylan's Art*. New York: New Press, 2003.

Marshall, Lee. *Bob Dylan: The Never Ending Star*. Cambridge, UK: Polity Press, 2007.

Matusow, Harvey. *False Witness*. New York: Cameron & Kahn, 1955.

McGregor, Craig, ed. *Bob Dylan: A Retrospective*. New York: William Morrow, 1972.

Partridge, Elizabeth. *This Land Was Made for You and Me: The Life and Songs of Woody Guthrie*. New York: Viking, 2002.

Paxton, Tom. *The Honor of Your Company*, ed. Milton Okun. New York: Cherry Lane Music Company, 2000.

Peer, Ralph. "Discovery of the First Hillbilly Great." *The Billboard*, May 16, 1953: 20–21, 35.

Pescatello, Ann. M. *Charles Seeger: A Life in American Music*. Pittsburgh: University of Pittsburgh Press, 1992.

Porterfield, Nolan. *Jimmie Rodgers*. Urbana: University of Illinois Press, 1992.

_____. *Last Cavalier: The Life and Times of John A. Lomax, 1867–1948*. Urbana: University of Illinois Press, 1996.

Prial, Dunstan. *The Producer: John Hammond and the Soul of American Music*. New York: Farrar, Straus & Giroux, 2006.

Radosh, Ronald. "Take What You Need." *New Republic*, June 18, 2001: 39–45.

Red Channels: The Report of Communist Influence in Radio and Television. New York: American Business Consultants, 1950.

Reuss, Richard A. "Folk Music and Social Conscience: The Musical Odyssey of Charles Seeger." *Western Folklore* 38, no. 4, October 1979: 221–238.

_____. "The Roots of American Left-Wing Interest in Folksong." *Labor History* 12, Spring 1971: 259–279.

_____. "Woody Guthrie and His Folk Tradition." *The Journal of American Folklore* 83, no. 329, July 1970: 273–303.

Reuss, Richard A., with JoAnne C. Reuss. *American Folk Music and Left-Wing Politics, 1927–1957*. Lanham, MD: Scarecrow Press, 2000.

Ricks, Christopher. *Dylan's Visions of Sin*. New York: Ecco, 2005.

Riley, Tim. *Hard Rain: A Dylan Commentary*. New York: Knopf, 1992.

Rinzler, Alan. *Bob Dylan: The Illustrated Record*. New York: Harmony, 1978.

Robbin, Ed. *Woody Guthrie and Me*. Berkeley, CA: Lancaster-Miller, 1979.

Robinson, David. *Chaplin: His Life and Art*. London: Grafton, 1985.

Rodnitzky, Jerome L. *Minstrels of the Dawn: The Folk-Protest Singer as a Cultural Hero*. Chicago: Nelson-Hall, 1976.

Rolfzen, B.J. *The Spring of My Life*. n.d.

Romalis, Shelly. *Pistol Packin' Mama: The Cultural Politics of Aunt Molly Jackson*. Urbana: University of Illinois Press, 1998.

Rosemont, Franklin. *Joe Hill: The IWW & the Making of a Revolutionary Workingclass Counterculture*. Chicago: Charles H. Kerr, 2003.

Rosenberg, Neil, ed. *Transforming Tradition: Folk Music Revivals Examined*. Urbana: University of Illinois Press, 1993.

Ruhlmann, William. "Peter, Paul and Mary: A Song to Sing All Over This Land." *Goldmine*, April 12, 1996: 20–50, 62–82, 142–150.

Russell, Don. "They Sing the Hard Hitting Songs That Belong to America's Workers." *People's World*, August 8, 1941: 5.

Sandburg, Carl. *The American Songbag*. New York: Harcourt, Brace, 1927.

Santelli, Robert. *The Bob Dylan Scrapbook, 1956–1966*. New York: Simon & Schuster, 2005.

_____, and Emily Davidson. *Hard Travelin': The Life and Legacy of Woody Guthrie*. Hanover, NH: University Press of New England for Wesleyan University Press, 1999.

Santelli, Robert, Holly George-Warren, and Jim Brown, eds. *American Roots Music*. New York: Harry N. Abrams, 2001.

Scaduto, Anthony. *Bob Dylan: An Intimate Biography*. New York: Grosset & Dunlap, 1971.

Schicke, C. A. *Revolution in Sound: A Biography of the Recording Industry*. Boston: Little, Brown, 1974.

Schumacher, Michael. *There but for Fortune: A Life of Phil Ochs*. New York: Hyperion, 1996.

Scobie, Stephen. *Alias Bob Dylan Revisited*. Calgary, Alberta: Red Deer Press, 2003.

Seeger, Pete. *The Incompleat Folksinger*. New York: Simon & Schuster, 1972.

_____. *Where Have All the Flowers Gone: A Musical Autobiography*. Sing Out! Publications, 3rd edition, 1997.

Shelton, Robert. *No Direction Home: The Life and Music of Bob Dylan*. New York: William Morrow, 1986.

Silber, Irwin. *Lift Every Voice*. New York: Oak, 1953.

Smith, Gibbs M. *Labor Martyr: Joe Hill*. New York: Grosset & Dunlop, 1969.

Sounes, Howard. *Down the Highway: The Life of Bob Dylan*. New York: Grove Press, 2001.

Spector, Bert Alan. *Wasn't That a Time: Pete Seeger and the Anti-Communist Crusade, 1940–1968*. Ph.D. diss. University of Missouri–Columbia, 1977.

_____. "The Weavers: A Case History in Show Business Blacklisting." *Journal of American Culture* 5(3) 1982: 113–120.

Spitz, Bob. *Bob Dylan: A Biography*. New York: McGraw-Hill, 1989.

Stavis, Barrie, and Frank Harmon, eds. *The Songs of Joe Hill*. New York: People's Artists, 1955 [paperback: Oak Archives, 2007].

Thompson, Toby. *Positively Main Street*. New York: Coward, McCann, and Geohegan, 1971.

Van Ronk, Dave, with Elijah Wald. *The Mayor of MacDougal Street: A Memoir*. New York: Da Capo Press, 2005.

Von Schmidt, Eric, and Jim Rooney. *Baby Let Me Follow You Down: The Illustrated Story of the Cambridge Folk Years*. Garden City, NY: Anchor Press, 1979.

Wald, Elijah. *Josh White: Society Blues*. New York: Routledge, 2002.

Weiner, Rex, and Deanne Stillman. *Woodstock Census: The Nationwide Survey of the Sixties Generation*. New York: Viking, 1979.

Weissman, Dick. *Which Side Are You On? An Inside History of the Folk Music Revival in America*. New York: Continuum, 2005.

Wilentz, Sean. "Mystic Nights: The Making of Blonde on Blonde in Nashville." http://www.oxfordamericanmag.com/content.cfm?ArticleID=254.

_____. "Notes for *Live 1964*." Bobdylan.com.

_____. "The Roving Gambler at Scenic Newport." Bobdylan.com.

Willens, Doris. *Lonesome Traveler: The Life of Lee Hays*. New York: W.W. Norton, 1988.

Williams, Paul. *Bob Dylan Performing Artist: 1960–1973 The Early Years*. London: Omnibus, 2004.

Wolfe, Charles, and Kip Lornell. *The Life and Legend of Leadbelly*. New York: Da Capo Press, 1999.

Woliver, Robbie. *Hoot: A 25-Year History of the Greenwich Village Music Scene*. New York: St. Martin's, 1986.

Yurchenco, Henrietta. *Around the World in 80 Years: A Memoir*. Point Richmond, CA: MRI Press, 2002.

Zwonitzner, Mark, with Charles Hirshberg. *Will You Miss Me When I'm Gone? The Carter Family and Their Legacy in American Music*. New York: Simon & Schuster 2002.

Archives

American Folklife Center, Library of Congress, http://www.loc.gov/folklife/archive. html.

Center for American Music, http://cam.music.utexas.edu/.

Center for Popular Music, http://popmusic.mtsu.edu/.

Experience Music Project, http://www.emplive.org/.

Folk Music Archives, http://folkmusicarchives.org.

Industrial Workers of the World, official depository for records, Walter P. Reuther Library of Labor & Urban Affairs, Wayne State University. http://www.reuther. wayne.edu/collections/iwwcollections.html

Institute for Studies in American Music, http://depthome.brooklyn.cuny.edu/isam/.

Labadie Collection. University Library. University of Michigan. Joe Hill file box.

New York Folklore Society, http://www.nyfolklore.org/.

Rock and Roll Hall of Fame, http://www.rockhall.com/.

The Ralph Rinzler Folklife Archives and Collections at the Center for Folklife and Cultural Heritage, Smithsonian Institution, http://sirismm.si.edu/siris/collection-cfch.htm.

Reuther Library Folklore Archive, Wayne State University, http://www.reuther.wayne. edu/collections/hefa_1731-wsu.htm.

Ronald D. Cohen Collection, 1914–2005, Manuscripts Department, University Library of the University of North Carolina at Chapel Hill.
Rosemont Collection, Newberry Library, Chicago, http://www.newberry.org/collec tions/FindingAids/rosemont/rosemont.html.
Southern Folklife Collection, http://www.lib.unc.edu/mss/sfcl/.
Wisconsin Music Archives, http://music.library.wisc.edu/wma/.
Woody Guthrie Archives, http://www.woodyguthrie.org/archives/archivesindex.htm.

Videos

Ballad of Ramblin' Jack. Director: Aiyana Elliott. New York: Plantain Films/Lot 47 Films, 2001.
Billy Bragg and Wilco: Man in the Sand. Director: Kim Hopkins. New York: Palm Pictures, 2001.
Bob Dylan Don't Look Back 65 Tour Deluxe Edition. Director: D. A. Pennebaker. New York: Docurama, 2007.
Bob Dylan The Other Side of the Mirror: Live at the Newport Folk Festival, 1962–1965. Director: Murray Lerner. New York: MLF Productions, 2007.
The Carter Family: Will the Circle Be Unbroken. Director: Kathy Conkwright. New York: *American Experience*, PBS, 2005.
Joe Hill. Director: Ken Verdoia. New York: PBS, 2000.
Lomax the Songhunter. Director: Rogier Kappers. New York: *POV*, PBS, 2004.
No Direction Home: Bob Dylan. Director: Martin Scorsese. New York: American Masters, PBS, 2005.
Pete Seeger: The Power of Song. Director: Jim Brown. New York: Jim Brown Productions/Concert Productions International, 2007.
Peter Paul and Mary: Carry It On — A Musical Legacy. Director: Jim Brown. New York: PBS, 2004.
Tales from a Golden Age Bob Dylan, 1941–1966. Director: Tom O'Dowd. New Malden, Surrey, UK: Chrome Dreams, 2004.
Tangled Up in Bob: Searching for Bob Dylan. Director: Mary Feidt. Santa Fe, NM: Feido Films, 2006.
A Vision Shared: A Tribute to Woody Guthrie and Leadbelly. Director: Jim Brown. New York: Showtime/Ginger Group Productions, 1988.
The Weavers: Wasn't That a Time. Director: Jim Brown. New York: George Stoney Associates/Harold Leventhal Management, 1982.
Woody Guthrie: Ain't Got No Home. Director: Peter Frumkin. New York: American Masters, PBS, 2006.

Selected Records and CDs

Almanac Singers. *Songs of Protest.* Prism, 2001.
Baez, Joan. *The First 10 Years.* Vanguard, 1970.
The Best of Broadside 1962–1988. Smithsonian Folkways Recordings, 2000.
Bragg, Billy, and Wilco. *Mermaid Avenue.* Elektra, 1998.
_____. *Mermaid Avenue, Vol. II.* Elektra, 2000.
The Carter Family, 1927–1934. JSP Records, 2002.
The Carter Family, Vol. 2, 1935–1941. JSP Records, 2003.

Cohen, Norm. *Folk Song America: A 20th Century Revival.* Smithsonian Collection of Recordings, 1990.

Cohen, Ronald D., and Dave Samuelson. *Songs for Political Action: Folk Music, Topical Songs, and the American Left, 1926–1953.* Bear Family, 1996.

Don't Mourn ... Organize! Songs of Labor Songwriter Joe Hill. Smithsonian Folkways, 1990.

Dylan, Bob. *Another Side of Bob Dylan.* Columbia, 1964.

_____. *Biograph.* CBS, 1985.

_____. *Blonde on Blonde.* Columbia, 1966.

_____. *Bootleg Series Vol. 1–3 Rare and Unreleased, 1961–1991.* Sony, 1991.

_____. *Bootleg Series Vol. 6 Bob Dylan Live 1964 Concert at Philharmonic Hall.* Sony, 2004.

_____. *Bringing It All Back Home.* Columbia, 1965.

_____. *The Freewheelin' Bob Dylan.* Columbia, 1963.

_____. *Highway 61 Interactive.* Sony, 1995.

_____. *Highway 61 Revisited.* Columbia, 1965.

_____. *Live at the Gaslight.* Columbia, 2005.

_____. *No Direction Home: The Soundtrack (The Bootleg Series, Vol. 7).* Columbia Legacy, 2005.

_____. *The Times They Are A-Changin'.* Columbia, 1964.

The Essential Ramblin' Jack Elliott. Vanguard, 1970.

Guthrie, Woody. *The Asch Recordings, Vol. 1–4.* Smithsonian Folkways, 1999.

_____. *Dust Bowl Ballads.* Rounder Records, 1988.

_____. *Woody Guthrie: Library of Congress Recordings.* 1964. Reissue. Cambridge, Mass.: Rounder Records Corp., 1988.

Cisco Houston: The Folkway Years 1944–1961. Smithsonian Folkways Series, 1994.

Aunt Molly Jackson Library of Congress Recordings, Rounder Select, 1990.

The Essential Kingston Trio. Shout Factory, 2006.

The Definitive Leadbelly. Catfish UK, 2002.

Newport Folk Festival 1964, Evening Concerts, Vol. 1, Vanguard 1964

20th Century Masters: Best of Phil Ochs. A & M, 2002.

I Can't Help but Wonder Where I'm Bound: The Best of Tom Paxton. Elektra, 1999.

The Very Best of Peter, Paul & Mary. Rhino, 2005.

Rebel Voices: Songs of the Industrial Workers of the World. Flying Fish Records, 1992.

Jimmie Rodgers Recordings, 1927–1933. JSP Records, 2002.

Seeger, Pete. *We Shall Overcome: Complete Carnegie Hall Concert.* Sony, 1989.

Springsteen, Bruce. *We Shall Overcome: The Seeger Sessions.* Sony, 2006.

Dave Van Ronk: The Folkways Years, 1959–61. Smithsonian Folkways Series, 1992.

Weavers, The. *Goodnight Irene: The Weavers, 1949–1953.* Bear Family, 2000.

_____. *Wasn't That a Time.* Vanguard, 1993.

Websites

Songs of the Almanac Singers: http://www.geocities.com/Nashville/3448/almanac.html.

The Joan Baez Web Pages: http://www.joanbaez.com.

Judy Collins: http://www.judycollins.com.

Bob Dylan: http://www.bobdylan.com.

Bob Dylan's Musical Roots: http://www.bobdylanroots.com/index.html.

Country Music Hall of Fame: http://www.countrymusichalloffame.com.

Ramblin Jack Elliott: http://www.ramblinjack.com.

Expecting Rain: http://www.expectingrain.com.

Official Woody Guthrie Website: http://www.woodyguthrie.org.

The Joe Hill Project: http://www.joehill.org/index.html.

Industrial Workers of the World: http://www.iww.org.

Aunt Molly Jackson: http://www.cmt.com/artists/az/jackson_aunt_molly/bio.jhtml.

Alan Lomax: http://www.alan-lomax.com.

Tom Paxton: http://www.tompaxton.com.

The Peekskill Story: http://www.fortunecity.com/tinpan/parton/2/peekskill.html.

Ralph Peer Remembers Jimmie Rodgers: http://www.silcom.com/~peterf/ideas/jr-rpeer.htm.

Pete Seeger Appreciation Page: http://www.peteseeger.net.

Peter, Paul, and Mary Website: http://www.peterpaulandmary.com.

The Sing Out! Pages: http://www.singout.org.

The Weavers: http://www.folkmusicarchives.org/weavers.htm.

Index